Creative Studi

for the caring professions

Creative Studies
for the caring professions

Edited by Denise Lyons

Gill & Macmillan

Gill & Macmillan Ltd
Hume Avenue
Park West
Dublin 12 **2010**
with associated companies throughout the world www.gillmacmillan.ie

978 07171 4768 7

Index compiled by Helen Litton
Design and print origination in Ireland by O'K Graphic Design, Dublin
Printed by GraphyCems Ltd, Spain

The paper used in this book is made from the wood pulp of managed forests. For every tree felled, at least one tree is planted, thereby renewing natural resources.

A CIP catalogue record for this book is available from the British Library.

Illustrations
Chapters 1 and 4; introductory illustrations, Chapters 1–17: Denise Lyons.
Chapter 2: Paul Timoney.

Contents

Section 3: Example Activities

Contributors

Pauline Brennan is the project leader of Bradóg Regional Youth Service in north west inner city Dublin. She has been working in the youth field for the last twenty years and has a background in art. As an artist, Pauline identifies with the role of the creative process in youth work. She still practises art in her spare time as well as being part of a great team of people who run a youth service for the young people of Dublin. Bradóg's youth work approach aims to develop young people as advocates for the next generation.

Pádraigín Caesar currently holds the Karel Seeldrayers Lectureship in Music at Carlow College, St Patrick's and works in both the Humanities and Social Studies departments of that institution. Her fields within the study of music encompass social care, catechetics and teaching. A highly accomplished musician, Pádraigín has achieved much in the field of musical performance and in academia. Having completed her primary degree (Bachelor of Music Education) at Trinity College Dublin, she continued her musical studies at Boston College, USA, as holder of the Fulbright Scholarship from the Ireland–United States Commission for Educational Exchange for Music. Pádraigín was awarded a master's degree in Ethnomusicology from the University of Limerick in 2008.

Sue Callaghan has a BA in Theatre Theory and Practice and an MA in English and Education. She recently completed an MA in Social Science and a Certificate in Therapeutic Play. Sue has been involved in theatre since she was sixteen years old, both professionally in the USA and with local theatre groups in Ireland. She has participated in the Re-inventing Culture Theatre Group, which works with young children and transition-year students to develop theatrical performances based on Irish culture. She is the staff advisor and director of the AIT Drama Society. She has worked with the Brothers of Charity in Roscommon, leading workshops for adults with learning difficulties, and with the HSE, giving workshops and summer camps in puppetry. In 2009 she had the pleasure of working personally with Dr Sue Jennings.

Mario R. J. Corbin is a lecturer in the Department of Humanities (Social Care) at the Institute of Technology in Blanchardstown, Dublin (ITB). His background is in cultural anthropology and sociology.

Jennifer Fawcett graduated from University College Cork in 2005 with an MA in Sociology. Her research interests lie in the fields of literature, social geography and cultural sociology. Since the birth of her first child in 2006 she has worked with young children in both informal and educational settings, with particular emphasis on developing literacy and enjoyment of reading through creative techniques.

Sinead Foskin and Fiona McSweeney. Fiona McSweeney is regional manager for the Irish Wheelchair Association (IWA) South region. She holds a master's degree in Education and has extensive experience as a social care practitioner specialising in the area of disability. Sinead Foskin is area manager for IWA South East and holds a master's degree in Health Care Management. She too has extensive experience of working with people with disabilities. Both authors are involved in the design, development and delivery of services, projects and programmes that enable people to engage in their communities and maximise their opportunities to live an independent life.

Lucy Hyland is a lecturer in Social Care in Carlow College. She has extensive experience as a social worker in the area of disability and in probation and has worked as a social care practitioner in the UK and the USA. She is currently a doctoral student at University College Cork. Joanne Seymour, Lucy's co-author, is a social care practitioner working in the area of intellectual disability. She holds an honours degree in Social Care from Carlow College. Her broad range of research and practice interests includes the provision of support initiatives for the child siblings of those with special needs and the development of enhanced social and occupational opportunities for adults with intellectual disabilities. Sheila Kissane, their co-author, graduated from University College Dublin with a degree in Social Science and later completed a Diploma in Applied Social Studies and a Certificate Qualification in Social Work. For the past fifteen years Sheila has been a social worker in community care in the area of intellectual disability.

Maria Kenneally is a lecturer in Spanish at ITB. Having completed her MSc in Latin American Sociology and Politics and her Postgraduate Certificate in Education at the University of London, she stayed on in London and worked for four years as a Modern Foreign Language teacher in an inner-city comprehensive school. She recently completed her Postgraduate Diploma in Drama in Education at Trinity College Dublin, and currently co-lectures on Creative Skills in the Social Care programme at ITB. In collaboration with Fingal Arts Council, Maria has also delivered Drama in Education workshops to children with Special Educational Needs and has guest lectured on the role of drama in language learning to MA students at ITB. At present she is co-ordinating a Theatre and Spanish programme for fifth-class primary-school students in the Dublin 15 area.

Denise Lyons is a social care worker, art therapist and lecturer for the BA in Applied Social Studies in ITB. Denise completed her MPhil in Social Care from the Dublin Institute of Technology in 2007, and graduated as an Art Therapist from Cork IT in 2003. Denise is Secretary of the Irish Association of Social Care Educators (IASCE) and an extern for the Creative Studies and Recreational modules for Athlone Institute of Technology (AIT) and Cork Institute of Technology (CIT).

Denise MacGiollari completed a BA in Design Products at Limerick School of Art and Design in 1993. After gaining experience in facilitating art sessions with marginalised groups and individuals in Limerick, between 1995 and 1997 she completed a Postgraduate Diploma in Art Therapy at Hertfordshire University. Denise spent many years working as an art therapist, sand play therapist and project worker with children at risk in education, children in foster care, single parents, people with acute mental health issues and people with disabilities. In 2002 Denise accepted a lecturing post with Athlone Institute of Technology to teach 'creative art' to Social Care students. In that capacity she continues to develop programmes that promote creativity as a vital tool of engagement within social care and for students' personal and professional development. Denise completed an MA in Art Therapy at Cork IT in 2008.

Kate McCarthy teaches Drama, Film and Live Art at Waterford Institute of Technology. She graduated with a BA in Drama and Theatre Studies and English, and an MA in Drama and Theatre Studies from University College Cork. Kate also holds an Associate and Licentiate Diploma in Performance from Trinity College London. She facilitates workshops with Little Red Kettle Theatre Company, Waterford, Waterford Youth Arts and Croydon Youth Theatre Organisation in London. Her research interests include drama/theatre-in-education, community drama, theatre history, performance practice as research, and the documentation of drama and theatre practices.

Gerry Morgan, MA (Dramatherapy), has lectured on the Performance Studies degree in DIT and is currently lecturing in Creative Studies, Drama and Psychology in Carlow College. He has worked in professional and community theatre since 1990, and has directed over twenty productions with Theatre of Joy and a number of other companies, including shows at the Dublin Theatre Festival and the Edinburgh Festival. He co-designed and worked on the Pathways Theatre Project for Schizophrenia Ireland (now Shine) and the Abbey Theatre from 1998 to 2000. He is a qualified drama therapist, working specifically with adults with mental health difficulties and with children. He is also artistic director of Theatre of Joy.

Una O'Grady is a stay-at-home parent of two children, aged ten and sixteen years. Among other jobs, Una worked as a teacher's assistant in a primary school with a senior infant class, which she found both personally and professionally rewarding. In college, Una studied Philosophy, Ethics and Developmental Psychology, and is still an avid reader in her spare time. She is currently working on an illustrated children's book with a philosophical theme and plans to write a novel in the near future.

Dr Carmel O'Sullivan is the Director of Postgraduate Teaching and Learning in the School of Education, Trinity College Dublin, and since 2004 has collaborated with Desmond McKernan, the Honorary Secretary of the Asperger Syndrome Association of Ireland (Aspire) on a creative arts research project entitled 'Building Bridges: An Exploration of the Use of Drama in Education in the Holistic Education of Young People with Asperger Syndrome'. Una MacNulty, Lesley Conroy and Anthony Walsh are teacher/researchers on that project.

Dr Sharon Phelan worked in community arts as Artistic Director of the Ionad Culturtha in Ballyvourney, Co. Cork, as dance education specialist with the Department of Education and as professional practitioner with Siamsa Tíre, the National Folk Theatre of Ireland. She has published numerous academic papers on dance in early childhood education and her PhD focused on dance in Ireland from educational and cultural perspectives. Sharon lectures in dance on degree programmes in Childcare and Social Care at the Institute of Technology, Tralee, Co. Kerry.

Paul Timoney has a BA (Hons) in Art and Design Education from the National College of Art and Design and an MFA from the Burren College of Art. He has worked as a creative group facilitator, specialising in art and drama, for a variety of community development and social care programmes for over ten years. He lectures on the Creative Studies in Social Care course at the Athlone Institute of Technology.

Abbreviations used in the text

BA	Bachelor of Arts
CACHE	Council for Awards in Children's Care and Education
CECDE	Centre for Early Childhood Development and Education
CSO	Central Statistics Office
DIE	Drama-in-education
DOH	Department of Health and Children
FETAC	Further Education Training Awards Council
HETAC	Higher Education Training Awards Council
HSE	Health Service Executive
IASCE	Irish Association of Social Care Educators
IDSF	International DanceSport Federation
IJASS	*Irish Journal of Applied Social Studies*
IT	Institute of Technology
IWA	Irish Wheelchair Association
MA	Master of Arts
MFA	Masters of Fine Art
OECD	Organisation for Economic Co-operation and Development
PLC	Post-Leaving Certificate
NAYD	National Association for Youth Drama
NCCA	National Council for Curriculum and Assessment
NDP	National Development Plan
NUI	National University of Ireland
NYCI	National Youth Council of Ireland
TCI	Therapeutic crisis intervention
TIE	Theatre-in-education
VEC	Vocational Education Committee

Introduction

The idea to write a creative studies textbook emerged from a frustration with the lack of relevant reading material about the benefits of using the creative arts, not as therapy, but within everyday experiences. The original group—Denise Lyons (ITB), Denise MacGiollari (AIT), Sue Callaghan (AIT) and Louisa Goss (Dundalk IT)—met in a rented house in the midlands of Ireland to write and to talk about the importance of using the creative arts. The more we talked, however, the less we wrote, and gradually the planned book fell to the bottom of our long list of priorities. That was until a chance meeting with Marion O'Brien from Gill and MacMillan, at the Irish Social Care Educators/National Digital Learning Repository Conference in May 2009, reawakened our enthusiasm, and the book was back on track. Since May 2009 many new names and faces have joined the original group of contributors, offering a variety of knowledge, experience and talent—and many more memorable conversations.

This book is a collaborative venture between lecturers, practitioners, teachers and parents and is intended as a textbook on the theory and practice of using the creative arts within the caring professions, which in our interpretation refers to social care, youth work and early childhood studies. These three professions were selected because they all use the creative arts of art, drama, music and dance in both training and practice. Creative studies, although presented under a variety of titles, is essentially a module on social care, youth work and early childhood care courses, thus the majority of chapters contain material relevant to the practice and theory of using the creative arts in all three caring professions.

Social care, youth work and early childhood professionals have discovered the potential benefits of using the creative arts within their practice. Creative activities enable the worker to interact in a non-directive way. Within education, students learn how to facilitate creative activities through participation in experiential workshops. The learning outcomes of the creative module include facilitation skills, communication skills and increased self-awareness. Being creative is fun, and students can relearn how to play and how to facilitate child's play through leading by example. Management and staff in the three caring professions have discovered that art, drama, music and dance are powerful tools, often proving a catalyst for direct work with people.

Chapter 1 introduces the reader to the three caring professions of social care, youth work and early childhood development. Within these professions creativity is used to help people develop social skills, to have fun, to learn new coping mechanisms, for relationship development and for personal expression, among other benefits. This chapter identifies the core principles needed to engage in creative activities: the belief that everyone is creative in their own way and that the focus of being creative should be on the process, not the end product. The final segment of this chapter explains the difference between using the creative arts as a therapist and using them as a caring professional.

In Chapter 2 students will learn how to facilitate creative activities with individuals or groups. Facilitation includes the ability to design a session that has a distinct beginning, middle and end. Before the worker can facilitate a creative experience, he/she must be aware of safety issues, class size, materials, how to plan, time management, clean up, endings and storage. This chapter guides the reader through this process in a clear and non-challenging way.

In Chapter 3 we look at the first of our creative activities: art. This chapter introduces the reader to the concept of creativity and how we can be creative in many different ways in our lives. The reader is directed through the wide variety of benefits that are derived through participation in art activities, including self-expression, psychological mastery, meaning-making, self-exploration and self-understanding, story-making, memory exploration, playful imaginative discovery, learning and having fun. Chapter 4, the second art-related chapter, describes how children use art and how their drawings change as they grow and develop. Understanding the meaning, structure and development of children's art is a topic that has fascinated many theorists and researchers, and this chapter focuses on the work of Lowenfeld and Brittain, Georges Henri Luquet and Rhoda Kellogg.

Chapter 5 describes how dance and movement are used in education to help students learn to use the body as a direct form of self-expression. Specific case studies are used to illustrate how dance can be useful: helping to develop self-esteem and trust; enhancing communication skills; establishing a broader movement vocabulary; and providing a greater understanding of different cultures and social issues. Dance in education can also enable the student to learn about trust and personal boundaries.

Chapter 6 begins our exploration of the role of drama-in-education and practice. Here the process of using drama-in-education and theatre-in-education is outlined. Theatre-in-education can bring about social change because it brings to life the story of the individual and the community. Through active participation students learn how to play, to have fun and to express themselves. Chapter 7 continues the discussion on the role of drama-in-education, looking in particular at the role it plays in supporting students. Maria Kenneally provides an example of how drama was used within social care education to help develop personal, group and social skills.

Chapter 8 examines the role of play in drama, which is especially important as it is the role of many caring professional to encourage and facilitate play experiences. This introduces the Embodiment-Projection-Role as fundamental to the dramatic development of children, where they learn the ability to play 'as if'. The links between creative drama and socio-dramatic play are also discussed, for example developing the social self, learning co-operation and working together, and providing a safe medium to explore life situations.

Chapter 9 introduces the reader to the role of storytelling in practice. Storytelling is an essential function of our everyday lives, from the fairytales our parents read to us at bedtime to the films we watch and the books we read as adults. Storytelling gives people an opportunity to tell their story and is therefore a less confrontational approach to talking through personal issues. In order to facilitate a storytelling activity, care workers need to have an awareness of their own stories and have the ability to listen and to empathise.

Chapter 10 starts from the reassuring premise that music is not exclusive to those with a music background, music education or musical talent. People can passively engage in music by listening, or can become actively involved through using traditional or homemade instruments. Music causes emotional responses and is also an associative cue to memory or experience. This chapter explains how students and practitioners can use music in their practice and provides several music workshop examples to illustrate the points made.

Chapter 11 discusses the role of play for children in residential care. Residential care provides a home environment for children who, for whatever reason, are unable to live at home. This chapter describes how play can help children in residential care to form appropriate attachments with the staff and also outlines the different types of play scenario and the role of game consoles in children's leisure time. Role play is also an effective tool in the training and education of social care staff and students. In this respect, the example of therapeutic crisis intervention training is used to show how role play encourages team cohesion and skill development.

Chapter 12 describes the role of creativity in early childhood education, focusing on the work of Maria Montessori, Jean Piaget and Lev Vygotsky, who have greatly influenced the practice and development of early childhood education, especially in the nursery and primary school areas. The role of creativity in early childhood education, from the crèche to the classroom, is examined and a selection of art-making activities is presented, for use in work with young children, or at home with your own children.

Chapter 13 presents an experience of facilitating 'Sibshops' for the siblings of children with a disability. This study starts with a description of what siblings experience when their brother or sister has a disability and the supports available for them. Sibshops provide an opportunity for siblings to receive peer support and education in a creative format. This chapter describes the types of creative activity that can be used, and concludes by presenting the views of siblings who participated in such workshops.

Chapter 14 gives the reader an insight into youth work with young people from disadvantaged backgrounds. Through the use of creative activities, youth workers have an opportunity to teach the soft skills of social communication, team work, time management, self-motivation and planning. In Bradóg Regional Youth Services, young people use digital media as a method for creative expression. This chapter concludes by examining the role of the student in the youth service, and how the experience of placement can be used to apply theory to practice in a creative way.

Chapter 15 describes a collaborative project designed to work with young people with Asperger Syndrome. The programme uses drama for social skills education. Drama-in-education is the core element of social skills training; it is designed to help young people understand the behaviour they are learning. This programme proved particularly beneficial for stimulating the imagination, turn-taking, maintaining eye contact, listening and responding appropriately to others, collaborating, working in pairs and small groups, visual literacy, reading and interpreting non-verbal body language and tone of voice, making presentations, changing routines and sharing space. In short, *understanding* was the key to the success of the project.

Chapter 16 highlights the role of the creative arts within services for people with physical disabilities. The Irish Wheelchair Association (IWA) uses a community development approach in its work, where engaging in creative activities provides opportunities for individual and community-based work. The *White Paper on Education* (2000) recognised that there was a need for arts education for people with disabilities. Thus, the Creative Arts programmes within the IWA are of primary importance for the social, developmental, educational and therapeutic needs of each person in the service.

Chapter 17 examines the use of drama practice in the area of mental health. It describes a drama programme for adults with schizophrenia, based on the work of Keith Johnstone (1989), Augusto Boal (1992) and Sheila Yeger (1990), and on the author's twelve years' experience as a professional theatre artist. Mental health issues reduce confidence and self-esteem, leading the person to seek to avoid being noticed and then feeling unable to return to the normal aspects of their life after treatment. Creative drama, broken down into manageable steps through the creative process, helps people to overcome their fears, increase their confidence and learn how to interact with others in the community.

Section 3 is a collection of workshops and ideas to use within your own practice as a caring professional. Engaging in activities is fun for yourself and others, so we want to encourage you wholeheartedly to give it a go. Remember that there is no right or wrong way to be creative and that everyone, regardless of ability or experience, can facilitate the creative activities and workshops presented in this book.

SECTION 1

Theory Underpinning Creative Practice

ONE

Introduction to Creative Studies in the Caring Professions

Denise Lyons

SNAPSHOT

▶ Early childhood care, youth work and social care—what they are, what the workers do, how they train.

▶ Creative Studies—what it is and why it is relevant to the caring professions.

▶ Process not product.

▶ Using the creative arts therapeutically, not as therapy.

Introduction

The term 'creative studies' refers to the role of creative activities—art, dance, drama and music—in the education and practice of caring professionals, especially social care, youth work and early childhood care. Engaging in creative activities is fun, but it is also beneficial in helping people to become more comfortable in their own skin while learning to be flexible and adapt to new experiences. Participation in creative activities can help everyone learn more about how they behave in a group, in different roles and when facing new challenges. Creative studies are based on the principle that everyone is creative in their own way and that creativity can be rekindled if people concentrate on the process,

rather than on the end product. Taking part in these sorts of activities encourages playfulness, and adults can relearn how to play and can facilitate child's play through leading by example.

The teaching of 'creative studies' in early childhood education, social care or youth work is varied in presentation, title and duration, depending on the course or college attended. In general, however, this discipline aims to: 1) enable students to rediscover their own creativity and playfulness through participation in art, drama, music or dance and movement workshops; and 2) provide a variety of creative experiences, in the form of ice-breakers, games, sessions and workshops, for the professional 'tool box'. These tools, when combined with facilitation skills and confidence, become a catalyst for relationship development with any age group or ability. It is through this relationship that teaching, demonstrating, modelling and caring can occur. Here, we shall discuss the role of creative studies in the caring professions, examining why the focus of this creative practice is on the process and not on the product; why the activity is therapeutic, but not therapy.

Defining Caring Professions

Sociologists argue that when society moved from agrarianism to industry, the quality of relationships between people deteriorated, leading to increased feelings of loneliness, isolation and mistrust of others (Chriss, 1999; Gibbs and Gambrill, 2009). According to Krueger (1999), this change influenced the emergence of helping or caring professionals, who now fulfilled the support function previously provided by family, the Church or voluntary organisations. Caring professionals are defined by their ability to care for vulnerable others who 'must be maintained by the helping professional throughout the process of helping' (Skovholt, 2005:82). Chriss (1999:3) states that the caring professions include all those who provide 'services to marginal groups and an assortment of distressed individuals'. The caring professionals referred to in this book include social care workers, youth workers and early childcare workers, and one of the key links between them is that they all use creative activities to teach, demonstrate, model, intervene, spend time, have fun with and learn about the other.

Setting the Scene: What is Social Care?

Social care is a generic term that defines the practice of providing physical, emotional and/or psychological support to people with a variety of needs. Throughout the years, social care was defined by the Department of Health and Children (DOH) and the Irish Association of Social Care Educators (IASCE) as including the following tasks: providing a safe environment; meeting the needs of vulnerable people; providing a quality service that is planned and performed by professionals (Task Force on Child Care Services, 1980; Joint Committee on Social Care Professionals, n.d.). This definition evolved to include the ability to work in partnership and an acceptance of the whole person in a holistic and individual approach to practice (Share and McElwee, 2005c; O'Connor and Murphy, 2006). It is through the relationship between the professional and other that acceptance, partnership, safety and care are demonstrated and experienced (Fewster, 1990; Garfat, 1999; Krueger, 1999; Kennefick, 2003; Byrne and McHugh, 2005). Social care, historically a female occupation, has evolved from a low-status 'vocation' of helping people in need to the current professionalism of social care, largely due to the introduction of the Health and Social Care Professionals Act 2005. Today, social care environments include care for the elderly, care for people with a physical or intellectual disability, community care, family support and residential care for children and adults, to name but a few.

Social care attracts a variety of people from diverse backgrounds and life experiences (Ricks and Charlesworth, 2003). As well as requiring an interest in people, Share and McElwee (2005b:10) identified the personal qualities necessary for social care practice as 'reliability and trustworthiness, altruism; empathy, compassion and maturity'. Byrne and McHugh (2005) outlined other essential personal qualities, which include the ability to listen and the capacity to be honest and open.

What do Social Care Workers do?

Social care practice is exceptionally varied, depending on the type of service and the specific needs of the individual or group in question (Williams and Lalor, 2000). Within the practice of social care, the worker performs 'direct and indirect care', where tasks are carried out with, for and on behalf of others (Ainsworth and Fulcher, 1981; Anglin et al., 1990). In general, 'direct' tasks revolve around meeting the physical, emotional, social, educational and spiritual needs, which for some includes the normal experiences of mealtimes, school, homework, family visits, personal care and activities (Byrne and McHugh, 2005). It is in the doing of normal life experience that the core of social care practice is performed. The key-working role, where one or two workers are named to assist in the promotion of personal and individualised care, encourages this sharing of life experiences between both the worker and other (Byrne and McHugh, 2005).

Indirect care, or 'organisational activities', relates to the organisational design, or the environment in which the individual receives the service. It includes adhering to policies and procedures, filling out forms, writing care plans, programme planning and communicating with schools, social workers and other related personnel (Ainsworth and Fulcher, 1981; Anglin *et al.*, 1990; Byrne and McHugh, 2005).

What Training do Care Workers Receive?

The current nature of social care training and education was greatly influenced by childcare legislation, in particular the *Tuairim Report* (1966), the *Kennedy Report* (DOH, 1970), the *Task Force Report on Child Care Services* (1980), and the Child Care Act 1991 (Share and McElwee, 2005a). The education of social care workers has evolved from a one-year course in Kilkenny in 1971 (Byrne, 2000; Share and McElwee, 2005a) to a Bachelor of Arts degree in Applied Social Studies in Social Care, available from the Institutes of Technology (Athlone IT, Blanchardstown IT, Carlow IT, Cork IT, Dublin IT, Dundalk IT, Limerick IT, Sligo IT, Tallaght IT, Tralee IT, Waterford IT), from Carlow College and from the Open Training College.

There is a history of collaboration between the social care colleges, beginning with the *Irish Journal of Applied Social Studies* (IJASS) and the formation of the Irish Association of Social Care Educators (IASCE) in 1998. In an attempt to encourage this collaborative process, Perry Share (Sligo IT) developed the IASCE website, with a link to the Irish Social Care Gateway (Courtney, 2003). This evolved in 2009 into a social care-specific website: *www.socialstudies.ie*. Along with educational advancements in terms of support, the individual colleges are constantly enhancing their social care programmes, aiming to further meet the needs of the student, the employer and future service users. This book is direct evidence of the collaboration existing between the social care colleges of IASCE, the creative studies lecturers who work in them and the practitioners working on the ground.

Creativity in Social Care Practice and Education

As discussed earlier, direct care includes building attachments, developing a relationship, listening, cooking meals and engaging in play and creative activities together. Using the creative arts within the area of social care is not a new phenomenon. Social care management and staff have long known that art, drama and music are powerful tools for developing and maintaining relationships. Vander Ven (1999) discussed the role activity plays within practice, which she defined as Activity Theory. These activities, or everyday life experiences, may include going for a walk, playing cards or playing a game of football. Through participation in activities, the young person learns new skills, interests and ways of interacting.

Prior to becoming a social care lecturer, I worked as a residential social care practitioner with teenagers. During this period I used creative activities to form relationships with the young people, as an intervention for challenging behaviour (Lyons, 1998) and as a way of sharing life experiences or just to have fun together. I worked this way because it made sense to me. In 2008 I decided to find out, via the social care services, whether I was alone in this approach, or if creative activities had a recognised role to play in current service provision (Lyons, 2008). Thirty-five social care services responded to a postal questionnaire, and all stated that they used creative activities as part of their service provision (eighteen from disability services, six residential centres for children, three youth work services, two high support units and one each of the following: family support, women's refuge, drug treatment, after-school project, community development group and a school for visually impaired children). These findings are presented in Chapter 3 (page 39).

Workers learn about social care skills in their formal education and training, in which creative studies plays a vital role. The creative activities of art, drama and/or music and movement are taught as a module in the majority of Irish social care colleges. The selection of creative activities depends on the college, with drama and art being the most common; Tralee IT is the only social care programme offering the creative activity of dance. Some colleges combine the creative activities with recreation or sport options. The creative studies module is an experiential course, where students participate in creative activities, supported by lectures on the therapeutic benefits of using the creative arts. For the social care student, participation in the creative arts can provide opportunities for self-awareness, especially when students are encouraged to express themselves in new and often challenging ways. The theoretical framework for the creative module includes, among other elements, the theory of creativity, activity theory, facilitation skills, children's development through art, reflection and self-awareness, and the therapeutic benefits of using the creative arts.

In creative studies training, workshops in art, drama and music are designed to give students practical creative skills and creative facilitation skills and to enhance students' self-awareness through creative expression. The creative studies course is considered an essential component of the overall training of the social care student in terms of their practical skill improvement, personal development and enhanced self-awareness. According to the Higher Education Training Awards Council's (HETAC) *Draft Document for the Award Standards on Social Care Work 2009*, creative and recreation practice is listed as an essential theoretical concept and students are required to demonstrate 'specialised technical, creative or conceptual skills or tools', to respond in a creative way to individual needs, and to perform 'creative and non-routine activities' (HETAC, 2009:5–11).

The following is an example of the content of a creative studies course taught over three years and incorporating the creative arts of art, drama and music.

1   Creative Studies, Year One: students learn about the various creative arts through participating in experiential workshops. The workshops are designed to encourage the development of interpersonal skills, communication and the skill of reflecting on practice. The drama element focuses on assertiveness, confidence and self-awareness, enabling students to practise standing up for themselves and leading others.

2   Creative Studies, Year Two: students learn to facilitate a creative experience with different groups, for example disabled people, young people or elderly participants. Each student is encouraged to draw on the experiences of year one, especially in how to design his/her programme plan.

3   Creative Studies, Year Three: the aim of this final year is to facilitate self-learning through participation in experiential workshops. The creative arts programme also aims to encourage students to become comfortable in their own skin in all situations, whether engaging with others on the first day of placement or facilitating a group experience. Learning to become comfortable requires self-learning through reflection, thus the student is asked to explore his/her personal journey through the creative process.

Setting the Scene: What is Early Childhood Care?

Early childhood refers to the development of children from 0 to 6 years of age, cared for in services that include: day care crèches (0–3 years+); nursery/Montessori schools (3–5 years); preschool, i.e. home playgroups and community play groups (3–5 years); Early Start programmes (3–5 years); and primary schools, both junior and senior infants (4–6 years) (Douglas and Horgan, 2000). Early Start was a government initiative set up to support early learners from disadvantaged backgrounds, and the Citizens' Information Bureau (2009) records that there are approximately 1,400 children attending Early Start programmes in forty primary schools across Ireland. According to the 2007 Quarterly National Household Survey, the percentage of pre-school children attending childcare increased from 42 per cent to 48 per cent. The most popular facilities include crèches, Montessori and playgroups, followed by relatives, a nanny or childminder (Central Statistics Office (CSO), 2009).

The discussion papers by Horgan and Douglas (1998) and by Douglas and Horgan (2000) gave recommendations for the development and recognition of early childhood, stressing the importance of early childhood education for young children's development. However, it appears that the sector is still 'at the crossroads' (Douglas and Horgan, 2000:192), with the proposed closure of the Centre for Early Childhood Development and Education (CECDE) in November 2009. The centre, established in 2002, was a joint project between the Dublin Institute of Technology and St Patrick's College, Drumcondra, for the development and structuring of essential early education services. This proposed scaling back of services is taking place against a background whereby Ireland recently appeared in joint last place in UNICEF's *Report Card 8* (2008), a league table outlining which of the top twenty-five OECD (Organisation for Economic Co-operation and Development) countries have implemented the ten early childhood education 'benchmarks' (Adamson, 2008). Ireland met only one standard on UNICEF's league table: 50 per cent of staff in accredited facilities are being trained to an approved standard. Early childhood care and education is a real experience for 48 per cent of Irish children, or 82,000 families, who are cared for and educated by early childhood workers (CSO, 2009). These workers carry out a multitude of tasks and deal with the range of experiences that arise when working with young children and their families.

What do Early Childhood Workers do?

Early childhood workers are employed in day care facilities, in Montessori schools, in play groups or in primary schools, either as teachers or as Early Start leaders. Caring for children between the ages of nought and six years is a very demanding role, one that requires a variety of skills and qualities, irrespective of the service. Ebbeck and Waniganayake (2003:206) state that the relationship formed between the child and the worker, or between the worker and the family, which they define as a 'sound relationship based on open communication, trust and confidentiality', is crucial for successful practice. It is through this relationship that the worker performs the many tasks of early childhood care, including teaching academic skills, language development, learning how children learn, dealing with challenging behaviour, working in stressful situations and developing solid relationships with children and parents. Encouraging the child's social and emotional development is also an essential task for the worker, and is achieved through social play, social skills training and direct one-to-one activities. Effective early childhood workers have an understanding of child development and anti-discriminatory practice, and can identify when a child needs extra assistance for their social, emotional or cognitive development.

Ebbeck and Waniganayake (2003:30) state that the essential qualities of early childhood workers include being 'kind, warm, friendly, nurturing, sympathetic, patient, self-aware, rational, logical, goal orientated, proactive, assertive, professional, confident, visionary and influential', because to the young people in their care they are a model, a guide and a mentor. Some of these qualities are intrinsic to the person, but others can be enhanced through quality education programmes that include supervised and appropriate placement experiences.

What Training do They Receive?

As well as a variety of early care facilities on offer in Ireland, there are also variables in the types of course and qualification open to workers in this field. The training courses 'are a mixture of care and education—the emphasis reflecting the philosophy of the core providers' (Douglas and Horgan, 2000:196). As a result, many different types of qualification are held by workers in crèches and playgroups, although primary schools and Montessoris require more specific training. Below is a sample of the types of training available, and the institutions where various courses are offered (see Table 1.1), to give some idea of the diversity and range of relevant programmes available.

- Primary-school teachers: BA in Education (Primary).

- Montessori schools: Nursery programme (for children aged 0–6 yrs); Junior Course (for children aged 6–9 years); Primary Teaching Course (for children aged 9–12 years).

- Early Childhood Education: HETAC, Levels 7 and 8; Further Education Training Awards Council (FETAC), Levels 5 and 6. There is a selection of programmes with similar titles to those offered at Levels 7 and 8, which are available in further education facilities all over Ireland. Athlone IT, for example, offers a Higher Certificate in Childcare Supervisory Management at Level 6, which is designed specifically for the managers of crèches and playgroups.

- Nursery Nursing: Diploma in Nursery Nursing from the Council for Awards in Children's Care and Education (CACHE).

Title of Course	University or Institute of Technology
Early Childhood Studies	University College Cork
	Waterford IT
	Dundalk IT
	Sligo IT
Early Childhood Care and Education	Blanchardstown IT
	Tralee IT
	Mary Immaculate College
	Cork IT
Early Childhood Education	Dublin IT
Early Childhood Education and Care	Carlow IT
BSc in Early Childhood Care, Health and Education	Letterkenny IT

Table 1.1: Early childhood care courses offered by third-level institutions.

As well as differences in awarding body, level of qualification and title of course, there are also discrepancies between the course durations, which modules are covered and to what depth, and how much placement experience is required (Douglas and Horgan, 2000). Despite the wide range of programmes on offer, one common theme that connects them is a recognition of the role of play and/or activity in the development of the early learner.

Creativity in Early Childhood Practice and Education

Children of all ages, and especially those under six years, engage in all kinds of creative activities as a way of exploring the world. According to Staples New and Cochran (2007:164), creativity is used in early childhood education as a 'vehicle for learning' and to help children 'develop social competence'. Curtis and O'Hagan (2003:viii) state that in modern early childhood education there is a move away from process learning towards 'end product' curricula for young learners, which is possibly due to a perceived requirement of showing the parent what the child has produced during the day. However, the authors stress that being creative through free play is essential for the child's verbal, social and intellectual development.

Before the age of two years, on average, children engage in solitary play. After reaching their second birthday they begin to socialise through play with other children, and by three years they can 'engage in dramatic play sequences' through role play, whereby 'they take on a whole range of characters both real and fictional' (Curtis and O'Hagan, 2003:119).

According to Smilansky and Shefataya (1990:22), this socio-dramatic play occurs when a child engages in the following six stages: 'child takes on a role, they make believe with toys, they verbally make believe on actions and situations, they stay in role for at least 10 minutes, interaction occurs with another child, and there is verbal interaction related to the play'. This socio-dramatic play is beneficial for children because it helps them to improve and enhance their concentration, communication, self-esteem, self-awareness, empathy, creativity and flexibility (Curtis and O'Hagan, 2003). It is also essential for emotional problem-solving and development, as it allows children to explore and resolve their issues and worries through play. Article 31 of the United Nations Convention on the Rights of the Child (1989) refers to the importance of activity and play in a child's life:

'Parties recognise the right of the child to rest and leisure, to engage in play and recreational activities appropriate to the age of the child and to participate freely in cultural life and the arts.'

'Parties shall respect and promote the right of the child to participate fully in cultural and artistic life and shall encourage the provision of appropriate and equal opportunities for cultural, artistic, recreational and leisure activity.'

The essential role of creativity is recognised in the education of students on the Bachelor of Arts (Hons) course in Early Childhood Education. Using the Dublin Institute of Technology as an example, in their first year students complete two creative modules: Art 1 and Drama 1. They then choose either Art 2 or Drama 2 for their second year, which they complete in year three: Art 3 or Drama 3. In this way the creative role is sustained throughout the training period as an important central concept and tool.

> **Task**
> *Can you remember any creative experience you had during your early years? What did you make or do?*

Setting the Scene: What is Youth Work?

Youth work is the practice of working predominantly with teenagers in services designed specifically to meet their needs. The Youth Work Act 2001 defined this practice as 'a planned programme of education for the purpose of aiding and enhancing the personal and social development of young persons through their voluntary participation' (Department of Education and Science, 2001b:7). Central to this definition is the educational emphasis, which aims to support existing education programmes in a 'non-formal or informal' way (Devlin, 2009), and the fact that the young people participate voluntarily. The Act defines young people as anyone under the age of twenty-five years; however, youth work focuses primarily on young people between the ages of ten and twenty years. The voluntary nature of participation is relevant to both the young people attending and to those running the service. According to the Youth Work Ireland *Annual Report* (2008), 75,000 young people are enrolled in 550 youth clubs, facilitated by 7,000 volunteer workers and 1,000 paid workers.

Youth work originally evolved from society's need to 'save' or 'rescue' troubled young people (Devlin, 2009). The focus on young people in particular was inspired by the desire to promote a 'way of thinking' into the future, which in the case of Ireland was a Roman Catholic ethos: 'Historically, the Churches set up most of the' youth associations ... including 'the various scouting and guiding organisations' (Devlin, 2009:367). The State played a secondary role to the Church, serving primarily as a funding agent. Examples of youth work organisations and representative bodies include Catholic Youth Care, Foróige, Youth Work Ireland, Ógra Chorcaí, Boy Scouts and Girl Scouts and the National Youth Council of Ireland (NYCI). These youth services are funded by the Department of Education and Science, although some organisations also apply for National Lottery funding or charity donations to subsidise the implementation of specific programmes. Youth workers may be found in youth clubs, youth information centres, drug services, Scouts and Guides and after-school projects.

What do Youth Workers do?

According to Devlin (2009:371), youth workers 'are primarily concerned with the education and development, personal and social, of young people'. As the young person's participation in the service is voluntary, the youth workers are reliant on the attractiveness and appropriateness of the programmes and activities on offer. The learning and development of young people is enhanced through planned activities, where the message is learned through participation in a relevant programme that is of interest to the young person. The relationship between the young person and the youth worker is central to the retention of voluntary participants. Youth workers develop programmes with the full involvement of the young people, which enhances the potential success of the programme and completion of the set outcomes. Youth workers focus on the process of encouraging young people to learn to work together, to communicate effectively and to develop empathy and self-awareness.

Possible programmes include health and nutrition, sexual heath, information technology skills, personal hygiene, parenting skills, art and craft activities and social outings. The programmes have an educational purpose, but also include social and emotional aims such as confidence-building, team work, self-esteem, self-awareness, self-advocacy, self-empowerment, social skills and communication skills. There is also a community and social dimension to youth work in that an awareness of society, pro-social attitudes and a sense of belonging to a community are all promoted (Devlin, 2009).

What Training do They Receive?

As discussed, the majority of youth workers are unpaid volunteers, which means the minimum training for youth work may be limited to in-house training programmes. In June 2009 the Ballymun Regional Youth Resource advertised for a youth worker to work through drama and specified a qualification in youth and community work or equivalent, or three years' experience. This shows that a recognised youth work qualification is desired, but not required, at this point. However, third-level qualifications in youth work can be obtained from various institutions, for example: BA in Youth and Community Studies from National University of Ireland (NUI), Maynooth; BA in Youth and Community Work Practice from Tralee IT; BA in Social and Community Development from Blanchardstown IT; BA in Community Youth Work from Dundalk IT; and BA in Youth and Community Studies from University College Cork. Youth work education is also provided at post-Leaving Certificate level and at FETAC Levels 5 and 6 throughout Ireland.

Creativity in Youth Work Practice and Education

The creative arts are very prevalent in youth work and are supported by government initiatives and funding. One such initiative was the setting up of the Arts Council in 1981, a national agency for the promotion, support and funding of the arts. The Arts Council is the vehicle through which community groups can apply for Irish and European funding for the arts. The NYCI Arts Programme was established as a result of the recommendations of a report published in 1993, *Making Youth Arts Work*. The Council acts as an advocate for youth arts in Ireland and has developed programmes to support the arts in non-formal settings, for example the Artist in Youth Work Scheme. Support for the arts in youth work was also ratified in the National Youth Work Development Plan 2003–2007, which stated that youth services should include 'creative, artistic, and cultural or language-based programmes and activities' (Department of Education and Science, 2003:21).

The extensive role of creativity and the arts in youth work practice is also reflected in the training of youth workers. In the Liberties College, Dublin, a student can study the Community Arts module as part of a FETAC Level 5 in Youth and Community Work. In NUI Maynooth, students of the BA (Hons) in Youth and Community Work study Community and Youth Arts in their first year. Students studying for a BA in Youth and Community Work Practice at Tralee IT undertake Creative Practice in each of the three years of their training.

The NYCI Certificate in Youth Arts is a one-year programme delivered in NUI Maynooth and is the first of its kind in Ireland. This training programme is a follow-on from the Youth Arts Programme, a collaboration between the NYCI, the Minister for Children and Youth Affairs and the Arts Council. The course is designed to provide youth workers with specific training in the arts in order to facilitate the development of creativity and appreciation of the arts in youth work practice. According to the course prospectus, students learn how to facilitate creative activities, how to plan, design and deliver programmes, to understand the role of youth arts in the development of young people and to become more self-aware and reflective.

> **Task**
>
> *Can you remember any creative activity you were involved in as a youth? Was it within a youth project? What did you make and what was the programme aiming to achieve?*

Creativity and the Placement Experience

Social Care, Early Childhood Care and Youth Work are all applied courses, thus the students must leave the structured environment of the college to apply their knowledge and practice their skills within an approved service. The practice placement gives students the opportunity to observe practitioners in their working environment, to perform supervised tasks and to learn the skill of reflecting on their experiences. Throughout the placement process the college tutor, student and placement supervisor 'are central to the student's placement experience and form a triad in practical and academic communication' (Lalor and Doyle, 2005:145). Learning is enhanced through the ongoing supervision provided by the supervisor/practice teacher (Batchelor and Boutland, 1996; Hanlon *et al.*, 2006).

While on placement, the amount of time spent working within the agency varies depending on which year the student is in, which course he/she is doing and which college he/she attends. As well as variations in the structure and length of placements, there are also inconsistencies in terms of what constitutes an appropriate placement, the level of supervision provided and the support provided to the student by the college (Byrne, 2000). Douglas and Horgan (2000) compared the placement hours of early childhood workers and outlined a vast difference in student placement hours, from zero hours on the Irish Preschool Playgroup Association's twenty-hour introductory training programme, to six to twelve hours per week for three years on the BA in Early Childhood Education, to 840 hours for the CACHE Diploma in Nursery Nursing. In the youth work sector placements range from 'observation visits' to youth and community settings, up to the two twelve-week, supervised placements in approved youth and community settings required for the BA in Community and Youth Work from NUI Maynooth. In social care, each of the Institutes of Technology has supervised placements, which consist of an average of thirty hours per week for twenty-five weeks during the course of training.

Doyle and Lalor (2009) state that the role of placements is to enhance a student's ability to relate, observe, communicate, understand needs, keep records and make decisions. One past pupil of DIT, Danielle, recalled her experience of placement (featured in Doyle and Lalor, 2009:175): 'I could not do certain aspects of the work, I could spend quality time listening and doing art and drama activities with the children.' Danielle's experience is not unique: the creative arts provide students on placement with an opportunity to develop relationships while sharing a creative experience. This is especially relevant in the first few weeks of placement, when students often feel unsure of their role. Engaging in creative activities encourages a 'getting to know you' phase without the pressure of asking questions. Being creative is potentially a fun and relaxing experience for both the student and the participant, which helps students to feel more at home and self-confident in this new environment.

Creative Problem-solvers

According to Carl Rogers (1961), the modern education system encourages conformity and undervalues creative and original thinkers. Furthermore, informal learning environments and recreation activities are becoming more passive, rather than active; therefore students are doing and thinking less than ever before (Rogers, 1961; Sternberg, 1999; Malchiodi, 2006). Working with people in any of the three caring professions is predominantly about problem-solving while working with individual needs in diverse situations. It requires that the worker be a creative thinker and problem-solver, with the ability to 'think outside' the situation, drawing on theory, a reflection on past learning and an understanding of self in the given situation, all while maintaining eye contact, displaying appropriate body language and remaining both physically and mentally present in the situation. Since a vast number of skills are required for this type of work, creative expression and creative activities are an essential part of the education of caring professionals in Ireland.

Process Versus End Product

In order to produce art, a process must be followed before an end is reached, which is referred to as the 'end product'. Creative activities can be process-based, product-based or both. Process-based refers to the practice of encouraging participants to explore the materials and to make decisions about the structure, content and finish of the art activity. Product-based activities are described in early childhood education as fixed activities, for example colouring in pages or using shaped cutting tools on clay or pastry. The participant does not make decisions regarding the stages of engagement in the activity and there is conformity in the finish. Product-based activities can be beneficial for some participants, especially those who require consistency or routine. They can also be used as an 'ice-breaker', affording the participant the time needed to gain the confidence needed for them to be able to engage in their own creative piece. In the caring professions, however, creativity is more about the process that the participant engages in than the product that is produced at the end.

According to Mayesky (2004), the main focus of all creative activities should be the process, which means the worker stays back and does not intervene with the image in order to make a 'pretty end product'. Caring professionals use creative activities purposefully, where the focus is not on the end product but on the potential benefits of engaging in the activity. The end product, if anything is produced, is the bonus, not the intention.

Assessment of Creative Studies

Creative Studies is assessed in different ways depending on the college and the year of study. The various tools of assessment include essays, reflective journals and exams. The reflective learning described within the 'reflective journal', often referred to as the 'creative journal', involves the process of contemplation, reflective skills and an understanding of the role of experiential learning (Jarvis, 1997). The role of this learning experience evolved through the work of Shulman (1988), Schon (1983) and Boud *et al.*, (1995). Reflective learning acknowledges that the worker will need to respond to unique situations and thus needs to understand how theory underpins practice (Schon, 1987).

In the reflective journal students are assessed on their ability to accurately reflect on the creative experiences in class as a prerequisite for completion of this learning module. According to Croton (2000:92), the journal provides evidence of the student's ability to transfer theoretical and personal knowledge to practice, but 'there must be clarity as to whether it is content or the ability to write that is being tested'. The ability to write competently about practice encompasses an ability to be self-aware in relation to reflecting on experiences. In order to participate fully in the Creative Studies module, students may need to undo some of the lessons from their previous creative experiences in

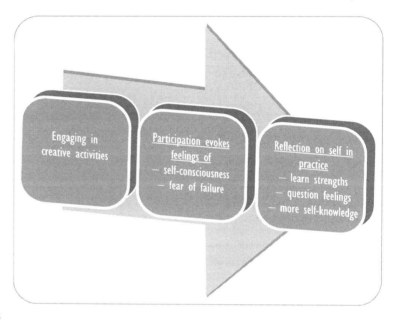

order to learn to accept that they are creative and that engaging in creative activities will help them learn about themselves.

You are Not Art Therapists!

As a social care lecturer I often visit students on placement, only to hear how they 'performed art therapy' on some unsuspecting and vulnerable individuals. Fortunately, in the majority of cases the student was merely trying to describe how he/she used art as an intervention, rather than actual art therapy, while on placement. So, to ensure that everyone is clear on the distinction between the two practices, they are discussed here in greater detail.

Social care, youth work and early childhood students and practitioners use the creative arts therapeutically in practice, which differs greatly from the practice of doing creative arts therapy, for example art therapy, music therapy or drama therapy. According to the *Oxford English Dictionary,* the definition of 'therapeutic' is 'connected with healing ... having a good general effect on the body or the mind' (Crowther, 1995:1238) and the definition of 'therapy' is 'Any treatment designed to improve a health problem or disability or to cure an illness' (Crowther, 1995:1238).

Caring professionals who are using creative activities in practice need to know what aspects of art-making can be used without straying into 'therapy'. Central to this understanding is the 'intention' behind the activity. Caring professionals intend for the participant to have a therapeutic experience, where they feel happy, have fun, express themselves, learn a new skill and gain confidence. In contrast, the 'intention' for creative arts therapists is to use the art materials as part of a specific treatment designed to address a set of symptoms or to deliver prescribed positive outcomes for the person. The intention of therapy is also for the participant to use the images created to learn more about themselves, in other words as a language to decipher their own psychosis. The differences between the two modes of practice are outlined in Table 1.2, below, under the following subheadings: aims/purpose; methods/interventions; outcomes/change; role of relationship; training.

	Aims/ Purpose	Methods/ Interventions	Outcomes/ Change	Role of Relationship	Training
Creative Arts Therapy	— Better understanding and awareness of self. — Exploring unconscious thoughts and feelings.	— Uses all art materials, dance, drama, movement and music. — Can be direct (with clear instructions given) or indirect (no instructions—free expression).	— New awareness of self. — Greater understanding of issues, feelings and thoughts. — New coping mechanisms emerge to deal with issues.	— Triangular relationship (therapist helps client to develop a relationship with his/her own images).	— Postgraduate training in art, drama or music therapy. — Training includes experience of personal therapy, theory on psychotherapy and use of creative material.
Therapeutic Use of Creative Arts	— Share life space while doing an activity together. — Purposeful use of creative materials as an intervention. — Have fun.	— Uses all art material, dance, drama, movement and music.	— Based on purpose of intervention. — Could include increased motor skills, relationships development with staff and peers, increased confidence, increased self-esteem.	— Activities used for relationship development between worker and participant. —Encourages communication, establishes rapport.	— Undergraduate courses in social care, community studies or early childhood care. — Courses that include modules in creative studies.

Table 1.2: Comparing creative arts therapy with the therapeutic use of creative arts.

Although caring professionals use the same materials as creative arts therapists, the aims, purpose, intent and outcomes are different. A caring professional and a young person in his/her care may spend the afternoon drawing pictures together. In this example scenario the aims of the activity are: a) to spend quality time together; b) to further develop their relationship; c) to explore how the young person is getting on at school and at home. The intervention (drawing pictures) directs the attention of the participant away from the one-to-one closeness of the situation. The two can sit together in silence, or chat away, but importantly the focus does not feel like 'information-gathering'.

The essential traits needed in order to engage in creative activities as part of your practice include patience, a sense of humour, confidence, problem-solving skills, facilitation skills, creative skills (i.e. knowledge of games and activities), flexibility and an interest in being creative. Creative training should provide the practitioner with creative skills and with a knowledge of the benefits of using these skills and also, and most important, with a clear definition of the difference between using the creative arts as a caring professional and using the creative arts as a therapist. The following chapters will provide information on creative facilitation skills and creative activities, but you, the reader, will have to provide the patience, confidence and sense of humour that are also needed yourself.

Chapter Summary

▶   The caring professions of social care, youth work and early childhood care are similar because they all use the relationship as a catalyst for practice, they are applied and hands-on in practice and they use creative activities to teach, share, have fun, relate, communicate and benefit those in their care.

▶   Creative Studies (art, dance, drama and music) is a module in social care, early childhood education and youth work courses.

▶   Creative studies teaches students to accept their creative expression without judgment, to facilitate creative experiences with others and to feel comfortable when faced with new people, varied experiences and challenging tasks and decisions.

▶   The 'Creative Studies' module is assessed through the reflective journal, which requires students to have the ability to reflect on their experiences and understand how these experiences have impacted on the self.

▶   Placement is an important component in the education of caring professionals because it allows students to practise how to engage creatively with others.

▶   To engage in the creative studies class students must understand and accept that the process is more important than the end product.

▶   Finally, on completion of the creative studies course the student will be a worker in a caring profession who has the skills to encourage creative expression in others. The student will *not* be a creative arts therapist, which is a separate and distinct type of practice.

TWO

Creative Group Facilitation

Paul Timoney

SNAPSHOT

▶ Introduction to creative group facilitation.

▶ Choosing a suitable activity.

▶ Preparation and planning.

▶ Presenting the activity.

▶ Reflection and personal evaluation.

Introduction

Art activities promote exploratory and experiential types of learning that encourage a diverse range of individualistic approaches to problem-solving. By engaging with materials in an effort to create visually expressive two- and three-dimensional objects, participants are afforded a forum for the attainment of knowledge through personal discovery. It is important that facilitators appreciate the value of processes that do not necessarily lead to 'finished pieces' and that they try to encourage the people in their care to do the same. The aspirations that ought to be most prevalent in the art activity are the

development of participants' curiosity, visual awareness, open-mindedness, physical and psychological well-being and self-esteem.

Good facilitators should be enthusiastic about the creative arts and have the ability to introduce activities within a context that is relevant to the group with whom they are working. The skill that is most integral to this process is communication, in particular the ability to assimilate information presented by participants both in their artwork and during discussion. Through recognition of the abilities and interests of one's 'clients', the caring professional can seek to devise projects that are both stimulating and challenging for those involved. This is why it is generally most effective to try to generate an atmosphere that is informal, industrious and calm. This kind of environment tends to be conducive to openness and creativity. Evaluation and reflection play important roles in creative group facilitation and can be utilised to reiterate learning objectives, to influence the direction of artwork and to explore any personal issues that may arise.

How to Prepare

Before you can create a space where those in your care can feel comfortable expressing themselves through the medium of art, it is important to prepare. You can begin 'getting to know' the people who will be participating in your activity before you meet them. Here are some questions that can help you to gather useful information about their interests and abilities. The answers to these questions will direct you towards the types of activity that will seem most suitable and enticing.

- How many people are in the group?
- What are their ages?
- What is their gender?
- Have they experienced art activities before?
- What have they enjoyed/not enjoyed?
- What sort of materials have they worked with?
- Can you see some of their artwork?
- Do they like music?
- Do they like sports?
- Do they like animals and nature?
- Do they have favourite books, magazines, TV shows or video games?
- Are they verbal and/or do they understand the language that you speak?
- Do they have intellectual, physical or psychological needs that you should consider?
- Do the group members know each other and get along well?
- Do they prefer to work individually or in small groups?

What do You Hope to Achieve?

Art activities can be used to achieve a variety of objectives. Try to identify the 'needs' of the people you are working with and then choose and adapt an activity accordingly. Would the group benefit from an activity that helps to promote team building, for example? Would it be useful to engage with something that would help to develop participants' fine motor skills or memory? Are there issues that they could explore, such as bullying, sexuality, grief, romance, health, safety, through the medium of art? Would it be advantageous to do something imaginative and fun? How about learning a new skill or technique and answering a creative challenge that could boost confidence and self-esteem?

It is important to set realistic goals for yourself and for the people you work with. Facilitating in care situations requires sensitivity and patience. Tasks that may seem relatively simple to many can require a great deal of effort and practice for others. To pour one's own paint, or to choose a particular coloured pencil, or to touch an unfamiliar material can be extremely difficult and worthwhile aspirations for some individuals.

When you have completed an activity with a group, you should evaluate your level of success in achieving your objectives. Reflecting upon your experiences in a focused way is key both to planning your next activity and your development as a practitioner.

Making an activity relevant

Imagine that you been invited to facilitate an art activity with a group whom you have not yet met. You are directed to explore the theme of 'personal identity'. You discover upon reading the answers to your 'questionnaire' that the participants are five children (three boys and two girls) aged between nine and eleven. They all indicate that they are fans of soccer. You could use this information to help you to begin a discussion around the topic of 'identity' by showing them examples of various soccer team logos and badges. You could talk with them about the images and colours that these designs utilise and consider what they suggest about the 'personality' or identity' of the clubs they represent. This kind of conversation could act as a starting point for an activity where the participants make a badge or a logo about 'themselves'.

If the group were apathetic towards soccer, they would hardly find that particular avenue of exploration stimulating. However, you could easily apply a similar formula to something else that they did like. So, if you discovered instead that they were interested in things to do with animals and nature, you could make 'animals and nature' your starting point. You could chat about various animals and their associated characteristics. For instance, lions are considered to be 'powerful' and 'majestic', while donkeys are supposedly 'stubborn' and monkeys 'playful' and 'cheeky'. This discussion could be an early step towards drawing, painting or sculpting an animal that represents some of each participant's personality traits. It could be a lot of fun to make up new animals using an amalgamation of already existing animal parts.

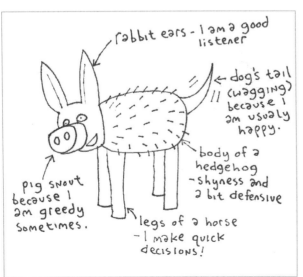

Both approaches lead to an exploration of the theme of 'personal identity'. Though they have different starting points that relate to the contrasting interests of the respective groups, they can manage to satisfy the same objective.

Activities to Avoid or to be Wary of

Information you gather via the questionnaire or through working with a group may suggest that there are certain themes you might best avoid or activities you should alter. If you find out that a member of your group is dealing with difficulties in their home life or is coping with grief over the loss of a relative, you have to be very cautious about introducing an activity with a family-related theme. If the group you are working with have issues with mobility, you might need to adapt an activity in order to make it workable. For example, Body Islands usually entails having individuals lie down on large sheets of paper while their partners trace around them. An alternative method of achieving a similar body shape, but which requires less physical dexterity, is to draw the outlines of shadows cast when people move in front of a strong light source. If you discovered that the people in a group did not get along very well, you should be wary of projects that emphasise working together. You could certainly try to address their issues through the medium of art and even try to progress towards activities that require ever-increasing levels of co-operation, but it would be important that you do so in a way that is careful and sensitive.

Working from your Strengths

One of the best ways to ensure that you facilitate effectively is to choose activities that genuinely excite you. Good, creative group facilitators should constantly aim to expand their repertoires and expose themselves to new activities by thinking, reading, learning, taking part in workshops and talking to other facilitators about their experiences. There will always be certain activities that appeal to you more than others. These are the activities that you should use. Convincing participants to embrace an activity that you like to do is much easier than trying to get them involved in something that you don't believe in. Also, when you know an activity well there is little chance of somebody asking you a question that you will not be able to answer.

Pitching your Activity

Learning to 'pitch' activities correctly so they are neither too easy nor too difficult is also important. If a task is overly simplistic, participants may feel bored, patronised and uninterested. If a task seems too difficult, they may be intimidated, self-conscious and disengaged.

Many artists and creative people describe their creative development as a journey. To a large extent your function as a creative group facilitator is to help those who participate in your activities to gain greater freedom to move along on their own 'creative journeys'. You can assist them to do so by offering skills, techniques and experiences that will develop their abilities and confidence to be expressive. For example, if somebody has only a little familiarity with painting and you teach them how to mix blue and yellow to make green, you have helped to broaden their 'artistic vocabulary' slightly because where before they may have had access to only two colours, now they have three. If, for some reason, they need the colour green in order to describe the appearance of a landscape or to express a feeling or emotion, they will now have it more readily and so they are freer to move along on their 'creative journey'.

The reason that correctly 'pitching' your activity is integral to the facilitation process is that it accounts for progress that a person has already made. If you were to try to show a very experienced painter something as basic as how to mix colours, he/she would probably not have very much interest in listening to you.

It is often the case, however, that the same activity can be approached in a variety of more or less sophisticated ways. It is important to note here that the term 'sophisticated' does not imply 'better', 'more beautiful' or 'more praiseworthy'. Some of the world's greatest art masterpieces are utterly unsophisticated. It simply means that there are countless creative approaches to most art activities and they may all be equally valid.

For example, if the task involved drawing a teacup, some people might enjoy using lines, perspective and shading to represent its shapes, forms, textures and proportions as accurately as they possibly could. Others might prefer to use expressive marks and random or imagined colours to create an image that may be exciting and full of energy … but bear only scant resemblance to the teacup.

They Would Never do That!

Gathering information about the group with whom you are working does not mean that you should fall prey to stereotypical assumptions about what they would or would not enjoy and benefit from doing. As you develop a trusting relationship with the people that you work with, they will be more likely to try things that might seem outside the bounds of usual age/gender/cultural expectations. A group of boys might love learning to knit or weave, for example. A group of elderly people might really appreciate an introduction to abstract found-object sculpture. It is essential to keep an open mind throughout.

Deciding on an activity—summary

The things to consider most carefully when coming to a decision about which activity or activities to choose are the group's interests and abilities, physical and psychological issues and your personal strengths and interests.

In fact, you can usually choose from any number of activities and they can all work well in an atmosphere where people feel secure and permitted to explore their own approach.

Here is an example an of an activity that I have used with groups (both children and adults) when meeting them for the very first time.

Activity example

CARS, ROADS AND SCRIBBLES (PLUS BUILDINGS AND BIRDS)

This is an activity in which participants make drawings and/or paintings that are attached together using glue and strong tape to make one large 'group landscape'. It is presented in language that one might use to address a group.

There are five separate tasks that each group member can choose from …

1. 'We need roads. You can make any type of road you wish—motorways, dirt tracks … straight, bendy, thin, wide … based on real roads or completely imaginary. The only stipulation is that they need to be drawn or painted from above. They will be cut out using scissors when you are finished, so there is no need to work on a background. Focus on the road itself.'

2. (I show an example of a pre-made car which is created using cut-out pieces of coloured card.) 'We also need plenty of cars and other vehicles. Again, they can be based on cars, trucks, vans, etc. that you have seen before … or you can invent some new and weird forms of transport if you wish. We will be gluing the cars onto the roads when they are finished.'

3. 'We also need scribbles. Lots of scribbles. These will be the background to the mural that we are hoping to make. Choose any colours that you like and use whatever materials you wish, but cover all the paper that you are scribbling on in scribbles. Leave no trace of the colour of the page.'

4. 'Buildings—again, these can be any type of building you wish. Schools, churches, hospitals, hotels, houses or huts. Can anyone think of any others? And they can be real or pretend.'

5. 'Finally—birds. The birds are also going to be cut out, so again there is no need for any background. As you have probably guessed, you can have any type of bird you like … except magpies … I really don't like magpies … I'm just kidding. You can make any type of real or made-up bird that you feel like making.'

The reason that this activity tends to work well is that it offers a wide range of options. People who feel reasonably confident in their creative abilities can begin by making 'roads', 'birds' or 'buildings'. 'Cars' can be done by participants who feel fairly secure, but who prefer to start with a task that is a bit more directed and therefore allows less scope for personal interpretation and self-criticism. Scribbles can be done by almost anybody and so offer a very safe initiation into the process of making art. This activity also tends to be a lot of fun and involves a symbolic bringing together of the people as their work is combined. As the activity progresses and 'scribblers' become more comfortable, they usually take on one of the other tasks. Also, people often introduce their own elements, such as roundabouts, traffic lights, animals, insects, spaceships, etc., and they can all become part of one large collaborative mural.

More on Preparation

Setting up the art room

If you are choosing a room in which to facilitate art activities, aim for a space that is sufficiently large, quiet and well lit. The presence of one or more sinks is a distinct advantage so that you have access to water for painting and cleaning. Non-absorbent floor coverings and tabletops are also desirable. If you are not sharing the room with any other facilitators, you may choose to allow the space to become a little bit messy. This can actually be conducive to the creative process. If the work area is pristine, participants may feel restricted by the implied expectation to keep it that way, but a few paint splashes here and there suggest that they do not have to be 'too' careful.

Useful things to have in the room are: plenty of materials; a large box containing odds and ends, such as scrap cloth, buttons, corks, bottle tops and other sundry stuff; a first aid kit; aprons or large shirts; disposable gloves; kitchen towels; baby wipes; hand soap; old magazines; newspapers and calendars; and a music-playing device of some sort.

The way you set up the workspace is significant. Placing tables or easels in a somewhat circular arrangement can help to convey an open, friendly and communicative atmosphere. It also provides a central focal point where you can set up a model or objects for a still-life. However, the centre of a circle is usually not a very useful place for you to deliver a demonstration or present visual aids (i.e. images or objects that can help participants to better understand an activity) because you can only face a few people at any one time. For demos and group discussions it is more advantageous for you to keep a space for yourself on the circle to ensure that everybody can see what you are doing.

Some activities work most effectively when people can operate together in separate, smaller groups, so you can re-jig the workstations accordingly for different projects.

A number of people make art most comfortably when they feel that they have privacy and so might prefer to segregate themselves somewhat. This is particularly true for those who are very sensitive to issues regarding personal space. It is not uncommon to meet such people whilst facilitating in social care situations. Some may even tend to react aggressively when others enter or linger within their close vicinity. It is very important to concern yourself with the safety and comfort of those who participate in your activities. If you feel restricted by the limitations of your designated art room, consider finding a more suitable alternative, including floor and wall spaces as potential work surfaces, or splitting up the group and seeing individuals or sub-groups at separate times.

Safety in the art room

Always keep a first aid kit in the art room. If you are facilitating with a group in a day care centre, hospital or certain other institutions, there will be medically trained staff nearby, so be aware of what procedure you should take in order to contact them quickly if you need to. Always keep potentially dangerous sharp or toxic materials out of reach on a high shelf or in a locked press, if necessary.

If you are working with people who have a lot of difficulty using scissors, prepare any 'cutting out' *before* the activity begins.

Working with other staff

In many 'care situations' you will have the opportunity to work alongside other staff who may be very familiar with the people with whom you are conducting your art activities. This can be extremely helpful, particularly if some of the clients require one-to-one assistance and encouragement in order to get the most from the activity. It is useful to explain to staff in advance what you hope to achieve and to indicate clearly what they can do in order to help you to meet your objectives. It is also important to listen attentively to any information that they have for you.

Sometimes well-meaning caregivers can end up doing the activity 'for' the people they are working with. This can be frustrating both for you and for the participants who are supposed to be taking part in the activity. You will be less likely to encounter this problem if you make your needs clear from the outset. The issue will also be easier to address if you do encounter it because you will be able to simply reiterate what you said before in a respectful and non-critical manner.

It can be great to invite willing staff to take part in art activities together with their clients. This process can be very enjoyable and beneficial for both parties and can also help to cultivate new, worthwhile and unexpected dynamics within their relationships.

Making a plan

Once you have decided upon the activity or activities that you are going to present to your group and you have a space to work in, it is very useful to write a plan. The process of writing can help you to really clarify both your objectives and the methods through which you intend to realise them. Having a strong sense of what, how and when you are going to do things will help you to facilitate with relative confidence and ease.

Here is an 'Activity Record Sheet' that will help you to plan your activity.

Title:

Aims and objectives:

Materials:

Visual aids:

Task:

Introduction/demonstration:

Timing:

Conclusion and Reflection:

Now, here is an example of a plan for the 'Cars, Roads and Scribbles' activity:

Title: Cars, Roads and Scribbles

Aims and objectives:
- To develop participants' confidence in working with several art materials by offering them a wide range of tasks to choose from.

- To develop participants' appreciation for working co-operatively in a creative, supportive and non-judgmental atmosphere by emphasising principles of effective teamwork during introduction and bringing everyone's art together to form a group mural.

Materials: poster paints, brushes, palettes, water containers, markers, crayons, coloured pencils, scissors, paper, coloured card, glue stick and duct tape.

Visual aids: after my 'car-making' demonstration I will show everybody three different examples of vehicles that were made using shapes cut from coloured card.

Introduction: introduce myself to the group. Ask everybody his or her name. Ask if they have done art activities before. Emphasise that our time together should be enjoyable. They do not have to think in terms of their work being 'good' or 'bad'. Their contributions through the art they make and the things they say are all welcome and valid. That we all agree to try to support and encourage one another.

Task: 'Cars, Roads and Scribbles'.

Roads—any type, drawn from above, to be cut out using scissors, so don't do background.

Cars—show visual aids.

Scribbles—emphasise importance of this task, scribbles must fill entire page.

Buildings—any kind.

Birds—any kind, also to be cut out, so no background.

Demonstration: quick demo on cutting out front headlight shape and sticking it on to car.

Timing: initial intro, 5–7 mins; task intro, 5 mins; demonstration, 3 mins; task time, 45 mins; tidy up, 5 mins; conclusion & reflection, 10 mins.

Conclusion and Reflection: did participants enjoy the activity? How did their feelings change throughout the activity? Was anyone nervous before we began? Has that changed? How do people feel about having their work incorporated into a large group mural?

More on Planning

Title

Sometimes a title exists simply to remind you of the content of an activity, but one that is interesting or catchy can be used during your introduction to stimulate interest and set the tone for what the group are about to do.

Title examples: Celebrity Costume Capers, Play With Clay, Moody-Judy.

Older more mature groups may (or may not) prefer titles that are less quirky.

Aims and objectives

The more specific you are when articulating your aims and objectives, the more likely it is that you will achieve them. When writing an aim or objective, clearly indicate how you hope to accomplish it. For example, 'To develop participants' self-esteem' or 'To develop participants' ability to express themselves' are worthy aims, but they are vague. Include words such as *by* and *through* to lead you towards the way that your intentions might be realised.

Example 1: To develop participants' self-esteem by teaching them techniques that will help them to overcome a series of creative challenges, from cutting the clay to making a pot, and acknowledging and praising their achievements.

Example 2: To develop participants' ability to express themselves visually through engaging with them in a group discussion on the relationship between colour and mood and offering them the opportunity to choose from a variety of different pieces of coloured paper to build a collage that describes a chosen mood.

Materials

It is important that you become familiar with the characteristics and qualities of many different art materials. The materials that you make available to your clients can greatly impact on the appearance of their work and so can mean the difference between more and less successful outcomes. For instance, in 'Cars, Roads and Scribbles' it is important that participants have access to a glue stick for the car-making element. If one were to use a liquid glue, such as PVA, it would moisten the card and cause the vehicles to appear crumpled. This would be a less pleasing result for the participant and would therefore leave him/her feeling relatively dissatisfied and unconfident.

You should personally try out any activity that you intend to introduce to a group using the materials that will be available to ensure that it will work properly. Poster paint is water-based and so will not stick to a plastic surface. As it dries it tends to peel away and flake. It is too late to make this kind of discovery when an activity has already started, so in order to avoid creating disappointment for participants and embarrassment for yourself, be sure that the materials on offer are suitable for what is required.

You can create a buzz of mystery and excitement in the art room by arranging materials in readiness for the appearance of your participants. It can be really appealing to the group to arrive at a space where something unexpected, such as blocks of clay or large sheets of paper taped to the ground with brightly coloured markers, crayons and brushes, lie in wait for them. It is wonderful when people enter and say, 'Oh wow! What are we doing today? What is this stuff called?' If you can instil that level of curiosity and enthusiasm from the outset, it will generate an energy that can really help to make the activity tremendous.

Visual aids

Visual aids are any images or objects that you show to participants in order to deepen their understanding of what an activity entails. You can use work that was made by a previous group that took part in a similar process, photographs, things you have made yourself or source material from books, magazines or the Internet.

Visual aids are particularly useful for showing people how a process that entails several stages (e.g. lino printing, ceramic glazing, puppet-making) might conclude.

Some individuals have a tendency to simply copy visual aids, particularly if they see only one, so show two or more if possible. Also consider how you pitch your visual aids. If they look too intricate and fancy, participants may feel as though they have 'failed' if their work compares unfavourably. If your visual aids are unattractive, on the other hand, then participants may feel uninspired.

Introduction

If you have met the group before, you can simply say 'hello' and engage in a little chat while everyone finds their place. If you are meeting a group for the first time, try to be extra welcoming. When everyone gets settled, introduce yourself and ask them to tell you their names. You may also ask people a couple of questions about themselves—particularly if the group is small—as this can help to ease awkwardness. Simple enquiries that allow individuals the option to give short or even yes/no answers are best.

At this point you may want to inform the group that you are there to *facilitate*. Your role is to help them to explore different ways to express themselves through their artwork. It is not like school, where their creative endeavours may have been judged and categorised as 'good' or 'bad'. They do not have to worry about 'being able to draw' and their verbal and artistic contributions will be welcomed and are valid. You may ask everyone if they are willing to respect this ethos.

If you are working with a group that could benefit from having very clear and explicit rules and boundaries, you could develop that conversation into an activity where you collaborate with the participants to draw up an 'art activity group contract' outlining an acceptable code of behaviour and some appropriate consequences for those who attempt to operate outside it.

In your plan you can indicate key points that you want to include in your introduction. Be aware of any details that might affect the success of the outcome for the participants. Some relatively simple interventions and instructions can make a huge difference. For example, in 'Cars, Roads and Scribbles' the scribblers are directed to 'fill the page with scribbles and leave no trace of the colour of the paper'. Although this doesn't make the task much more difficult, completely covering the page adds greatly to the aesthetic quality of the finished mural and also to the satisfaction experienced by the participants.

This is another reason why it is such an advantage for you to have already done the activity yourself. You will be sensitised to the nuances and fine points of the task and will therefore be in a position of some expertise when you explain it to your group.

If you are afraid that you might forget an important point, it is a good idea to keep your plan in front of you during your introduction. It is better not to 'read out' or even 'learn off' what you are going to say, though, because it might prevent you from interacting with the participants. If you memorise what you want to say word for word and then somebody interrupts you with a question or comment, you may find it difficult to reply or resume.

If you do feel yourself becoming nervous or excited at the prospect of facilitating, you can practise your introduction alone or with companions. Sometimes you can learn a lot from viewing a recording of yourself made using a video camera. However, the potential difficulty with doing so is that looking at the same footage of oneself several times can tend to make for an overly critical self-assessment. It is much more advantageous to watch once or twice before deleting because re-watching several times and deconstructing every detail of your delivery, gestures, appearance, etc. will only make you feel more apprehensive than you were to begin with.

Anxious facilitators have a tendency to rush through their introduction, perhaps in an effort to get it over with. If this is an issue for you, try to be aware of it, and even write a note in your plan reminding yourself to speak slowly. Also, take some time in the room by yourself before the participants arrive so that you can breathe in and out gently and be as calm as possible. Also, be aware that most people are nervous at first and you are going to be fantastic!

Demonstration

Indicate on your Activity Record Sheet whether or not you intend to conduct a demonstration. Demonstrations should be quite short and succinct. If you are teaching somebody a new skill, it is best to do so in manageable fragments that they will be able to follow and remember. It is okay to perform several separate demonstrations throughout the course of an activity if needs be.

Be sure that everyone can see you properly and invite people to move closer if they need a better view. It can be fun to involve a client in a demonstration and doing so can generate more interest from the rest of the participants, while giving you the chance to see if a member of the group can manage to perform the procedure that you are trying to teach.

Timing

Work out a schedule for your activity. Practise your introduction and demonstration alone or with friends to get a realistic sense of how many minutes they will take. It is important to communicate information clearly to your group without rushing, but remember that the art activity is foremost about 'doing', so ensure that there is plenty of time allotted to the task itself. Allocate space in your schedule for tidying so that you have a sufficient period for reflection before the end.

Finally, while you are facilitating be sure to tell people how long they will have with particular tasks and update them on the time there is left at appropriate intervals. Say when there are ten, five and two minutes to go so that participants are not forced to finish their work abruptly.

The tidy-up

Clearing the workspaces and cleaning art materials is very important, especially when you are working with different groups in quick succession. There can be few worse beginnings to an activity than having to deal with a barrage of complaints because the new group has arrived to find wet paint on their chairs and desks or that the paintbrush bristles have become hard because they were not cleaned properly.

Paintbrushes should be cleaned one at a time. It is not sufficient to merely rinse a bunch of them together under running water. Rub the bristles back and forth to be sure that the inner ones do not have paint/glue on them.

If you are using acrylic paint, it is vital to wash brushes immediately after use. It is essential to be thorough in this because acrylic paint will not dissolve in water after it has dried, so brushes cannot be rescued. If water-based poster paints dry on brushes there is still hope, so do not discard them. Simply soak them for a few hours in water and when the bristles soften, give them a good wash. When brushes are wet, place them bristle side up in a container so that the hairs do not become bent. It might be necessary to conduct demonstrations to ensure that your group learns how to clean items properly.

You can make the tidy-up much easier by planning ahead. If you are using a material such as clay, do not work directly on a table surface. Instead use wooden or plastic boards on top of the tables ... and keep the boards solely for clay activities. If you are doing other 'messy' activities, you could lay down newspaper or plastic sheets, which can simply be recycled or discarded when the activity is over.

When organising the tidy-up, try to delegate tasks fairly. With some groups it may be helpful to draw up a roster so that participants take it in turns to sweep the floor, wipe the tables, put materials back into the presses, etc. after each activity.

It is best to make the tidy-up a feature of your activity the first time you meet with a new group because developing the habit of reorganising the room will make your facilitation much easier. It is also generally good for participants to learn to take responsibility for the upkeep of the art space, the materials in it and the experience that they share with all other groups that use the room. Be sure to show your appreciation for people's efforts.

Conclusion and reflection

Leave time after the task and tidy-up for participants to reflect upon and discuss their experiences during the activity. Some people might like to talk about what they enjoyed most or least. Others might want to mention something about what they learned about art or their own creative process. Sometimes personal issues can arise that individuals might wish to share.

It is useful to write some questions in your plan that could help to open a forum where people can talk freely. It is important that you do not ask intrusive questions or make individuals feel obliged to say something if they do not want to. The initial questions can be quite simple: 'Can anyone tell me what we did today?' or 'What materials did we work with?' or 'How would you describe the material?' You will quickly get a sense of how comfortable the group is to engage with you in conversation. It is important to be attentive, calm and also patient.

If these questions are met with enthusiastic answers, you might sense that it is okay to probe a little deeper. You could ask how people felt during the task. Did they find it relaxing or frustrating? Did their work bring up any memories? Are there any stories that they would like to tell about their work? Did they pick up any new skills? Would they be more confident if they had to approach this kind of task again in the future?

Of course, in real-life situations your questions can be less generalised and based more specifically on the things that the group has made: 'Can you tell me why the man in the picture is smiling? What might he be thinking about?' 'Is this dog you made out of papier-mâché based on your own dog at home? What is he called?' etc.

Conclusion and reflection can also be structured in unusual and fun ways. For instance, if you have done a puppet-making activity, you could conclude by doing a mock television interview with each person's puppet, asking it questions such as: 'What is your name?' 'Where do you come from?' 'What are you made of?' 'What is your favourite food?' etc.

Really good reflections can be therapeutic because they give participants the chance to consider and share what they have learned—about their art and about themselves—during the activity. A person's artwork is a piece of evidence that is a record of their creative process and their ability to express themselves in a visual and tactile way. When clients assimilate and articulate their experience through discussion and reflection, they can become more aware of their ability to face challenges and meet objectives in creative ways, which in turn can boost their confidence and self-esteem.

You can also use art activities as a starting point for all sorts of conversations. An activity such as making a pinch pot from clay, which is done in a few simple steps—roll the clay into a ball, make an impression in the ball using your thumb, pinch the clay between finger and thumb to form a bowl shape—can be used to start a meaningful chat about 'individuality'. You can point out that although everybody has followed the same procedure whilst making their pot, all the pots are quite different. Sometimes having a thing or things to look at and refer to can really help people to understand a concept.

One-to-one interactions

The art class offers an excellent opportunity to talk to people on an individual basis about their work. One-to-one interactions give participants a chance to discuss their ideas, to enlist your expertise as they try to master the fine points of particular skills, to tell 'stories' relating to their art and to reflect on personal issues that they might like to share.

Effective one-to-one interactions are largely dependent on the level of rapport that you have with the people in your group. Rapport tends to happen when people feel connected to you, and people tend to feel connected to you when you behave and communicate in a manner that demonstrates that you care for them.

The effort that you put into planning your activity, the manner in which you prepare the art room, the way you interact during your introduction and the level at which you engage with their artwork will impact on how 'cared for' your participants feel, and the extent to which they trust and speak to you.

Your relationship with the people you work with will evolve over time and it is important to allow that to happen organically. If you attempt to rush participants into 'deep and meaningful' conversations, they are likely to respond by either becoming silent or acting out.

Incorporating one-to-one interactions

When you have completed your introduction/demonstration, you should allow your participants time and space to 'psych themselves up' and decide how they wish to begin the activity. Be available to answer any questions, but do not initiate interactions unless you strongly sense that it is necessary to do so.

After a little while, you can walk around the room and have a look at what everyone is doing. At this juncture you may notice that there are individuals who might require some assistance or encouragement. It is better not to assume that this is always the case, however. Just because somebody appears to be struggling, it does not mean that they are. Some people simply like to work slowly, methodically and almost gingerly. You can ask individuals how they are doing, or enquire from the group generally if anyone needs your help, but do so in a way that is unobtrusive.

If participants seem content and busy, then let them be for another spell. Continue to be available and observant in case your input is required, but remain apart if it is not. After another few minutes you should wander around again to see how people's artwork is developing.

What to say

It is best to begin with questions that are easy to answer and are not too personal. You could ask about how they mixed a particular colour of paint, or what method they used to create an effect. These kinds of questions are good because they indicate to the participant that you have engaged with their artwork and they can give you a factual answer.

If you started by saying something like, 'tell me about this picture…', that would be a far more difficult thing to respond to (unless, of course, you had already established a strong rapport, in which case it could be a good way to begin an interaction). 'Tell me about your picture…' is too vague a request for somebody that you are only getting to know because it puts pressure on them to interpret and to try to gauge what you mean. This may make them feel awkward and wary in case they say the 'wrong' thing and sound stupid.

A question to avoid is: 'What is that?' Even if an image seems hard for you to decipher, its meaning may be perfectly clear to its creator and he/she may be insulted by your inability to discern it. It is also possible that the maker of the image wants its meaning to remain a secret or that they do not know its meaning or that it does not have a meaning. All these possibilities are perfectly valid and it is important that you do not say anything to imply that that is not the case.

As mentioned in the 'Conclusion and Reflection' section above, many of the most effective questions arise from your engagement with the artwork itself. If somebody has drawn a car, for example, you might ask them to tell you if they know who owns the car, where the car is heading to and so on.

Be sensitive in your approach. Sometimes people reveal more about themselves through their artwork than they may realise, but it is not your place to try to interpret their creations and explain the meanings back to them. Your one-to-one interactions should draw more from your ability to listen than to speak and your focus should remain on the development of participants' curiosity, visual awareness, open-mindedness, physical/psychological well-being and self-esteem.

If an issue does arise during the art activity that concerns you, then you should share it with a colleague or supervisor. Remember what you learned in Chapter 1 and ensure that you are using the creative arts therapeutically and not trying to deliver an art therapy session.

Personal evaluations

When you have completed your activity, take the time to reflect upon and examine how successful you were in meeting your objectives. It is very helpful to write a personal evaluation because doing so will really help to clarify your thoughts.

Consider the areas of the activity that you think went well and those that didn't. Bear in mind the feedback that you received from the group during the conclusion and reflection on the activity.

Any areas that you identify for consideration should be developed. It is not enough to say that the participants didn't understand the introduction. You have to identify reasons why this was the case. Perhaps they could not hear you properly, or the language that you used was too sophisticated? How could you possibly address these problems? It might mean that you need to speak more clearly, or more simply, or ask the group some questions during the introduction to ensure that they are understanding you.

Pay attention to any practical matters. If you were doing an activity that involved the use of clay and some people said they did not want to touch it because they thought it was dirty, you could consider ways to respond to this issue in future. You could offer participants disposable gloves and ensure that you have soap at the sink, or you could spend more time allowing participants to 'get to know' the material gradually.

You should also take note of factors that helped the activity to go well. If the participants were very excited as they entered the room because you had the materials set up in an interesting way, then you need to acknowledge that. Perhaps you could also imagine ways you could use this knowledge to help with planning future activities.

Every time you do an activity you will have the opportunity to learn something new that will give you the chance to develop as a practitioner.

Here is an example of a personal evaluation written by a student who facilitated the 'Cars, Roads and Scribbles' activity with a group of people in their early twenties.

Personal evaluation

I was generally very pleased with how the activity went. Everyone got really into it and the feedback during the reflection was very positive ... people said that they really enjoyed drawing and painting and that they liked the variety of things they had to do ... so I do feel that I met with my first objective, which was to encourage participants to work with a range of materials.

I probably spent too long on the introduction. I intended to just ask everybody their names and get a quick sense of whether or not they had experienced art activities before ... but my interactions with some individuals went on for too long and I noticed some of the other participants becoming fidgety ... which probably made me rush my demonstration. I think that I let myself get involved in 'chat' because I was nervous. I think that is fair enough because this was my first time facilitating by myself. In future I don't think that I will get that nervous ... but if I do, then I will try to do some slow breathing exercises before the group arrives.

Everything got a lot better as soon as the task started and it was great to hear everyone laughing, enjoying themselves and encouraging one another. I let everybody get on with their work for about seven minutes ... because they seemed engrossed. Then I reminded them that they could switch tasks if they had finished their first thing. I think that I chose a good time to do that because some of the 'scribblers' were finished and wanted to make space on their desks so that they could try doing roads, birds, buildings, etc.

I then collected some of the participants' pictures and started to lay them down on a big space on the ground. It was amazing how quickly the mural seemed to be coming together and I could hear people saying 'wow' and 'that's brilliant', which I personally found very encouraging ... and the group did too ... which relates to my second objective, which was to develop participants' appreciation for working co-operatively in a creative, supportive and non-judgmental atmosphere by emphasising principles of effective teamwork.

I went around to people and asked them how they were getting along. One of the women said to me that she was enjoying herself, but that she was embarrassed because she thought her work looked like something a child would make. I told her that I think children's artwork is often very beautiful and that lots of artists focus on trying to recapture the freedom and expressive quality of a child. I told her I would bring in a book about the painter Matisse next week so I had better remember to do that, because she seemed really interested. In fact, I think I will probably keep a little library of art-related books in the art room.

The reflection was really great. Lots of people said that they were quite nervous before the activity began because they felt they 'could not draw' and it had been many years since they did anything like this ... but they said they really enjoyed the activity and that they were really excited about the prospect of coming back next week. A couple of people said that they were going to make some pictures at home because 'they had gotten the bug'.

I was really pleased with how the activity turned out. I have stuck the mural together using strong glue and duct tape at the back. I have pinned it to the wall and it does look very impressive. Looking at it now, I think it could be really good to continue to build on it next week so I am thinking about inviting the group to build the mural 'up' towards outer space, or 'down' into the ocean.

Chapter Summary

▶ Creative group facilitation is concerned with helping people to develop their abilities to express themselves through the medium of art.

▶ Choose an appropriate activity that takes into account the interests and abilities of the group.

▶ Know and plan the activity thoroughly and be very clear about your objectives.

▶ Your confidence in speaking in front of a group and delivering demonstrations will grow as you become more experienced.

▶ Be attentive to the needs of your group and engage with them through their artwork and in discussion.

▶ Always be encouraging and caring.

▶ Try to incorporate some reflection at the end of an activity. This will help to deepen participants' understanding of what they have been doing.

▶ Evaluate each activity, identifying things that went well and things that could be improved.

▶ Each time you facilitate you will have an opportunity to learn something new, which will give you the chance to develop as a practitioner.

Good Luck!

THREE

The Benefits of Using Creative Art

Denise MacGiollari

SNAPSHOT

- The value of creativity.
- Encouraging creativity.
- The value of art in society.
- Art and self.
- The benefits of art.

Introduction

Creativity should not be underestimated—it lies at the heart of humankind and is the spark that ignites life itself. Art and creativity have the capacity to bring forth personal change and something *new*. Art has been part of our collective human history because it provides a very special, yet natural way to channel our innate creativity. Art is also part of our national identity: the artefacts of our history and the works of art emerging from modern Ireland express our cultural identity, our origins and our history.

This chapter sets out to address the nature of creativity and its benefits, and how to encourage it. It explores the relationship between society and art, and the historical evolution of art, as a means of communication and as an expression of the self. Art is explored from a number of perspectives, focusing on the functions and benefits of its use. The benefits described are supported by data collected by

Lyons (2008) from thirty-five caring professionals using creativity within their practice. This section will introduce a number of contemporary rationales and theoretical concepts that underpin art engagement and its practical uses.

Creativity: Global and Personal

In common usage, 'creativity' describes something new and novel. Amabile and Tighe (1993) stated that the created idea or object must be different from what has gone before and be 'appropriate, correct, useful, valuable, or expressive of meaning' (Amabile and Tighe 1993:9). As a general concept, creativity means different things to different people. Its meaning varies according to the culture in which a person lives and the general associations that become attached to the word and concept. For example, 'artists' are generally seen as creative, but scientists are not, even though they can be just as creative. Ordinary creativity that flows from within everyone often goes unrecognised, and perhaps undervalued, by society.

Howard Gardner (1993) attempts to differentiate between the two areas of creativity—personal and global. He categorises creativity under two separate terms: 'little c' and 'Big C' (Gardner, 1993:28–47) 'Big C' is the creativity that has the capacity to create 'change' on a global scale. It is an '... achievement of something remarkable and new, something which transforms and changes a field of endeavour in a significant way' (Feldman,1994:1). Creativity at this level requires momentous effort, sustained commitment and vision. Only a few people can hope to make a significant contribution to their field and change it in the process.

'Little c' is the creativity each person is capable of in their everyday lives (Gardner, 1993:32). The way a person decorates their house, or combines clothes to make an interesting ensemble, can be an expression of the 'little c'. The 'little c' is part of an ordinary pursuit that is altered or changed in accordance with the individual's unique desires and inspiration.

Boden (2003), who summed up a wealth of research, suggests that:

'Creativity draws crucially on our ordinary abilities; noticing, remembering, seeing, speaking, hearing, understanding language, and recognizing analogies: all these talents of Everyman are important.'　　　　　(Boden, 2003, cited in Florida, 2002:32)

Thus, creativity can be seen as combination of ordinary abilities that together bring about something new.

The Benefits of Valuing Creativity

Creativity helps us to make the most of our lives. When we use our creativity, we make use of our available resources and are not 'bound by the past, nor fixed to the limits of the present' (Moustakas, 1977:2). Richards (2006) stated that creativity can be valued as a way to live more productively, to cope with difficulties, to discover possibilities, to produce constructive activities for self and the world and to develop 'new resilience, perspective, aliveness in the moment, joy, and purpose in life' (Richards, 2006:353).

Richards (2006) goes on to state that living an 'ordinary life' creatively can '...improve one's physical and psychological health, decrease visits to the doctor, improve one's sense of personal well-being, and, as seen with expressive writing, even boost immune function' (Richards, 2006:353).

Nickerson (1999) agreed that creativity has the capacity to bring joy and *well-being* and added that its benefits can be far-reaching for the individual and for the people who inhabit their environment and society:

> '... creative expression is generally desirable, because it usually contributes positively to the quality of life of the individual who engages in it and often enriches the lives of others as well.'
>
> (Nickerson, 1999:392)

How can we Encourage Creativity?

A considerable amount of research has identified the key barriers to and promoters of creativity.

The factors that can promote creativity include:
- rewarding effort (Nickerson, 1999:418);
- setting clear boundaries;
- encouraging freedom (Maslow, 1959, cited in Lee *et al.*, 2005:463);
- a balance between too little and too much structure (Runco and Okuda, 1988, cited in Nickerson, 1999:418);
- the room layout being physically safe (Malchiodi, 1998);
- an environment that is fit for purpose (deSouza-Fleith 2000:149);
- allowing time for creative thinking (deSouza-Fleith, 2000:149);
- a non-repressive atmosphere (Nickerson 1999:392).

The factors that can inhibit creativity include:
- fear of failure (Amabile, 1989:88; Jackson, 2005b:1);
- fear of making mistakes (Bowkett, 2005:4);
- lack of spontaneity (Malchiodi, 1998:12);
- belief in 'one right answer' (Oech, 1983, cited in Sternberg and Lubart, 1999:5);
- lack of tolerance of ambiguity (Adams, 1974, 1986; Oech, 1983, cited in Sternberg and Lubart, 1999:5);
- unchallenged habits of thinking (Bowkett, 2005:13);
- lack of self-awareness (Jackson, 2005:5);
- overly judgmental attitude (Bowkett, 2005:13);
- resistance to change (Bowkett, 2005:13);

- lack of risk-taking (Nickerson, 1999:418);
- lack of persistence (Craft, 2001:6);
- lack of motivation (Craft, 2001:6);
- embarrassment (Malchiodi, 1998).

The creative facilitator can promote creativity by:
- promoting freedom (Nickerson, 1999:418);
- encouraging playfulness (Nickerson, 1999:410);
- building confidence (Nickerson, 1999:413);
- being non-judgmental and allowing autonomy (Amabile 1989:87);
- having an open mind and promoting thinking about the thinking processes (Starko, 1995, cited in deSouza-Fleith, 2000:149);
- promoting working knowledge (Amabile, 1989:87–8);
- establishing purpose and intention (Nickerson, 1999:408);
- encouraging risk-taking (Craft 2001:6; Sawyer, 2006:311);
- encouraging multiple solutions and ideas (deSouza-Fleith, 2000:149);
- questioning assumptions (Sternberg and Williams, 1996, cited in deSouza-Fleith, 2000:149);
- reducing competition (Amabile, 1989:75);
- accepting failure as part of learning (Ansdell, 2001:2);
- providing a psychologically safe space (Hunt and West, 2006:165);
- placing less emphasis on evaluation and assessment (Amabile, 1989:72);
- rewarding creative behaviour (Amabile, 1989; deSouza-Fleith, 2000);
- building motivation (Nickerson, 1999:411);
- creating an atmosphere of friendship and partnership and offering choices (Amabile, 1989:72–91);
- supporting non-conformity (Amabile, 1989:89).

Task
What might inhibit your creativity?
Identify a person who you think is creative. Why do you believe this?
How would you encourage others to be creative?

Art and Society

Dissanayake (1995) asked, 'what is art for?', and argued that art has a biological origin. She states that art is, and always has been, part of every society and that it serves an important function. She points to the fact that:

> 'All over the world people enjoy making music, singing, dancing, reciting or listening to poetry recited, telling or hearing tales told, performed or watching performances, making beautiful things, and so forth.'   (Dissanayake, 1995:24)

The arts, she argues, are a force of nature that can unify participants, performers and their audience, thus bringing together the community. The value of the arts lies in engaging in the rituals to unite a group and gain a sense of belonging. The arts as entertainment can 'enjoin people to participate, join the flow, get in the groove, feel good' (Dissanayake, 1995:24).

Keating (2008) supports the belief that our artistic faculty is integral not merely to the development of society but to human nature, and offers the observation that in Ireland today art has become separated from ordinary people. Creativity has instead been redirected towards making life easier through technology and 'so art has lost its primacy in daily discourse' (Keating 2008:7). The arts have therefore become a *niche industry* and a field of speciality divorced from society. Keating does indicate, however, that there has been a cultural shift away from *consumption* of art to *creating,* as an antidote to the consumer society. She points to the use of the arts as means of helping minority communities to contemplate their experiences. She points also to the importance of the arts in education in 'shaping the growth of the individual mind' (Keating, 2008:7).

The challenge for the arts is to normalise creativity by making it relevant to the ordinary person. Instilling creativity as a value, as well as a skill, may encourage non-artists to take a more active role in creative endeavours on a personal level, as well as on a community level.

Task
Think about what art means to you. What do you believe art is for?

Historical Origins of Art For and About the Self

According to Carroll (1999), the eighteenth-century art objective of creating imitations or representations of the external world gave way to the Romantic movement in the nineteenth century, which focused on the subjective experience of the artist through the exploration of the inner self and the emotions. From this point on, art shifted focus from the reproduction of images from the external world to the expression of the inner world of the self. The artwork is used to capture an emotion and communicate it to the viewer. With the era of modern psychology, artwork has provided a useful medium for exploring the self and communicating with others. For the worker who wants to use art in his/her practice, the question is: what are the benefits of art in the caring professions?

The Benefits of Creative Art

Art for expression

For children, art can provide them with a wonderful way to express themselves. It offers an opportunity to express their 'thoughts, feelings, interests, and knowledge of the environment in creative expressions' (Lowenfeld and Brittain, 1987:7). Mark-making for children offers a unique opportunity to make a permanent mark that exists outside themselves. Art also becomes a way for children to express and make sense of their world.

Children's artwork is often self-directed and thus provides an expressive outlet that is free from direct external control. They can make choices and decisions in relation to the artwork that allows autonomy and ownership of their expressive capacities. In this way, their expression can become truly their own. Art expression in children can involve the whole body. They experience the world with vigour: through the senses, in the movement of their bodies, in their thinking, through their emotions and from their memories. As children become more cognitively aware of their creative abilities, the more likely they are to be positively or negatively influenced by the values and attitudes expressed and communicated to them by adults and significant others. You will learn more about children's experience of art and the role adults play, positively or negatively, in this process in Chapter 4.

> **Task**
> *Observe a child involved in art. What do you notice?*
> *How do they use their body? Do they speak?*
> *How do you value children's art process and products?*
> *Do you consider all art made by children to be 'good' and worthwhile?*

Art for symbols

In our dreams we *see* things in our mind's eye, played out like a disjointed movie. The objects and circumstances of our dreams, if they reach consciousness, have meaning and significance for us. The mind uses visual information, often gathered during the previous day, to play out our concerns and preoccupations. The objects and circumstances become personal symbols as they are invested with personal meaning and emotion that might not be so obvious to another person. Personal symbols are therefore useful as a means to understand ourselves, our relationship with others and the world. Artwork also uses symbols. The artwork can be viewed as using marks and colours that are invested with personal meaning and thus come to be used as a personal symbolic language.

Art as a tangible object

Storr (1980:52) wrote about the *distancing effect* of the artwork, in other words the artwork as an externalised, concrete object that is available for inspection (Storr, 1980:52). The artwork can be seen as an object that exists outside the self, but its origin and meaning have come from inside the person. As an object it can be invested with meaning, either simple or profound. As the object exists outside, it can be looked at from different perspectives and its meaning may fade over time or it can become more significant, depending on the circumstances and associations attached to it. The continued existence of the art object, after its creation, makes possible a continued dialogue between the maker and the object.

How the artwork is treated post-creation can have meaning and implications for the maker. The participant may wish to destroy the artwork, put it in the bin, bring it home or have it looked after by the facilitator. If the artwork is invested with personal symbols that are alive with personal meaning regarding the self, then how the artwork is treated could be seen by the maker to be representative of how the self is treated by others. Accordingly, the clearance or storage of artwork needs to be considered in consultation with the art-maker.

> **Task**
> *Imagine you are seven years old. You have spent an hour constructing an artwork sculpture. It reminds you of lots of early memories and you love the colour pink that has been poured over the top. It gets put aside to dry, but when you return a few days later, it has been thrown in the bin. What are your thoughts? How do you feel?*

Art for free association

Art can be used to bring to light associations or links to other ideas, thoughts, emotions or experiences. A drawing of a boat, for example, can be freely associated to by saying or writing what comes to mind as the artwork is being made or when the work is finished. The art-maker needs to be in a relaxed state, without the pressure of time or the pressure to find the 'right' answers. The key is allowing the mind the freedom to say or write the words without conscious judgment.

> **Task**
> *Paint or draw an image. Respond to it by writing words that come into your mind; try not to censor the words as they emerge.*

Art for interpretation

Interpretation of art is where an individual, either the art-maker or a skilled professional, makes suggestions as to the meaning of the artwork. The concept of interpretation can be misrepresented when a person believes that their artwork can be *read* and understood instantly by another person. This simply does not happen. The person who is best placed to *interpret* the artwork is the art-maker, as the maker is the expert with inside information.

Storr (1980) warns the novice of the danger of any form of external or suggestive interpretation (Storr, 1980:52). An art facilitator can offer feedback and a questioning style that supports the process of self-interpretation by the art-maker. The facilitator does not assume an 'expert' role, but rather offers this role to the art-maker.

Art for meaning-making using the emotions

No object or experience has inherent meaning, only the meaning we give it. Life is experienced though the senses and meaning is assigned in accordance with the disposition of the meaning-maker and his/her previous experiences and associations in relation to the culture and society in which he/she lives (Ferszt et al., 1998:73). As humans we do not have complete control over our circumstances, but we are free to choose the meaning of our actions, our response and reactions (Corey, 1991, cited in Artz, 1994:11). Experiences are then given meaning and value according to our emotions (Artz, 1994:11). Emotions are attached to both old and new experiences and are given meaning and value.

> **Task**
> *Do you remember the first day at primary school, secondary school or college? Do you remember the emotions you felt?*
> *Did it remind you of other situations you experienced previously? Close your eyes and think about an important experience you have had; now think about an object that symbolises this experience for you. Paint, draw or make this object. Reflect on its meaning for you.*

Art-making offers an opportunity to explore the personal meaning of experiences. Searching for meaning through the art process and the art products inevitably involves the emotions. Emotions point to areas of importance for us and therefore must be viewed as a valuable element of the art-making and meaning-making processes. Emotions tend to be seen as a messy and unnecessary part of human exploration, when in fact they can be the key to finding meaning. Powerful feelings, such as anger and sadness, instead of being viewed negatively, can be seen as 'powerful ways of knowing' and understanding rather than as irrational feelings to be handled, controlled or eradicated (Artz, 1994:15). Fear of disintegration and social non-conformity often lie behind the resistance to exploring at this level.

> **Task**
> *How do you view the expression of emotions?*
> *How do you respond to other people's expression of emotions?*
> *Are you aware of how you are feeling right now?*
> *Can you visualise it? Paint or draw it.*

Art for personal development and self-actualisation

The creative act of making art may help to facilitate the growth and development of the self and provide a creative channel to direct our natural motivation towards self-actualisation. As May (1980:38) states:

> 'The creative process must be explored not as the product of sickness, but as representing the highest degree of emotional health, as the expression of normal people in the act of actualising themselves.'

Self-actualisation is only possible, according to Maslow's psychology of health, when a healthy person has met the hierarchy of basic needs, which is described as follows.
1   Physiology.
2   Safety.
3   Belongingness and love.
4   Respect and self-esteem.
5   Self-actualisation.

The concept of self-actualisation can be seen as a motivation that is common to all and that helps a person to reach his/her utmost potential. Maslow (1971) linked creativity to self-actualisation when he stated that: 'The concept of creativeness and the concept of a healthy, self-actualizing, fully human seem to be coming closer and closer together, and may perhaps turn out to be the same thing' (Maslow, 1971:55). Using art as a creative act can reach the authentic self and thus facilitate growth[1], self-acceptance and change within the individual.

Art for meaning-making and perception

The mind is constantly seeking meaning and as we create art the mind is interacting on many levels to direct the process towards integration and understanding. The four psychological functions of perception that Carl Jung speaks about—sensing, thinking, feeling and intuiting—come together to inform action (Sharp, 1991). The artwork could be said to be an externalisation of the art-maker's internal mental process. Being in the art process can involve the art-maker's perceptive functions reaching equilibrium, where no one function dominates another. This state can be described as '*flow*', being a state in which the person becomes so engrossed in the art-making that he/she '*loses*' themselves in it, time flies by and even bodily functions such as hunger are ignored (Collins and Amabile, 1999).

> **Task**
> *Can you remember an occasion when you lost yourself in a task or in artwork? Describe the feeling.*

Art for meaning-making and communication

'There are some kinds of general purpose (*goals*) that are extremely pervasive among us … such as the goal of understanding or making sense of things and the goal of communicating with one another.'
(Donaldson, 1992:1)

In conversation we employ mental strategies to understand each other. We listen carefully and may check information with the person so that we can understand fully. We check our own thoughts and feelings that are being expressed and we empathise. We ultimately attempt to find meaning in relation to what we know about ourselves and the other person. Artwork can also be produced to communicate with others.[2] The art-maker may seek to be understood in a straightforward or profound way. Showing genuine interest through authentic dialogue around the artwork ensures that the artwork is given a voice and this provides an excellent way to find meaning and foster understanding.

Art for silence and contemplation

The world can be a noisy place and as art-making is a solitary pursuit, even when undertaken in a group, it can offer the chance to experience calm,[3] silence, silent contemplation and reflection. The solitary position allows the participant to direct his/her attention inwards in the pursuit of self-knowledge and to appreciate his/her own uniqueness. According to Nadeau (2008), this brings inner peace.

> Task
>
> **When was the last time you were in a silent environment? How did it feel? What did your mind do?**
> **Paint your vision of silence and reflect what it means to you.**
> **Paint the colour of silence and reflection.**

Art for reflection through visual art journalling[4]

Reflection is the process that, through writing, seeks to understand the self by looking closely at our attitudes, motivations and responses to our experiences. Reflective examination reveals hidden motivations and attitudes and as these new perspectives become conscious, the new information becomes available to inform future responses and actions.

Visual art journalling offers an opportunity to combine written expression with visual expression. The art-making process as a sensory act can tap into aspects of the self that are often beyond cognitive and verbal reach. Making visual art in a journal and responding to one's own visual expression with the written word can reveal emotions and personal meaning. Further exploration from different perspectives can, for example, help to alter the person's understanding of the experience and thus new meanings can emerge for consideration and contemplation.

> **Task**
>
> *Doodle or paint in a sketchbook and respond to the visual expression with writing. Allow a day or two to pass and review the entry. Think about what you have written and paint or doodle in response. Continue this cyclical response.*

Art for group work

Artwork can be created collectively by the group, or by individuals as part of the group. Artwork created by individuals in a group situation acknowledges, supports and witnesses the individual's artwork as part of the group. The individual's artwork can be influenced by the general milieu, the context and the purpose of the group. Artwork that is created by the group encourages the participants to make collective decisions, generates creative ideas and helps to foster a sense of togetherness.[5]

Group artwork can be used, for example, to explore the individual within the group as an expression of the individual's place in society, and to look at how the group's rules apply to their organisation. Generally, themed artwork works best for novice group art projects as total freedom of expression may give rise to feelings of fear and apprehension. Artwork can also be used as a warm-up activity in a group setting. It can provide a fun way to help the group engage with each other.

Here is one student's account of how a warm-up art activity encouraged interaction in a new group:

'I had only been at college three days, I kinda felt lost, a tiny bit alone, scared and there was so many questions to be asked in order for me to find my bearings. Once we had drawn something on the sticker, making our way round the circle each person would explain their picture. In a strange way this made me feel at ease, as many of the other people in the group felt the same way I did, I didn't feel alone anymore.'

Student A: Reflective journal entry (MacGiollari, 2008:6)

> **Task**
>
> *Warm-up art activity: using stickers, write your name and draw a symbol to represent something interesting about yourself. The group members can attempt to guess the interest and the facilitator can award points for correct answers. Alternatively, in a paired activity each partner can introduce the interests of their partner to the larger group.*

Art to occupy the body and mind

Art, as an occupational activity, has been widely prescribed for use with people in many settings with the primary aim of occupying the mind and body.[6] Views vary in the literature as to the benefit of this approach. Art activities such as painting by numbers may limit the freedom of the participants to apply their own creative ideas. These activities may be successful in achieving an art piece, but the art-maker may lose out in the expression of their own unique creativity. The activity may occupy the body and perhaps the mind but, as Howard (1980) suggests, may turn out to be *busy work* that fails to recognise and utilise the power of creativity as a precursor to change. However, in the right environment art as an occupation can encourage the mind to become thoughtful and reflective and can give a sense of accomplishment (Howard, 1980). Furthermore, artwork designed to occupy can be useful to pass the time and distract the mind away from pain or other troubling emotions and thoughts.

A simple example: a friend of mine broke her leg and was faced with many long weeks of recuperation. She decided to occupy herself with a pre-designed rug-making kit. She soon became absorbed in the activity, and the time flew by. By the time her leg was healed, she had a lovely hand-crafted rug that takes pride of place in her sitting room. The rug was a productive and positive outcome of the confinement. Indeed, the subject of the rug—a broken-down house—became a symbol of meaning for the maker.

Art for rehabilitation

Art for rehabilitation is used as a prescription for an ailment of mind and/or body. For example, painting may be used as an activity to help co-ordinate and strengthen fine motor skills,[7] or clay maybe used to aid sensory discovery, to build skills and aid learning.

Art as recreation

Art can be a hobby that is undertaken as a way to relax. For many people painting and other forms of artworks are fun and productive ways to spend their spare time. Active retirement groups enjoy using art as a recreation activity.[8] According to Bedding and Sadlo (2008), retirees value artwork as it gives satisfaction, offers a challenge, a sense of achievement, productivity, a boost of confidence and transforms time. Artwork produced in retirees' group setting offers a social outlet that promotes a sense of belonging through shared social activity.[9] The group setting can also be stimulating and offer an opportunity to learn from the other members (Bedding and Sadlo, 2008).

Art as story

Just one art image can ignite a story or narrative. The story can be factual or fictional and offers an opportunity to explore life through a creative lens. The imaginative story can suggest new ways to view reality, communicate our own life stories, find commonality and empathise with others' stories, and find solutions to life's struggles.

Interestingly, when viewed after a lapse of time the narrative artwork can be altered as the associated story fades and a new, perhaps unexpected narrative emerges, with new meanings.

The life story can be produced using a creative art approach. According to Hewitt (2000), the life story is used by carers of people with disabilities to 'get to know the person, to define the person and to display the personality of the person' (Hewitt, 2000, cited in Markwick & Parrish, 2003:100). The life story can also become a record of the person's history. You can learn more about the role of storytelling and the life story book in Chapter 9.

> Task
>
> *Cartoons are visual stories. Create a cartoon storybook about where you live using photographs. Write a brief story and take posed photos or use photocopies of old ones. Don't forget to add the fun speech bubbles!*

Art as observation

In a busy world humans *edit out* the unnecessary and the known. Our eyes grow accustomed to seeing the world at a glance. The details we see all the time are often scanned over. Artwork brings to life the joy of seeing anew. Art-making allows the participant to take the time to stop, focus and concentrate on those details. Seeing the world with new eyes brings discovery and childlike delight.

> Task
>
> *Look around you and imagine you are seeing your surroundings for the first time. Take the time to see things. What catches your eye? Can you describe the detail in your mind? What is it about what you are seeing that interests you? Draw, paint or photograph what you see.*
>
> *Viewfinders (cards with window-like cut-outs) can be used to find a section of a view for drawing. This may break down the view into manageable pieces. Also, a large Perspex sheet may be used to copy a view on to the clear surface.*

Art for memory

Our brains work by making synaptic connections between neurons. We are born with billions of neurons that are connected together by synaptic nerves in response to our genetic make-up and environment. Although the synaptic connections decrease more rapidly in later life, according to Howard (2000) the aging process itself is not totally responsible for the decline of brain function.[10] Remaining active in body and mind in later years[11] seems to slow down the rate of mental and physical degenerative decline (Howard, 2000).

Reminiscing about the past is one way to stimulate the mind and engage the body of a person in later life. Rousing memories of past times engage the mind, while working creatively using the memories can engage the body. Creative engagement, by its very nature, creates links between memories, ideas, thoughts and mental images. This active use of the mind ensures that the established synaptic neural pathways remain open and active. Reminiscing can help with change and loss, with communication, with gaining a positive sense of self, with finding meaning and making sense of the past, with hearing and recording cultural and family history and with simply enjoying the past by reliving it with a willing listener (Sheridan, 1991).

An art activity can be based on a past occupation, on places where a person lived or on past interests and achievements. For example, pictures of a soldier's uniform could be used to cover a book about a person's life in the army, a map of the area a person lived in could be used as a background on which to place collages and photos, or a picture could be created using items that represent achievements in a person's lifetime.

Task

Go back through old photos and memorabilia, perhaps with a person who also remembers those times, and notice how you feel. What memories come to the surface? Does one memory ignite another? Paint or draw a memory.

Art for guided imagery

Guided imagery takes the participant inside his/her mind as an imaginative exercise. According to Edwards (2006: 71), 'guided images are planned experiences, read or spoken by someone other than ourselves, that provide stimulus words or suggestions during a state of relaxation.' In a relaxed state[12] the participant hears the story of a journey or a scenario and, using his/her imagination, memories and internal imagery, brings the images to life inside their mind. Using guided imagery with participants can help them to *see* images in their mind's eye before they begin to express them externally.

According to Edwards (2006), guided imagery with children has the advantage of being able to tap into the unique experiences and imagery of the child, which means the art production is more likely to spring from the true depths of the child. Edwards (2006) suggests four phases or steps to be followed when undertaking guided imagery with children (Edwards, 2006:71).

- Centring—'to be quiet, to reflect, to pause, or to center ourselves – simply to "be..." a place of inner stillness'.

- Relaxing with awareness—'focusing on your breath while practicing being alert and aware'.

- Imagining—'the process of using our imagination, or mind's eye, to create mental images'.

● Processing—'sharing your experience with others ... a time to draw, paint, or dance the images that have emerged'.

> **Task**
> *Sit in a comfortable spot and close your eyes. Imagine you are taking a journey to find treasure in a far-off land. Where do you go? What do you see, hear, smell, touch and taste? Who is with you? What does the treasure turn out to be? Write the journey or paint, draw or sculpt an aspect of the journey.*

Art as a controlled process

The artwork comes into existence through a process of ideas, thoughts and decisions; the art process is under the control of the maker. The maker can make something happen, stop and start at will, adapt and respond to its existence, while all the time making decisions based on many complex interactions.

Art as imaginative play

Many adults either lose the ability to play or do not fully engage in any play processes as adults. Adult play, through a creative art activity, is a valuable means by which a person can reconnect with the joy of discovery and with their imagination. Children play naturally, but adults' playfulness becomes dulled through the seriousness and the heaviness of life. The ability to play and a playful attitude makes possible artistic discovery and imaginative linkages. Without play, creativity cannot be fostered and developed. Duffy (2006:25) states that 'play promotes the flexibility and problem-solving skills that are needed to be creative'. You will learn more about the ability to play being used as a professional tool in Chapter 11. Playing in art facilitates self-expression, develops creativity, engages the imagination, allows freedom to discover and develops an ability to learn by doing.

> **Task**
> *Collect lots of junk materials, for example yoghurt cartons, egg boxes, cereal boxes, wool, cotton wool, magazines, sticks, sand, shells, etc. Have good-quality PVA glue or a low-heat glue gun to fix the pieces together.*
> *Choose a few items from the junk collected and using your imagination begin to construct a sculpture on any of the suggested themes:*
> > *Future robot;*
> > *Space machine;*
> > *The house that Jack built.*
> *Use acrylic paint as it can be used on plastic.*
> *Enjoy! It's fun.*

Art as a means of engagement and relationship-building

Creative art can be used as a means of engagement with a participant or group.[13] The artwork becomes a component of the relationship and through a dual purpose and goal between the participant/s and the facilitator, a genuine and intentional partnership emerges. Creating art can help to develop relationships because it provides a wonderful way to interact,[14] to build trust between the facilitator and participants and between the participants themselves. Sharing space, time, tasks or a goal can foster a sense of belonging and value.

The artwork provides a focus, a task and a purpose for engagement. The relationship can be less personally threatening as attention is directed towards the artwork and not towards the participant. The challenges that emerge through the art process can offer opportunities to explore issues in an abstract form or through symbolic dialogue. Direct communication of difficult issues can be redirected instead into symbolically profound verbal and non-verbal communication. The art process can thereby become a mechanism by which overt and hidden communication can emerge. Frank and Frank (1993) supported the view that art can stir the emotions and offer a *new way* to relate to another person or persons.

Art as fun

Art activities can be fun and enjoyable.[15] When the participant is enjoying the activity, he/she feels relaxed and at ease. The normal psychological defences, such as avoidance and withdrawal, often employed to defend against the unknown can be lowered by fun art activities. As these defences are reduced, the person can become more authentic and more available to engage with others.

Art as a means of expressing personal uniqueness

When undertaken using personal creativity and with the intention of producing authentic expressions, art-making is a unique *fingerprint* of the person (Nadeau, 2008). Every person creates art from a distinct position or perspective. Creative language, so to speak, has evolved out of an exclusive interaction between the internal and external worlds of the unique person. Creative activity thus gives people's *uniqueness* a concrete form.

Art for self-esteem

Self-esteem is a concept relating to the person that places either a negative or a positive evaluation upon the self. According to Gecas (1982, cited in Cast and Burke, 2002), there are two dimensions involved in self-esteem: competence and worth. Competence relates to the degree to which you see yourself as 'capable and efficacious' and worth refers to how you view your value as a person (Cast and Burke, 2002:1042). Torrance (1962:169) linked creativity and self-esteem when he stated that 'self-esteem is a human need which ranks high in man's hierarchy ... Self-esteem is most likely to flourish when others feel pride in one's creativity.' Art can make an important contribution to the self-esteem of a person by fostering and encouraging feelings of success.[16] By focusing on the positive outcomes of the art-making process confidence will increase[17] and fear of failure will be reduced. Achieving a creative goal can be very rewarding, bringing with it self-confidence, pride and hope.

Art as learning

In a sense, all experiences can bring new knowledge, skills and competencies. Art as an experience can challenge the maker to adapt and learn something new.[18]

Art can be a natural and wonderful way for children and adults to learn. The objectives of their learning can be directive and non-directive.

Here is one student's experience:

'Today's class went really well! We worked individually and as a team as a result of working together, I have made friends with people who I have never spoken to before … I was very pleased with my folder at the end of the class. I didn't copy anyone else's ideas. I originated something by my own use of creative thinking. It surprised me actually how easy it can be. I think creativity is a good means of releasing any emotions you may have repressed in the past. The use of colours and textures is a good way to just let your emotions flow. Creativity is free and can only occur if you try! I am going to keep this in mind all along and hopefully by the end of this year I will have a more honest in depth picture of myself and how I may appear to others.'

Student B: Reflective journal entry, September 2007(MacGiollari, 2008:6)

> **Task**
> *The learning lists for adults and children, below, are not exhaustive. Read back over the chapter and identify areas that could be looked upon as learning. Can you add any points to these lists?*

Children learn about:

- art materials, as well as other materials and how to use them;
- bringing elements together to make something new;
- how one action can lead to another and the consequences of those actions;
- how to verbalise and use language;[19]
- colours and textures;
- how to move and control their bodies;
- making marks: pattern, shape, line, tone, form, space and proportion;
- how to represent their ideas;
- how to problem-solve;

- working independently and in groups;
- expressing feelings;
- enjoying art-making as a process rather than as a product.[20]

Please add to this list:

_____

_____

_____

_____

Adults can learn how to:
- represent the world as they see it;
- express an emotion, idea or experience in a visual form;
- activate their imagination and see possibilities;
- communicate with others.

Please add to this list:

_____

_____

_____

_____

Chapter Summary

▶ Creativity is an ordinary ability that can be used to make the most of our lives.

▶ Encouraging creativity in oneself and in others is a worthwhile pursuit.

▶ Art can be viewed as a means of societal expression and as a means of joining society together.

▶ Art is beneficial as a means of self-expression, psychological mastery, meaning-making, self-exploration and self-understanding.

▶ Art can help to communicate with others, build self-esteem, encourage relationship-building, occupy the body and mind and help a person to relax and see the world differently.

▶ Art can facilitate story-making, memory exploration, playful imaginative discovery and learning.

▶ Art is fun and enjoyable.

ENDNOTES: CHAPTER 3

1. Research found two respondents who felt art helped service users 'express themselves' and 'release hidden talent' (Lyons, 2008).

2. Research found two respondents who felt art helped service-users with communication (ibid.).

3. Research found two respondents felt art was a good calming technique for service-users (ibid.).

4. Further reading on Creative Journalling: Makin, S. *Therapeutic Art Directives and Resources. Activities and Initiatives for Individuals and Groups,* London and Philadelphia: Jessica Kingsley Publishers, 2000; Capacchione, L., *The Creative Journal for Children: A guide for parents, teachers and counselors,* Boston & London: Shambhala, 1989.

5. Research found three respondents who felt art was used for 'building relationships', 'social interaction' and to 'interact together' (Lyons, op. cit).

6. Research found two respondents who felt art 'stimulated' and made the service users 'active' (ibid.).

7. Research found one respondent who felt art helped the 'development of coordination, motor skills and sensory skills' (ibid).

8. Research found one respondent who felt art helped service users as a recreational activity (ibid.).

9. Research found one respondent who felt art helped with 'socialisation' (ibid).

10. Howard names other factors that influence this decline: 'medication, chronic disease, extended grief over personal loss, alcohol, the absence of a stimulating partner, an unfavourable living environment, an inflexible personality style, a sedentary lifestyle, high blood pressure especially in middle age, lack of stimulation, a low educational level and absence of curiosity or a desire to learn, malnutrition and depression.'

11. Research found one respondent who felt art helped the elderly (Lyons, op. cit).

12. Research found two respondents felt art helped with 'relaxation' (ibid.).

13. Research found two respondents who felt art was useful in helping to engage with service users (ibid.).

14. Research found two respondents who felt art helped service users 'develop their relationships' and 'meet their social needs' (ibid.).

15. Research found three respondents who felt art was fun and enjoyable (ibid.).

16. Research found two respondents felt art helped service users to 'build self-esteem', and two respondents who felt art gave a 'sense of achievement' (ibid.).

17. Research found one respondent who felt art helped with 'self-confidence' and three respondents felt art gave the service users' 'confidence' (ibid.).

18. Research found one respondent who felt art helped to 'learn different things' (ibid.).

19. Research found one respondent who felt art helped improve 'poor language skills' (ibid.).

20. Personal conversation with Inez Finn, primary school teacher.

FOUR

Children's Art—Meanings, Methods and Maturity

D e n i s e   L y o n s

SNAPSHOT

▶ Key theorists on children's art.

▶ Stages of development.

▶ Critique of stage theories.

▶ Encouraging children to draw.

Introduction

'It has taken me a whole lifetime to learn to draw like children' (Gardner, 1980:141).

All children begin to draw and make marks by two years of age, and by four or five years they will be making images that represent people and objects in their lives (Cox, 2005). For children, drawing is a means of self-expression, skill development, motor control and a way to visually represent the world around them (Kindler, 2004). As children grow and mature they learn new skills, and this is reflected in their art-making. Adults can potentially play a part in either encouraging children's development through art or inhibiting it. In drawing, children learn about the world, they solve problems and express feelings in a natural and safe way, and being aware of this helps us as caring professionals to prolong their engagement in this process. This chapter explores the characteristics of children's drawings as they grow and develop, beginning with the first scribble, the tadpole-type representation of the human figure, and leading to the realistic drawings made by teenagers. It commences with an overview of the various perspectives and studies on children's drawings and the stages they go through, and concludes with suggestions on how to encourage children to draw.

What the Experts Say

Children's art is an extensively researched subject and the wide variety of texts on this subject includes references to why children draw, what the marks mean, whether there are identifiable characteristics in drawings by children of similar ages and whether drawings can be used to examine intelligence and development. The subject is so vast that only a limited selection of those key questions can be addressed in this chapter. Gilbert Clark (1993:72) completed a 'time-line' of the principal theorists on the subject of children's art over two centuries, and his list comprised 'almost 200' names. Table 4.1, below, lists my top twenty theorists on children's art, these being the writers who have influenced the way I understand children's art and how the characteristics of their drawings change as they grow and mature. They also represent the central theorists referred to within this chapter.

Name	Year	Theory	Reference in Bibliography
1. Jean-Jacques Rousseau	1712–1778	Childhood is important, and studying childhood and children's art is important for society.	Kelly, 2004
2. Ebenezer Cooke	1837–1913	Drew attention to developmental stages in children's art.	Kelly, 2004
3. James Scully	1896	Collected data on children's drawing looking at perceptions, memory and imagination. 'Sought an evolutionary and scientific theory of image making.'	Kelly, 2004:8
4. Georg Kerschensteiner	1903–1905	Collected thousands of drawings over two-year period. Noted for child drawing classifications: 'a) schematic, b) visual or ideoplastic drawings – based on visual appearance – and c) three-dimensional drawing'.	Kelly, 2004:94 Dorn, 1999:109
5. Georges Rouma	1913	Extensive studies of children's drawings, in Le langage graphique de l'enfant. Noted for six stages of development in drawing the human figure: preliminary stage 'tentative' and 'pre-tadpole'; tadpole stage (transitional stage); representational; transitional stage between full face and profile; profile.	Dorn, 1999:109 Di Leo, 1996:5
6. Karl Bühler	1913	Three stages: 'preliminary stage of drawing, the schema, and the realistic drawing'. Scribbles linked to motor movements.	Kelly, 2004:94 Cox, 2005
7. Cyril Burt	1921, 1933	Noted for his 'seven stages of development: a) scribble stage, b) line stage, c) descriptive symbolism stage, d) realism stage, e) visual realism stage, f) depression stage, and g) artistic revival stage'. Children's scribbles are purposeless.	Malchiod,1998i Dorn,1999:109 Cox, 2005
8. Florence Goodenough	1926	First test to evaluate children's drawings of the human figure. Looked at measuring children's intelligence from their drawings in the 'Goodenough Draw a Man Test'.	Golomb, 2004
9. Georges Henri Luquet	1927	In his book Les dessins d'un enfant he studied his daughter Simone's drawings. He developed four stages of realism: fortuitous realism; failed realism; intellectual realism; and visual realism.	Luquet, 2001

Name	Year	Theory	Reference in Bibliography
10. Norman C. Meier	1929	Random scribbling takes on recognised forms. Meier-Seashore Art Judgement Test linked the ability to judge art to intelligence.	Di Leo, 1996
11. Helga Eng	1931	First longitudinal study of niece's drawings from 1 to 8 years, exploring developmental stages.	Kelly, 2004
12. Lev Vygotsky	1934/1962	Children develop 'psychological tools' to deal with, and express their knowledge of, their own environment – which includes image making.	Cooke et al., 1998:10
13. Herbert Read	1943	Study of using art at core of primary education curriculum. Role of 'chance' in image making. Stages in development include: scribble 2–4 yrs, line 4 yrs, descriptive symbolism 5–6 yrs, descriptive realism 7–8 yrs, visual realism 9–10 yrs, repression 11–14 yrs, artistic revival 14 yrs.	Di Leo, 1996 Kelly, 2004
14. Viktor Lowenfeld, Lowenfeld and W. Lambert Brittain	1947, 1957, 1964	Stages of development – scribbling stage 18 months to 4 yrs, pre-schematic 4–7 yrs, schematic 7–9 yrs, stage of dawning realism 9–12 yrs, pseudo-naturalistic 12–14 yrs, period of decision 14–17 yrs.	Lowenfeld and Brittain, 1987
15. Dale Harris	1963	Revised the test completed by Goodenough (1926) in 1963. As children develop, they include more detail in their images.	Clark, 1993
16. Rhoda Kellogg	1970	Studies of drawings from children 6 months–3 yrs. Identified 20 basic scribbles. Stages of development include scribble stage 2 yrs, combine stage 3 yrs, aggregate stage 4 yrs, pictorial stage 5 yrs.	Golomb, 2004 Kelly, 2004
17. Rudolf Arnheim	1974	Stages in tadpole drawing 'pre-tadpole, tadpole, transitional and conventional'.	Willats, 2005
18. Norman Freeman	1980	'System used by children in drawing could be applied to how they develop other skills, sequencing, organisation, and orientation.'	Willats, 2005
19. Annie Vinter	1999	Did a study of 209 children between 6 and 10 years, and 40 adults, looking at the relationship between the 'what and the how' of drawings.	Vinter, 1999
20. John Matthews	2003	Longitudinal studies (1970s–1980s) of three children 'Ben, Joel and Hannah' – studies show the process of development. Action representations – children show things as they are happening/moving. Developmental process – 1st, 2nd and 3rd generational structures.	Matthews, 2003

Table 4.1: The author's choice of the top twenty children's art theorists.

Children's Development through Art

It is argued that children's art evolves through identifiable stages, beginning with scribbling, moving on to the early human form, and then gradually progressing to detailed images of familiar people and places (Malchiodi, 1998). The idea of children's development through art being age-related emerged through the work of Cooke, Scully, Kerschensteiner, Rouma, Bühler, Luquet, Eng, Read, Lowenfeld and Kellogg (see Table 4.1). They described the development of drawing from meaningless or meaningful scribbles, to deliberate mark-making and on towards the ultimate goal of *representational* images (Matthews, 2004). According to those theorists, as children grow and develop their creative processes also change and develop. This is reflected in the images, the forms, the materials and the colours they choose to create their artworks.

This discussion of children's art will focus on the work of Luquet, Lowenfeld and Kellogg.

Stage Theories

Georges Henri Luquet's book *'Les dessins d'un enfant* (1927) presented an understanding of the representations in children's drawing and the stages of progression evident in these images. Luquet's work was based on the drawings produced by his daughter, Simone. Although the book was written over eighty years ago, Luquet's contribution towards understanding children's development has recently taken centre stage again due to a translation of his work by Alan Costall (Luquet, 2001). According to Luquet, children's art progresses through four stages of realism: fortuitous realism, failed realism, intellectual realism and visual realism. Thus, all the images made by children are motivated towards the ultimate goal of producing a realistic representation.

Viktor Lowenfeld and W. Lambert Brittain's (1987) first edition of *Creative and Mental Growth* was published in 1947 and described the development of children's art through six identifiable stages:

- *scribbling stage* (18 months–4 years);
- *pre-schematic stage* (4–7 years);
- *schematic stage* (7–9 years);
- *stage of dawning realism* (9–12 years);
- *pseudo-naturalistic stage* (12–14 years);
- *period of decision* (14–17 years).

Lowenfeld maintained that 'children's art experiences both reflected and supported their emotional, intellectual, physical, perceptual, social, aesthetic, and creative development' (Staples *et al.*, 2007:494).

Rhoda Kellogg, an early education teacher, carried out extensive studies of children's drawings between the ages of six months and three years. Kellogg (1970) identified four stages of development:

- *scribbling stage*;
- *combine stage*, when children put basic scribbles together to form diagrams;
- *aggregate stage,* when children combine two or more diagrams;
- *pictorial stage*, when the child completes a representational drawing.

Collectively, these three theorists studied thousands of children's drawings from the 1920s to the 1960s. Their views are presented here, structured using the stages of development as defined by Lowenfeld, i.e. scribbling, pre-schematic, schematic, stage of dawning realism, pseudo-naturalistic stage and the period of decision.

Stage 1: Scribbling stage (12 months–4 years)

Scribbles are the first marks made by children from twelve months old. At this age children are pulling, pushing and grabbing objects and moving themselves around independently. Also, hand-to-eye co-ordination is improving, which is evident in their ability to make marks with crayons and markers. Kellogg (1970) was particularly interested in the scribbles of young children of this age and she recorded twenty basic marks that she referred to as 'building blocks' for all other shapes used in drawing (Golomb, 2004:12).

According to Kellogg (1970), children make these marks without looking at the page, and they quickly begin to group the basic scribbles together to form *emergent diagrams* (Mayesky, 2009). Examples of such diagrams include 'the rectangle, the oval, the triangle, the Greek cross, the diagonal cross, and the odd shape – a closed though irregular shape' (Golomb, 2004:13). Children then begin to draw several diagrams together in deliberate actions (Kellogg, 1970). 'When a shape incorporates two diagrams it is labelled a *combine*, and when it incorporates three

1	Single vertical
2	Multiple vertical
3	Single horizontal line
4	Multiple horizontal line
5	Single diagonal line
6	Multiple diagonal lines
7	Single curved line
8	Multiple curved lines
9	Dots
10	Roving open lines
11	Roving enclosing line
12	Zigzag or waving line
13	Single loop line
14	Multiple loop line
15	Spiral line
16	Multiple overlaid circles
17	Multiple line circles
18	Circular line spread out
19	Single crossed circle
20	Imperfect circle

(Adapted from Kellogg, 1970:15)

Table 4.2: Twenty basic scribbles.

or more such units it is called an *aggregate*' (Golomb, 2004:14). According to Golomb (2004), children do not progress through the twenty basic scribbles as identified by Kellogg. Instead, Golomb found only two examples of Kellogg's scribbles in children's drawings: whirls and loops, and multiple densely patterned parallel lines (Kelly, 2004).

According to Lowenfeld and Brittain (1987), there are distinct parts to the scribbling stage, beginning with *disordered scribbling*, which occurs in the drawings of children between eighteen months and two years. During this stage children have limited control over their movements and the marks made relate in size to the motions made by the full arm. Children will look away from the drawing and appear not to connect the mark to their activity. Thus, the marks may not be confined to the page and may appear on the table as well. How children hold the crayon will also impact on the marks made: 'The crayon may be held upside down or sideways, it may be grasped in the fist or held between clenched fingers'

(Lowenfeld and Brittain, 1987:189). Sometimes the scribbles will happen in other places, for example while playing in the mud or on the sand, or on the kitchen walls.

The child's scribbles become controlled by the second stage, *longitudinal scribbling*. Children have greater control at this stage and they use the lower arm rather than the whole arm, thus the marks are more defined. Children appear more interested in the marks and want to repeat the lines made on the page. This was described by Lowenfeld and Brittain (1987) as a move from disordered or accidental scribbling to controlled movement. Controlled scribbling will include lines, circles and dots as the children have now learned to lift the crayon off the page and start again in a new place. Now the child enters the third stage; circular scribbling. They are also

Disordered scribbling

more motivated and enthusiastic to fill the page with marks, and will spend longer on the drawing. Lowenfeld and Brittain (1987) view the presence of controlled scribbles as a sign that the child is developing cognitively; however, they warn parents not to see this as a sign of premature genius.

The final stage is *named scribbling*. Lowenfeld and Brittain (1987) described this phase as a milestone in human development: birth—named scribbling—adolescence—death. It is at this point that children recognise the relationship between the marks on the page and the objects or people in their world, which represents 'a change from kinaesthetic thinking to imagination' (Lowenfeld and Brittain, 1987:193). Now the scribble is more than an active movement—it has a meaning. Children are more interested in image-

Longitudinal scribbling

making at this stage and will spend more time drawing. Children will introduce the meaning of the image to their parents or caregivers: *This is my bike*, or *Ringo has the ball and he is running in the park*. Lowenfeld and Brittain (1987) stress that it is important not to rush children towards named scribbling because in trying to please the adult, *false naming* may occur.

Lowenfeld and Brittain's *named scribbling* stage is similar to Luquet's (2001) first stage of children's development through art, which he defined as *fortuitous realism*. In this stage children scribble away until they randomly begin to notice similarities between their scribbles and objects in reality. The similarities between the image and the reality may be difficult for adults to determine, and children may not find similarities in each scribble. Luquet (2001) claimed that any likeness between the object and the images

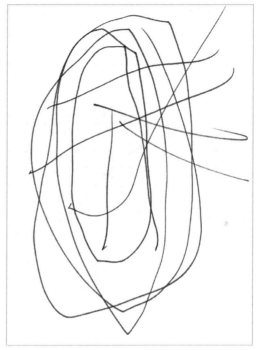

Circular scribbling

made by children was accidental. Children experimented with drawing materials and the

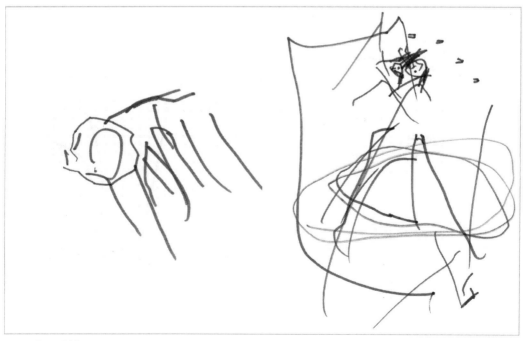

Named scribbling

result was a mark. Read, cited in Goodway (1998), viewed any representational marks as occurring by chance, where children stumbled upon marks that resembled some objects in their world. Yamagata (1997) argued that children were more intellectual than Luquet or Read gave them credit for, when they re-make and perfect these found marks (Cox, 1993).

In Luquet's second stage, 'failed realism', three-year-old children state beforehand what they are going to draw, but the image may not be recognisable due to their lack of motor control. In young children the eye moves from detail to detail, rather than trying to encompass the whole image (Willats, 2005) or take in the whole view. As children begin to accept the *realism* in their scribbles, they will gradually begin to intentionally try to create a realistic representation in their drawing (Jolley, 2009), and realism will become the inspiration from then on.

Meaning in scribbles

Children are introduced to mark-making tools by their caregiver and they learn, mostly on their own, how to make marks (Matthews, 2004). The majority of views on these early marks (Cooke, Scully, Kerschensteiner, Rouma, Bühler, Luquet, Eng, Read, Lowenfeld and Kellogg) agree that the drawings represent the mastery of a tool and have no deeper meaning. However, Matthews (2004:255) believes that the earliest marks and scribbles made by very young children are not random and disordered, but are 'in fact the beginnings of visual expression and representation' and thus not to be disregarded as trivial. Studies carried out by Golomb (2004) revealed that children were able to draw finer details when provided with slim markers rather than bulky crayons, leading her to argue that some of the primitive, *disordered* images produced by young children may be due to the material used rather than the development level of the child.

Stage 2: Pre-schematic stage (4–7 years) and the evolution of the human figure in children's drawings

According to Lowenfeld and Brittain (1987), children of pre-schematic age tend to represent images that they can name and describe verbally. One of the prominent images to emerge is the human figure and, due to the egocentricity at this stage, they may try to represent themselves. Rudolf Arnheim (2004) writes about this very common image that children first produce when they are drawing representations of themselves or others. This is the *tadpole person*, so named, or '*misnamed*' (Arnheim, 2004:197), because the body is contained initially within the circle, with the legs and arms, if any, extending from the circle (see page 66). Tadpoles are a direct development from the named scribble, where children use controlled movements and purposefully select how they will represent a person. Kellogg (1970) argued that the *combined* drawings of the *sun schema* and *mandala* were the beginning of drawings of the human face. However, Golomb's and Whitaker's studies of children's drawings, completed in 1981 (Golomb, 2004), found that the 'face' and 'sun' appeared at the same time (Kelly, 2004) as the tadpole person drawing.

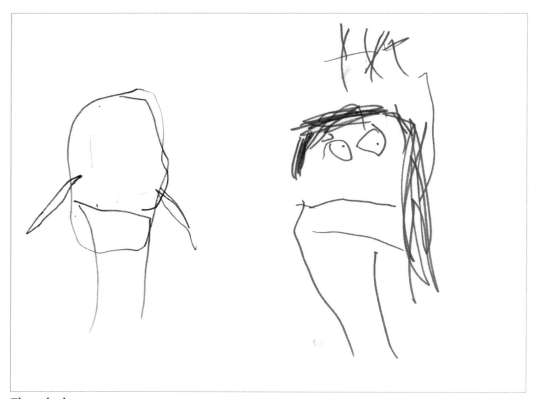

The tadpole person

Why are the bodies missing?

In studies by Golomb concerning the *puzzle of the tadpole man*, she asked children aged from three to seven years to draw a man. The 'majority of children drew scribbles, global humans and tadpoles' (Golomb, 2004:40). She then presented the children with a pre-drawn image of a head, with facial features inside, and asked the child to complete the image. The majority of children (69 per cent) included more details, for example the body and limbs, than had been included in the first *draw-a-person* task (Golomb, 2004:40). According to Golomb, children know about bodies and the relevance of the body as well as the head, and can point out the body inside the global image (circle drawing) or tadpole drawing, if asked. Golomb's rationale was that children leave out the body because it is too much detail to remember when drawing (Cox, 1993). However, Luquet (2001) argued that the bodies were not drawn because at that stage they were not viewed as relevant.

Norman Freeman thought that children made *drawing errors* when drawing their first people, errors he felt were based on their competence to reflect accurately and see the full person or on their level of control over their motor and graphic skills (Freeman, 2004; Willats, 2005). According to Freeman, the bodies are missing because children do not focus on the body as much as the face. They know about the body, but do not think it is important; therefore the head and body are contained in the one shape (Freeman, 2004). Imagine you are a small child and your parent is bending down to talk to you. What is predominantly in your vision? It is the face. Another suggestion, by Jolley (2009), is that the details are missing from the tadpole drawings because of the difficulties encountered in trying to master the crayon.

Later drawings in the pre-schematic stage

According to Lowenfeld and Brittain (1987), during the pre-schematic stage, as well as drawing tadpole people, children also draw objects from their environment. Children have now discovered a relationship between their drawings and the outside world. These mental pictures of people and objects were defined by Lowenfeld and Brittain (1987) as *concepts*. When the concept is turned into a drawing, it is called a *schema*. During this stage children are trying out different schemas to represent all the people and objects in their environment that are important. As yet they have not developed visual perception; therefore distant, close, big and small may appear similar in size in their drawings.

In later drawings, pre-schematic children will begin to change schemas and will include more details. The drawing below demonstrates the changing schema of *Mammy*. According to Lowenfeld and Brittain (1987), children may also exaggerate parts of the image if these parts are of particular interest, for example if they have a sore right ear, the right ear will appear larger in a self-portrait. Children will also make references to ownership and belonging—*my dog, my mammy*—and are aware of colours but are not trying to use them realistically.

Stage 3: Schematic stage (7–9 years)

Children repeat the chosen schema once they have decided that this is the way they want to represent the people and the objects in their lives (Lowenfeld and Brittain, 1987). Children in this age group attend school and their relationships with friends and peers have become more important to them. They are also developing a sense of belonging to a community as well as to their family. The images produced during this stage demonstrate a marked improvement in graphic skill. There is a *base line*, so the images are grounded in the picture as opposed to *floating* in open space, as in earlier images. There may be two base lines, for example when a drawing includes two sides of a football pitch, and especially in the drawings that look *folded over*.

In Luquet's third stage, 'intellectual realism', six-year-olds are able to include more detail, but they still have no ability to demonstrate perspective or foreshortening. Perspective is when there is depth in the picture, for example an image of a road getting smaller as it disappears behind a hill in the distance. Foreshortening refers to the technique of drawing things smaller if they are further away, but it requires an ability to draw what you see, even if it looks *wrong*, rather than what you know.

Although Luquet's 'intellectual realism' stage was posited as appearing a year earlier than Lowenfeld's 'schematic stage', the features of both the *schematic stage* and the *intellectual realism stage* are similar. The characteristics of intellectual realism include *rabattement* (a term coined by Luquet (1921)), which describes a drawing folded over showing two or more views in the one image (Willats, 2005). Another feature of this stage is *transparencies* or *X-ray images*, which occur when the drawing shows everything inside and outside of the object, for example being able to see inside the body, or to see a man driving a car with his hands on the steering wheel and feet on the pedals. Here children are trying to present the facts, knowing rather than seeing, which is called *object-centred image-making* (Marr, 1982, cited in Willats, 2005). As children develop, however, they begin to realise that their drawings do not really represent how they see the object, so they become dissatisfied with their image (Jolley, 2009). The picture provides an example of rabattement, X-rays and two base lines.

Task

Look at the drawing above and decide to which stage the drawing belongs. Find other drawings by children you know and see how they relate to the stage theories presented. Do they contain the same characteristics? Does the age of the child relate to the age of the stage?

Stage 4: Dawning realism (9–12 years)

During this stage children are changing and developing into young adults, and friends and clubs are becoming more important than family. With regard to drawing during this stage, children will pay close attention to detail in order to create a realistic image; thus the looseness of their previous images may be lost. Boyatzis and Watson (2000) examined peer influences on children's art, focusing on primary school children (8–11-year-old boys and girls). In their findings, boys differ from girls in subject matter, technical form and meaning. Boys draw themes of power, competition and depersonalised aggression, such as monsters, vehicles and weapons, with lots of movement and action in their drawings. The characters in the images are drawn far apart, and they often include angular technical shapes. There was also a strong conformity to each others' style: the children would wait until the popular boy began to draw, and then the rest would copy or try to imitate the style and content chosen by him.

Girls, on the other hand, drew static images, in natural settings, with people and animals together or separate. The people were drawn in an inactive frontal view, face on, and the face could be the main theme of the drawing. Girls also favoured curvy organic shapes. For both boys and girls there was a concern to get the picture *right*, which meant mistakes were not tolerated, were rubbed out or torn up and thrown away. Boyatzis and Watson (2000) presented a rationale for the differences between the developing genders. In the development of young adults the role of the peer group increases. Peers are now viewed as important role models and socialising agents, and young people are more aware of belonging within the group. Peers influence the content and process used in drawing, as children show their drawings to other children in the group. Comparisons are made between the *good* drawing and the *weak* drawing, and evaluations of each others' work are shared openly.

Stages 5 and 6: Pseudo-naturalism and period of decision (12–17 years)

In Luquet's final stage, *visual realism*, children begin to stop including transparencies and folded-over techniques and instead become interested in the technicality of the drawing. They begin to learn perspective, shading and occlusion (Luquet, 2001; Jolley, 2009). When children have mastered the skill of occlusion in art they are able to draw one object blocking another, drawing what they see rather than what they know. The pseudo-naturalism stage marks the end of art as a spontaneous activity as young people become focused on the end product, on producing a realistic drawing that demonstrates technical and artistic ability. Young adults are very critical of their own work and the more self-conscious they are in front of others, the less they will engage. The final stage or period of decision generally marks the end of facilitated sessions in art, when the majority drop out and consider themselves non-artists.

Critique of the Stage Theories

Luquet, Kellogg and Lowenfeld and Brittain all agree that children pass through stages of development in their art and that there are recognisable characteristics in each stage. If this is true and children pass through identifiable stages with definable skills and archetypal symbols, there should be similar images produced by children from different countries. Brent and Wilson (1982, in Willats, 2005), asking the same question, compared children's drawings of the human figure in Europe and America. The results were not conclusive, but according to their findings there was a vast difference between the drawings made by children in Italy and those made by children in America. They concluded that American children's drawings contained more images from printed media, whereas the European children's images showed a naturally drawn face in the frontal perspective (Willats, 2005).

Matthews (2004:260–61) argues that children's development may be defined by *moment-to-moment time* rather than *developmental time*. In other words, a child may change sporadically, based on what is going on for them and what they are exposed to, rather than evolving from one drawing technique to another. Boyatzis and Watson (2000) also criticised the rigidity of the stage theory as an over-simplification of all the processes that occur as children grow and develop through their art. Boyatzis completed a longitudinal study of drawings by 'Janine' over a six-year period, concluding that children can return to earlier stages and are more likely to display a variety of skills and characteristics in each drawing than described by the stage theorists (Boyatzis and Watson, 2000).

Lowenfeld and Brittain's theory starts at the scribbling stage, 12–16 months, and ends at seventeen years with the period of decision. The characteristics identified by Luquet appear to have similarities with Lowenfeld's stages, but are posited at earlier ages. From the personal experience of facilitating art experiences for young children and teenagers, I feel that the ages presented by Lowenfeld and Brittain are outdated and that children are progressing through the stages at a greater speed than earlier stated. Kindler and Darras (1997) view the scribbling stage as still being relevant when describing the drawings of pre-school children. However, they argue that children's art is now influenced by advancements in computer technology and educational aids: 'Stage theories are founded on a culture-free assumption and either neglect to consider the implications of the cultural and social context, or view any extraneous influences as detrimental to the natural, biologically defined process of development' (Kindler and Darras, 1997:19). It is only through further research in this area that we will truly know how cultural and social influences have impacted upon the content, methods and progression of children's art. However, if children are opting out of drawing at an earlier age, it is crucial that adults encourage children to engage in art-making for as long as possible.

Encouraging Children to Draw

From the moment that first crayon is placed in a child's hand, his/her natural journey of expression through mark-making begins. Children draw at home, in playgroups and as part of their formal education. Examining children's drawings offers us a window into how they view the world (Anning and Ring, 2004). Light (1985) believes that it is our understanding, or misunderstanding, of the role that art plays in children's development that influences how we 'plan learning experiences for children' (cited in Matthews, 2004:267). In the education system, children are taught to make realistic representations of the world around them (Matthews, 2003) and in doing so a value is placed on the *realism* of the image, rendering it a *good or bad* drawing, or one containing faults. For the majority of children their creative journey begins to dwindle through primary education, gradually declining in confidence and fluidity by eleven or twelve years of age.

Golomb (2004) stated that children will attribute a meaning to their drawings if asked by an adult (Cox, 1993). Lowenfeld and Brittain (1987) argued that all children would continue to develop as artists if they did not encounter cultural interference from parents, teachers and peers. Children draw more images with greater detail when encouraged to do so by a parent (Yamagata, 1997). This was called the 'zone of proximal development' by Vygotsky, and it measured the gap between the images that the child could make on their own and the details they could include when encouraged by an adult (Cooke *et al.*, 1998:10). Di Leo (1996:25) recommends that adults should not ask children what it is that they are drawing for the following reasons: 1) by asking, adults are 'establishing a premature connection between two areas of development that are at different levels of maturity', in other words, children have language skills, but may not have the visual or graphic skills to accompany their vocabulary; and 2) before naming has begun naturally, children are still learning about perception from touch and feel experiences and, according to Di Leo (1996:25), forced naming 'deprives children of the visual-motor experience'.

According to Boyatzis and Watson (2000), children will draw an image that the adult approves of. Here is a relevant example from the movie *Sixth Sense* (1999) by Hollywood Pictures:

Cole (boy):	We were supposed to draw a picture. Anything we wanted. I drew a man. He got hurt in the neck by another man with a screwdriver.
Malcolm (psychologist):	You saw that on TV, Cole?
Cole:	Everyone got upset. They had a meeting. Mom started crying. I don't draw like that anymore.
Malcolm:	How do you draw now?
Cole:	I draw ... people smiling, dogs running, rainbows. They don't have meetings about rainbows.

As a caring professional, your role is to encourage spontaneous drawing, where the child is not interested in the realistic end product but is drawing 'by and for themselves; drawing which serves their own intentions, and through which they understand the world' (Matthews, 2003:3). Children draw what they are interested in, what they love, what moves them, what upsets them, in other words what they see and feel every day. Children tell their life story in their own way, using images as well as words. Finally, many theorists have recommended that parents, teachers and those in the caring professions should avoid using colouring books or getting children to copy from pre-drawn images as both experiences create boundaries on imagination, on creative expressions and on the choice of materials that can be used.

Chapter Summary

▶ Children make marks naturally from around twelve months old, or when the first crayon is placed in their hand.

▶ As children grow and develop, the content and style of their drawings change.

▶ Hundreds of theorists have written about children's drawings and how they evolve through identifiable stages of development.

▶ Lowenfeld and Brittain describe children's art as passing through six stages.

▸ Stage theories are criticised as being out of date, over-simplified and not taking into account the process involved in growing and developing.

▸ Most children begin to lose interest in drawing as they reach their teenage years. It is important for caring professionals to prolong this activity because it promotes personal awareness, problem-solving and creative expression.

FIVE

Dance in the Caring Professions

Dr Sharon Phelan

SNAPSHOT

▶ Creativity.

▶ Trust, self-confidence and interpersonal skills.

▶ Cultural understanding and cultural integration.

▶ Dance and disability.

▶ Dance and society.

Introduction

This chapter recognises and explores the importance of dance in the caring professions. Initially, it places dance within a creative context, then illustrates how dance can benefit certain groups in society. Primarily, dance is presented as a means of gaining trust, confidence and promoting interpersonal skills. Following from this, the ways through which dance can promote cultural understanding and cultural integration are explored. The notion of dance and disability is examined—from visual, hearing, mobility and intellectual perspectives. Finally, this chapter describes ways in which participants can use dance to explore social issues. Each section provides sample tasks that might prove useful in these various contexts.

Creativity

Often perceived from physical perspectives, dance can be regarded as a 'talent', an innate gift.

However, this section adopts an alternative viewpoint when it presents dance as a creative art form, an interpretation that refers to the theories of Hungarian dancer and dance theorist Rudolf von Laban. Laban placed the participant at the core of the dance process and encouraged individuality of expression: 'Dance art works are not only publicly acknowledged professional dance performances but also the dances that (participants) make for themselves' (Laban in Smith-Autard, 2002:1). Laban's movement themes were based on the use of space; the body; interactions (self/others/objects); and dynamics. His stimuli were broad-based: tactile, conceptual, narrative, visual and auditory. (Please refer to the samples cited at the end of this section.) The dancers' responses were spontaneous and original, existing movement patterns were broken and something instinctive and untaught transpired. Even if other dancers had performed the movement skill or phrase before, it was immaterial. The participants were unaware of the fact and they perceived their movement phrase to be their own unique dance works.

Several factors contributed to making the session a positive experience. As participants improvised, there was a transfer of power: the carer became a co-worker and the participants retained power over their dance works. The atmosphere was less intimidating as the pressure to dance 'correctly' was lifted and error became a natural part of the learning process. Working individually or in small groups, participants of weaker technical ability were less obvious and as the teacher circulated, each participant received individual attention. Comparisons between participants' works were difficult as the dance compositions were unique. Finally, performance was not always an end goal.

There are many advantages to the adoption of this creative approach to dance in caring situations. The next section will relate Laban's approach to the teaching of pre-school children. Younger children's energy levels are high; they want to move freely and use large body actions. The child carer challenges the child physically when he/she analyses the natural movement patterns of the child according to his/her age and stage of physical development. Laban commented that 'what is interesting to the investigator of dance is the great resemblance of the first stirrings of the human being to the first dancing jump which a child attempts a few years later' (Laban: 1963:14). He noted that babies often stretch out from a closed position and that they use two-sided body actions that are strong, direct and fast. They also move rhythmically and employ large body actions. He therefore adopted these movement principles with younger children and he chose to avoid light, curving, sustained, isolated movements.

Children can explore other dance types from a Laban-based perspective. For instance, many folk dance techniques are inappropriate for the young child's stage of physical development. The fine motor skills are restrictive and often too difficult to master and the child becomes disheartened. However, this does not prevent young children studying folk dance. Laban compared the dance actions of younger children to the 'primitive dances of adults' (Laban, 1963:14). Therefore, primitive folk dances will suit pre-school children and these dances are as much a part of the folk dance tradition as more recent folk dances.

A Sample Class

A group of pre-school children wait for their folk dance class to begin. The aim of this class is to allow them to respond to traditional rhythms, to reflect nature and to use large body shapes as they dance. The ice-breaker sets the tone: the children play a game of statues. The teacher controls the game using a percussive instrument (refer to Chapter 10 for examples of how to play a beat). After exploring basic elements, such as fire, water, trees and animals, with their bodies, the class improvises to reel, jig or hornpipe rhythms. The fun element returns when they dance together to bongo drums, in a communal fashion, at the end of the class. Afterwards, the children discuss the class with their teacher and with each other.

Sample tasks for social care and early childhood care

Use of space

- Imagine you are a seed and grow into a flower/ You are a snowman and you are starting to melt. (Personal space/ levels in space)
- You are a leaf on the ground. The wind blows you into the air and down again. (General space/ levels in space)
- Imagine you are a balloon and the teacher is blowing you up. You have burst and you are flying everywhere. (Personal space into general space)
- Dance a simple four-hand reel. (Directions: forward, backward, sideward, curved)

Use of the body

- You are a puppet: let the teacher pull the strings. Head, shoulders, knees and toes game. (Body parts)
- Imagine you are in the jungle. Imitate a tiger, a snake, etc. (Body actions)

Time

- March in time to the beat of the bodhrán, drum, etc. Dance to a regular beat. (Set rhythms)
- Put your hand on your heart. Tap your feet to the beat. (Organic rhythm)
- The statues game. (Fast and still)

Interactions

- Write your name in the air with your hands and then with other parts of your body. (The self)
- As above, except this time find a partner and write your names together. (Partners)
- Make up a dance, in groups of four, based on Christmastime. (Groups)
- Find a toy sword and make up your own war dance. (Objects)

Types of stimulus: examples

- Touch a hedgehog or a hot stove. Walk on ice or gravel. (Tactile)

- Dance in silence, to a tambourine, to the sound of the sea, to a jig tune. (Auditory)

- There are shapes on the ground, walk, skip, jump round them. (Visual)

- Dance a dance based on a specific season, a colour, a mood. (Conceptual)

- Choose/make up a nursery rhyme/short story and tell it using your body. (Narrative)

Trust, Self-Confidence and Interpersonal Skills

'The dancer with self-conviction has power; many a dance of poor power has been put across just by the superb belief of the performer in the work … if you believe in yourself probably everybody else will too.'   (Humphrey, 1951, cited in Taylor and Taylor, 2002:37)

Blom and Chaplin suggest that 'improvisation during performance' is a means of gaining 'trust' and confidence (2000, 54–6). During improvisations participants are provided with an opportunity to reveal their inner thoughts and feelings. A simple example might involve the participants' use of personal and general space. Initially, the less confident dancer will work within personal space, and then he/she will move into general space as his/her confidence develops. Having 'struggled' with his/her 'creative impulses, blocks, ruts, fears and cautions' (Blom and Chaplin, 2000:55), he/she will create a unique movement piece and from this a feeling of self-satisfaction and self-esteem will transpire.

Contact improvisation is another dance type relevant to those in the caring professions. Pioneered by Steve Paxton in the 1980s, it originally catered for dancers with visual difficulties. (Today, contact improvisation is used among many marginalised groups to promote social inclusion.) During their improvisations, dancers make contact with other dancers' bodies and they maintain this contact as their source of inspiration. It is a sensitive process and self-contact precedes contact in pairs and groups. (Please refer to the tasks cited at the end of this section.) Contact improvisation develops a sense of trust. As participants take responsibility for each other's bodies, they '*bank*' on each other to be there, to support or lift them. Contact improvisation also develops the participants' social skills as completed works are 'derived from a diversity of tempos, rhythms and moods' and the success of the works depends on 'the relationship of the people in the group to the group as a whole' (Preston-Dunlop, 1980:11).

Sample tasks

- One partner shadows the body actions of another partner—then the situation reverses.

- As before, except this time the partners mirror each other.

- Support your own body using different body parts (e.g. handstand).

- Support each other's bodies (e.g. falling forwards/backwards, the 'Trust Circle').

Cultural Understanding and Cultural Integration

Dance has an innate capacity to promote participants' identity and belonging within their social context. The approach used in this chapter is twofold: it advocates the use of native Irish dances as an indigenous part of our culture, but it also suggests ways in which folk dance can function as an intercultural tool, by crossing cultural boundaries and promoting relationships between participants from different cultural backgrounds. Before acknowledging other cultures, participants (irrespective of nationality) need to examine their immediate surroundings. This supports the notion of Irish dance sessions. (Local dancers can provide workshops and it is also probable that expertise may be present within the group.) This provides participants with an opportunity to appreciate their immediate environment and it also introduces people of other cultural backgrounds to Irish culture.

However, the teaching of Irish dance alone is a suspect concept. Exposed to just one dance type, participants will assume its importance over other folk dance types—an inappropriate assumption in a multicultural society. When participants receive exposure to a wide range of dance types, cultural boundaries can be dissolved. For example, ballet dancer Peter Brinson adopted this policy when he took ballet to the people of East London in his 'Ballet for All' project (Preston-Dunlop, 1979:155). Prior to Brinson's initiative, ballet was rarely experienced among the working classes in that part of the city.

Dance provides other ways of uniting participants from different cultures. They can compare their respective folk dance types, noting the differences and searching for common features. Specific features will unite their folk dance types, thus revealing connections between their respective cultures: 'tree worship dances, animal dances, work dances, war dances, courtship dances and recreational dances' are familiar to most cultures (Whelan, 2000:8). Participants can also receive novel folk dance sessions (cha cha, rumba, salsa). Proceeding from the same learning point and following the same learning curve, they will unite to achieve the same goal: the dancing of the dance as a unit at the end of the session. As dance is a language, the participants can converse using their bodies. This is a dialogue that proves particularly important in a session where participants have poor command of the English language.

While this section concentrated on dance as a tool of social inclusion, all performing arts can fulfil the same purpose. Initiatives that involve swapping, fusing and exploring differing dance forms will integrate participants from different social backgrounds. As the participants experience each others' traditions, they will recognise the value of each tradition in the Irish cultural hybrid.

Sample tasks

- Teach each other your native dance forms (Irish, African, etc.). Fuse them into a performance piece using percussion, sound effects, silence or music as accompaniment.
- Ask teenagers to research a traditional Irish step or group dance using the knowledge

of elderly members of the local community.

- Let young children sing 'The Wheels on the Bus go Round and Round' as they travel to different places in their immediate locality. They can also travel from country to country as birds or fish, or on airplanes.
- Research a specific dance form and place it into its cultural context.
- Invite a local dancer to give a workshop.

Dance and Disability

'Dance is the hidden language of the soul ...'   (Martha Graham, *The New York Times*, 1985).

Often, dance is associated exclusively with young, able-bodied people. This study addresses the notion of disability and dance. It suggests ways in which able-bodied people can dance with people with disabilities, including dancers with mobility, visual and hearing difficulties and dancers with Down Syndrome.

Many dance companies include dancers with wheelchairs, such as AXIS Dance Company, (Oakland), Full Radius Dance, (Atlanta), Bildwerfer (Vienna) and Dancing Wheels (Cleveland). In addition, the International DanceSport Federation (IDSF) supports dance competitions for wheelchair-users. The dances include waltz, slow foxtrot and quickstep; Latin-American dances include the cha cha, rumba and jive. The competitions have different structures. Duets and group dances involve able-bodied dancers and wheelchair-users, and wheelchair-users alone. Wheelchair-users also perform solo dances and duets.

While most dance forms involve the feet, wheelchair-users dance their dances in their own unique ways. Some dance using their wheels as their 'feet', while others dance the dance in their wheelchairs, using other parts of their bodies to represent their feet. A famous piece performed by Siamsa Tíre, the National Folk Theatre of Ireland, utilises this idea. Founding Director Pat Ahern composed a piece entitled 'The Chair Dance', which reflected a traditional dance master at different stages of his life. Here, the dancers represented the dance master as an elderly man, for example when they danced sitting down or using the backs of chairs to support themselves.

Naomi Benari explored the relationship between dancers with hearing difficulties and dance. In her book *Inner Rhythm*, she emphasised that a deaf dancer's apparent lack of physical ability is often due to low self-confidence. However, people with hearing difficulties can learn dance pieces in a variety of ways. The carer can communicate the dance using his/her body and participants can imitate the movement and its set dynamic. Resources such as DVDs, mirrors and large television screens can also prove useful. It is probably best that those participants with hearing disabilities receive one-to-one attention at first, but after a while there is no reason why they cannot join a class with many participants. There, able-bodied people will dance the movement phrase or technique and those with hearing difficulties can shadow, mirror or reply to their able-bodied partners. Finally, silence is a valid form of accompaniment in dance and particularly relevant in this context.

Benari focused on the advantages of folk dance for people with hearing difficulties. These dances have basic rhythms and steps, which can be further simplified if necessary, and they involve repetition, which most dancers enjoy. Dancers with hearing difficulties can often have poor interpersonal skills, but as the nature of folk dance is sociable, the dancers will interact as they create and perform together (Benari, 1995). The rhythm of the dance can be transferred to the participants with hearing difficulty in many ways: they can feel the vibrations of the dancers' feet when they place their hands on a dance floor and they can also feel vibrations from a sound system, an Irish bodhrán and other similar percussion instruments. If the participants are capable, they can read music and transfer the rhythm to their feet

So far, the focus has been on dancers with physical difficulties, but dance is also beneficial for participants with intellectual difficulties. For example, dance counteracts the tendency towards poor fitness levels and abdominal obesity among people with Down Syndrome and it also improves their balance and co-ordination. Daniel Vais (2008), director of The Love Spotter (an Irish dance troupe made up of dancers with Down Syndrome), explains that 'the average person with Down Syndrome will need a longer time to reach a certain level as many have motor system and hearing problems and others have communication problems'. In a mixed situation where some participants do not have Down Syndrome, those with Down Syndrome can receive one-to-one tuition from their classmates. The learning experience will challenge participants' patience and discipline as they aim at their common goal. Once the dance has been mastered, the length of time it took to acquire it becomes irrelevant as all participants will have achieved the same goal.

Sample tasks

Visual difficulties

- A person with full visual ability leads the person with visual difficulty around the dance studio. Initially, he/she holds the participant's hand, then he/she uses a piece of ribbon or rope.
- Pairs clap their hands and move their feet in response to each other's rhythm.
- One person uses a bodhrán, tambourine or shaker to create a rhythm and his/her partner responds with the feet and other parts of the body.
- The able-bodied dancer moulds the dancer with hearing difficulties into a set shape.

Mobility problems

- Dancers in wheelchairs can use different body parts to 'dance the dance'. For example, the wheelchair-user can dance an Irish step dance using his/her hands instead of feet.
- Dancers can roll their chairs in different directions to a specific beat.
- Crutches and wheelchairs can become a focal point to which dancers can relate during contact improvisation.
- Dancers can tap their wheelchairs and crutches to a specific rhythm.

Hearing difficulties

- Follow the Leader.

- Shadowing and mirroring and replying to specific body actions.

- Let the participants:

  ▶ respond to their inner rhythm and move accordingly.

  ▶ feel an established rhythm: on the floor, on a piano, on a drum, on a bodhrán—anything that provides vibrations.

  ▶ use different resources, screens, mirrors, etc., as they will provide for necessary repetition.

  ▶ use silence as accompaniment.

Down Syndrome

- Participants can create a circle, moving forward and backward to a set beat using a stamping and a marching action. (Participants with Down Syndrome often prefer gross body action and they enjoy a set rhythm.) Progress to using fine motor skills.

- Let the participants perform the same movement technique/phrase following the teacher and subsequently in pairs and in groups. Improvise and compose a piece around this phrase of movement. (This will allow for necessary repetition.)

- Activities such as 'Statues', 'Mirrors' and 'Head, Shoulders, Knees and Toes' will refine participants' motor skills and improve balance.

Dance and Society

'Behaviour and attitudes are not fixed but are affected by cultural practices and social contexts'   (Adair, 1992:38).

As mentioned previously, participants can examine dance in 'different social contexts: in mainstream popular cultures and in sub-cultures' (Thomas, 1995:2). Certain social issues may have specific relevance. Stimulated by this issue, the participants compose a dance sequence pertaining to it. As the participants work on their piece, they will gain insight into the relevant social issue.

Participants can also analyse how social issues manifest themselves in dance works and in the development of dance. Stereotyping and racism are cases in point. For instance, dance is often viewed as a female art form. In addition, dance can also be linked with homosexual men. (It does not help that homosexual men previously sought shelter in and self-expression through dance.) In this particular instance, the social carer's mission is twofold: to illustrate instances where stereotyping occurred in dance and to remove the social prejudices that arose from this stereotyping. This will involve participants examining different dance types in workshops and on stage.

For instance, male and female participants might note the categorisation of men and women into stereotypical roles in dance shows: the virgin and the whore in Michael Flatley's *Lord of the Dance*, the nineteenth-century virgin-like ballet dancer and the strong macho man in *Grease* or *Footloose*. (Many of the males never danced: the moves were deemed 'effeminate' and thus their 'bodies quietly absented themselves' (Coward, in Ramsey, 2007:12).) The carer can introduce the participants to the works of dancers who confronted gender issues. For example, famed contemporary dancer Martha Graham was a staunch feminist—and she celebrated her womanhood in her famous piece *Diversion of Angels* when she travelled through female stages in love (romantic love, erotic love and the love shared between mature men and women). She also indicated a power shift in the sexes when she challenged Franco in *Deep Song*.

A caring professional can also introduce the participant to social inequality. For instance, in South Africa the history of dance reflects the country's transformation from a colonised territory into a multicultural democracy. Ballet was the main dance type studied in schools during the British colonial period. While it remains part of the present curriculum, native dances now receive equal emphasis. This broad-based perspective promotes an awareness of diversity in a post-colonial setting, where social equality and social integration are paramount. Many other social issues can be explored using dance: class distinction, nationalism, gender inequality, colonialism. By exploring such issues the carer will provide his/her participants with a deeper understanding of society, thus liberating their minds and bodies to develop freely in an informed way.

Task

Watch a traditional ballet piece and a contemporary dance piece. Analyse how women are portrayed, using styles of movement as criteria for assessment,
Learn basic rumba. Analyse its elevated position in post-colonial Cuba. (This notion applies to native dances in most post-colonial societies.)
Compose a dance sequence, basing it upon the societal issue of your choice.

Chapter Summary

▸ There are many ways in which dance can support typical goals of the carer: the development of self-esteem and trust; the enhancement of communication skills; an establishment of a broader movement vocabulary; a greater understanding of different cultures and social issues.

▸ Some consider dance the most effective tool of expression in the arts because it uses the body as its instrument of expression—and therefore is a direct expression of the self.

▸ Dance caters for all ages and both sexes in individual and group situations, yet young children and marginalised people are often denied the opportunity to dance.

▸ While the obvious advantages of dance are starting to receive recognition among the caring professions, there is still a need for further development in the area.

SIX

The Drama Workshop: Towards a Change in Understanding

Kate McCarthy

SNAPSHOT

▸ Drama-in-education, theatre-in-education.

▸ Applied drama, applied theatre, the arts in Irish education.

▸ Defining the workshop.

▸ The drama warm-up.

▸ A drama workshop in practice.

▸ Winding-down and reflection.

Introduction

This chapter is concerned with the use of drama applied in a workshop setting for the personal and professional development of students of the caring professions. The discussion suggests the validity of drama as a possible pathway or intervention for facilitators in the caring professions to utilise with workshop participants. I will begin by briefly delving into the rich artistic and pedagogic history that has influenced applied drama and some of the theoretical underpinnings that have informed this history. The latter part of the discussion explores a sample drama workshop that further considers aspects of drama, illustrating the application of theory to practice. I propose that (especially for practitioners of the caring

professions) there are innovative tools to harness within the creative arts that provide participants with diverse opportunities to learn about themselves as individuals and in whole group settings. However, to reduce drama education to the 'practising of life-skills' is too functional because it is also vital that the facilitator offers participants an opportunity to become 'agents as well as recipients of the experience' (Bolton, cited in Jackson, 1993:40 and 41). It is participation and reflection on the experience that lead to an understanding of our community, of the society we live in and of ourselves in the world.

Drama-in-Education and Theatre-in-Education

You may already be familiar with the terms drama-in-education (DIE) and theatre-in-education (TIE) from drama/theatre exercises introduced by a teacher/facilitator, or perhaps a theatre company visited your school to perform a theatre-in-education play on a social issue. In the UK drama-in-education and theatre-in-education grew in popularity after the Second World War, when 'a comprehensive state education system and non-hierarchical teaching methods became an important symbol of post-war democracy' (Nicholson, 2009:13). Within these new teaching methods drama had an important role to play in developing the participants' sense of play and their imagination through collaborative learning methods. The progressive education movement, influenced by American philosopher John Dewey, also had an impact on DIE and TIE practices. This particular movement 'stressed the centrality of the child in the learning process' and encouraged all children 'to express themselves spontaneously and freely, without fear of social constraints' (Nicholson, 2009:14).

Anthony Jackson's *Learning through Theatre* (1993) offers a historical account of the development of TIE worldwide. He traces the origins of TIE from its early beginnings with the Belgrade Theatre Company in 1965 to the developments of the 1970s, when 'children were put right at the heart of the events with responsibility to investigate, interrogate and make decisions that had repercussions for the characters involved' (Jackson, 1993:23), and on to the 1980s and its funding issues. Practices of the 1990s highlight TIE programmes that take place in site-specific spaces alongside the traditional school setting. Although the term theatre-in-education was coined during the 1960s, many of its key principles were already popular in the writings of educationalists and philosophers, such as Dewey. TIE's primary objective is 'to use theatre as a tool to explore ideas, feelings and values rather than to teach children how to put on plays … to participate in theatre as a learning medium and as a vehicle for social change' (Nicholson, 2009:24 and 19).

Gavin Bolton and Dorothy Heathcote greatly influenced the educational and artistic use of drama in the primary-level classroom and are synonymous with DIE. The focus of DIE is on classroom drama. DIE serves a dual function in that its objectives serve the educational system and the world of drama: 'its potential to achieve change of understanding (a pedagogic objective) along with improvements in drama skills and knowledge of theatre (an artistic objective)' (Bolton, cited in Jackson, 1993:39). DIE and TIE are similar in their objective to bring about this change in understanding; however, in the DIE process the participants are the 'agents as well as recipients of the experience' (Bolton, cited in Jackson, 1993:40). In DIE the facilitator/teacher and the participants are on the journey together, as a community of learners. Often, you will find the teacher-in-role technique (developed by Heathcote) at work: 's/he is at a fictitious level, joining in with them, but at an educational level or aesthetic level s/he is working ahead of them' (Jackson, 1993:41). As well as encouraging participants to take part on these levels, there is much to be gained from classroom drama in terms of personal and social development where the group can learn to deal with 'group interaction, discipline, language usage, self-esteem or movement skills' (Bolton, cited in Jackson, 1993:44). The participants are also working on their understanding and application of theatre skills within certain parts of the drama, which is a key issue for critics of DIE (see Hornbrook, 1998; and Fleming, 1994).

Applied Drama and Applied Theatre

The terms 'applied drama' and 'applied theatre' seem to have originated in the UK in the 1990s. Initially, these terms explained 'forms of dramatic activity that primarily exist outside conventional mainstream theatre institutions, and which are specifically intended to benefit individuals, communities and societies' (Nicholson, 2005:2). Applied theatre encompasses many types of practice 'that take participants and audiences … into the realm of a theatre that is responsive to ordinary people and their stories, local settings and priorities' (Prentki and Preston, 2009:9).

Bertolt Brecht, the German theorist and playwright, was influenced by Marxist theories and believed that theatre should not be mere entertainment but rather a tool for instigating social and political change. In addition to Brecht, Brazilian philosopher Paulo Freire and the aforementioned progressive education movement also influenced applied theatre. Freire advocated 'the possibilities of learning as a way of transforming the lives of students in a process that depends upon the establishment of a genuine dialogue between students and teacher' (Prentki and Preston, 2009:13). The authors acknowledge that this 'notion has much in common with ideas around facilitation practices' (Prentki and Preston, 2009:13). Augusto Boal is a central figure in the tradition of applied theatre and community drama worldwide. Boal was greatly influenced by Freire and Brecht, developing, amongst other practices, participatory theatre, for example forum theatre, where the audience become 'spectactors' and can physically engage with the play and improvise a possible solution to the characters' situation (Boal, 1992).

Helen Nicholson identifies three theatre movements that have directly influenced the development of applied drama: theatres of the political left (those with liberal and radical views), DIE and TIE, and community theatre. The common intentions of these 'traditions' lie 'in furthering educational, social and political' objectives (Nicholson, 2005:8), as well as artistic objectives. The intentionality of practitioners in these traditions is 'to use drama to improve the lives of individuals and create better societies' (Nicholson, 2005:3), while maintaining an approach to creating work that is more process-based than product-based. Alongside equal participation and collaborative working methods, 'what is emphasised in applied drama is its concern to encourage people to use the experience of participating in theatre to move beyond what they already know' (Nicholson 2005:166), bringing about a change in understanding. These ideas are echoed by drama educator and practitioner Cecily O'Neill: 'The long-term aim of drama teaching is to help the student to understand himself and the world he lives in ... and should extend pupils in their thinking *beyond* what they already know' (O'Neill *et al.*, 1976:7).

The Arts in Irish education

In the Irish context, applied theatre entered the scene in 1970, when Joe Dowling founded the Young Abbey, Ireland's first TIE group. Unfortunately, the Young Abbey was dissolved in 1974, but practitioners associated with the company created TEAM, an educational theatre company based in Dublin. The acronym TEAM maintains its affiliation to the Abbey Theatre in its title: Theatre-in-Education Amharclann na Mainistreach. Its aims include the provision of an 'authentic experience ... that challenges [children and young people] to feel, think, interact and do within the dramatic context' (TEAM, 2009). Graffiti Theatre Company in Cork, founded in 1984, is another leading educational theatre company that is 'dedicated to the provision of high quality educational theatre performance, workshops and resource materials' (Graffiti, 2009). Interestingly, Graffiti is also involved in the provision of training through its outreach department, which comprises Activate Youth Theatre, Physically Phishy, Fish Tank (a 2010 initiative), a Drama Training Programme and specialised workshops for their outreach work in schools. The National Association of Youth Drama (NAYD) was established in 1980 'to increase young people's involvement in drama and the arts ... It encourages youth theatre leaders to use drama in a way which helps young people to develop personally, socially and artistically' (Cronin, 2001:12–13).

The creation of the Young Abbey in 1970 certainly cemented the educational merit of the arts, in particular drama and theatre, and reflected the need for such a company. As so blatantly stated in Ciaran Benson's 1979 report, *The Place of the Arts in Irish Education*: 'The arts have been neglected in Irish Education.' The Benson report emphasises the unquestionable usefulness of the Arts: 'a familiarity with the arts can provide a form of language which can assist communication across the divisions of class, religion and nationality' (Benson, 1979:1.28). As well as providing the reader with a history of the arts in Ireland, he advocates the importance of arts training, which 'could be a useful aspect of training for social workers, youth leaders, adult and community educators' (Benson, 1979:41). There have been welcome improvements in the Irish system, such as the National Education Convention in 1993, which called for a more 'holistic' and 'balanced' curriculum, especially at second level, in the paper *Education for a Changing World*. However, the Education Acts of 1998 and 2000 only marginally make reference to the arts in education. Government bodies such as the National Council for Curriculum and Assessment (NCCA) endeavour to include arts education at primary level and for junior and senior cycles (McCarthy, 2004). The most recent report addressing the topic is *Points of Alignment*, the Report of the Special Committee on the Arts and Education (2008).

What is a Workshop?

As suggested in the introduction to this chapter, the creative arts can provide diverse opportunities for participants, and it is within the workshop space that participants and facilitator can explore and bring about changes in understanding. The drama workshop has many guises, and much depends on the context of where the workshop is taking place: a third-level classroom, a primary school, a family centre or a day-care centre, etc. The context will indicate to the facilitator the range of participants to expect and the type of planning that needs to take place in terms of age range, client group, the physical/emotional level of activities, timing of workshop session(s), the rules that need to be discussed, etc.

According to NAYD, a workshop is 'a sequence of activities designed with specific aims and objectives in mind. Each session has a beginning, middle and end' (Cronin, 2001:26). Other definitions highlight the interpersonal nature of the workshop: 'A workshop should promote collective learning, where a group of people spend time together using certain materials and, more importantly, each other as resources to explore ideas through interaction' (Hahlo and Reynolds, 2000). Although these definitions are not specific to the drama workshop, they do serve to highlight some of the key ideas for facilitators wishing to utilise the creative arts. First, collective learning is paramount to the creative arts process and it is vital to the practitioner as it involves teamwork, co-operation, communication and the ability to compromise, to listen and to participate. Second, the exploration of ideas through interaction may take various forms—music, dance, art, drama—but what is important is the interaction within the group, making participants aware of 'the fun to be had from social play' (Hahlo and Reynolds, 2000:xiii).

Preparing for your Workshop

Let us imagine that as a practitioner in the caring professions, you have been invited to give a drama workshop. How do you prepare for your workshop? Visit the space you will be working in, so you can easily plan for the layout allocated to the workshop. Try to arrive at least fifteen minutes before the workshop begins to give yourself time to move tables, chairs and other obstacles. Often, chairs and tables can become energy drainers as participants can lean against them in between, and during, warm-ups and exercises. Chairs and tables can also act as barriers towards building the ensemble by creating sub-groups and reinforcing the hierarchy of the traditional classroom approach. On your visit, you can also make enquiries as to the facilities in the building/space, i.e. the canteen, toilet facilities, first aid, nurse, etc.

It is important to find out an approximate number for your session (between ten and twenty is appropriate). As the numbers get larger, it is easier for participants to become disengaged from the process. The opposite is also undesirable, as too few participants will make people feel self-conscious. Before you undertake any creative arts workshop, it is important to ascertain the level of abilities within the group. These can be dependent on a variety of factors: age, specific client group, language, etc. Ascertaining this information indicates a level of respect for the prospective participants, as well as allowing you to plan your activities appropriately and to think about the best strategies and techniques to achieve your objectives: techniques that 'will stimulate the participants to release their energy, to free their body and their voice, to listen, to think, to be creative, to engage in focused exchanges with other people, to take risks and to watch others' (Hahlo and Reynolds, 2000:xii).

The Warm-up

One of the common elements within the drama workshop is the warm-up. This element always occurs at the beginning of the session. Generally, it lasts between forty-five minutes and an hour, depending on the type of session. In my experience as a drama facilitator and participant, the warm-up can often be the most challenging part of the workshop. As a facilitator, you will have to work your hardest at the very beginning to motivate participants. As a participant, you may experience feelings of self-consciousness and find it challenging to self-motivate in the early workshop exercises. Alongside motivation, the facilitator also needs to ensure the safety of the group at all times, plan and facilitate the workshop accordingly, be familiar with the space, side coach, improvise, have an awareness of group dynamics and deal with any initial resistance or, rarely, workshop sabotage.

Why do we warm up?

One of the main functions of the warm-up is to help the participant to contract into the work at hand, dispersing 'the daily clutter' (Hahlo and Reynolds, 2000:5), allowing themselves 'an opportunity to play, exchange ideas and exercises, and share the enjoyment of making a dramatic event together' (Hahlo and Reynolds, 2000:xvi). Participants have the opportunity to learn in a non-traditional way. The content of a drama warm-up often consists of theatre games. I find it useful to try to cover at least one exercise in each one of these sections: physical, vocal, ensemble and imagination. Augusto Boal's practice advocates specific games for the development of the senses as part of the warm-up. Boal's *Games for Actors and Non-Actors* (2002) is a great resource for both workshop games and illustrative stories from his workshop practice. Chris Johnston, author of *House of Games: Making Theatre from Everyday Life* (2005), proposes four initial focuses for the warm-up: attention, energy, imagination and communication. Indeed, some practitioners/directors argue the irrelevance of warming up, but the aim should be to include activities that relate directly to the later work of the workshop, or theme, as opposed to including games just for the sake of playing a game. The warm-up can be thought of as 'a ritual bridge', helping the participants to move from 'a world of conventional behaviour into one where rules are altered' (Johnston, 2005:117). Theatre games can also help the facilitator 'to assess the social health of the class' (Morgan and Saxton, 1989:109) and promote a positive atmosphere from the outset.

What might an applied drama warm-up look like?

Keeping words such as 'energy', 'imagination', 'ensemble', 'positive atmosphere' and the 'ritual bridge' in mind, how is a warm-up constructed? The planning of the warm-up will depend on the aims you have set out at the beginning of your workshop(s). I have chosen to discuss one of the applied drama workshops I have facilitated with first-year students who are studying Applied Studies in Social Care. The workshop is designed for an educational context, and the ages of the participants range from 18 to 65 years. The workshop takes place in a large room, with plenty of space for a group of twenty to twenty-five participants. Because of the context and age range of possible participants, I anticipate that there may be some who have prior knowledge of drama. The aims of all drama workshops for first-year students in semester one are as follows:

- to develop the students' imagination, creativity, communication skills and self-confidence through drama activities;
- to foster group skills and team-building through collaborative group projects;
- to encourage students to reflect on their personal development and in-class practice.

I would advocate some form of workshop planning, as it takes many years of experience to have the confidence to enter the space without a plan. In early workshops there needs to be a lot of structure in place so that participants can learn to trust the facilitator, each other and themselves. Trust is very important in order to allow them to commit to the work at hand, leaving self-consciousness behind and learning to re-engage with their imaginations. Although facilitating a trust exercise will not generate an immediate sense of trust, these exercises allow participants to move from working individually to working in pairs or smaller groups. While planning is very useful, do not be afraid to deviate from the plan if an exercise is not working or if an exercise becomes more interesting. Timing is another key responsibility for the facilitator, and includes the amount of time given to a particular exercise/activity as well as the duration of one particular session, and the time scale of the workshop programme.

A more detailed outline of the workshop explored below and the exercises discussed is available in Section 3 of this book (see page 229). The warm-up embodies a variety of activities to continue to develop the participants' imagination, communication skills and self-confidence and to foster group skills and team-building. In general, it is good practice to open the drama workshop with unchallenging exercises in which the whole group can participate, but allowing each participant to work on an individual level.

Observing the Space

Observing the space is an example of an unchallenging exercise that helps to take the focus off the individual while allowing each person to begin to contract into the work. Initially, participants will move in different directions, but quickly fall into the same step/same direction, so it is important to ask the group to change direction from time to time. This allows the participants to mill about between each other, becoming aware of their presence in the space together in a non-threatening way. As a facilitator, I think it is important to participate in this type of exercise as you are also a part of the drama workshop: 'As Dewey points out, it is absurd to exclude the teacher [or facilitator] from membership of the group' (O'Neill and Lambert, 1990:13). You can also use this exercise to observe the group dynamics at an early stage. As the exercise develops, it allows the participants to begin to make eye contact and get used to being looked at: 'Performing is all about looking at other people and also about allowing yourself to be looked at—feeling comfortable knowing others are looking at you' (Hahlo and Reynolds, 2000:xvii). This exercise also encourages the breakdown of physical barriers between participants, something to which beginners need to adjust.

Name Games

There does come a point in workshop sessions where name games become obsolete as the participants have become familiar with one another. In my experience, this familiarity takes a few workshops to establish. I learned the following game in a workshop facilitated by Raymond Keane of Barabbas Theatre Company, Dublin. As with most theatre games, this is only one variation of the game that can be played. When playing name games, it is important to encourage the participants to use a louder voice, as this also helps to begin to warm up the voice by combining physical action with projection. This physical game involves the creation of a sequence by throwing juggling balls from one participant to another. Inevitably, there can be a lot of laughing, shouting and confusion in the space. A lively discussion often takes places afterwards regarding the group's reactions, which indicates that participants are forgetting their self-consciousness and being heard. Hahlo considers this an 'unselfconscious use of the voice' (Hahlo and Reynolds, 2000:8), which brings the participant another step closer to feeling more relaxed in the workshop. I ask, 'How can we play this game better?' The participants begin to name the rules of the game: eye contact, using a loud voice, waiting until someone is ready, being calm, etc. This allows the group to establish the rules of the game, encouraging them to make their own version of the game's simple process. It also introduces in a subtle way the concepts of playing by the rules and co-operative team playing.

Mime it Down the Alley

The group have begun to contract into the work of the session and have certainly begun to work as a team. The next game is based on the idea of copying and showing, introducing one of the ideas for the main exercises of the workshop: watching and learning from others and interpreting those actions. As a facilitator you will find it necessary to introduce activities that fall into particular categories: name games, trust games, improvisation games to develop spontaneity, etc. It is a good idea to start collecting these activities so that you always have an intervention to hand. Again, I emphasise the importance of choosing an activity for a specific purpose, and stating the relevance of the activity to your workshop.

Status Games

Sociologist Erving Goffman drew on theatrical metaphors in analysing how humans communicate in society; thus the use of the term 'social role' (Giddens, 2009:264) comes into play to describe the way people act in different social settings. Max Weber believed that 'Markers and symbols of status—such as housing, dress, manner of speech and occupation—all help to shape an individual's social standing in the eyes of others' (Giddens, 2009:441). Keith Johnstone, whose name, alongside Viola Spolin, has become synonymous with the development of theatre improvisation, suggests that 'Our behaviour (reinforced by our appearance) signals our importance, or lack of importance' (Johnstone, 1999:219). In my drama and theatre studies training, the following status exercises were utilised to examine status at play within scripts. The status exercises illustrate how actor-training exercises can be adapted and applied in the workshop/classroom. As Bolton discusses, it is important to improve the participants' skills in theatre, as in setting up the drama workshop you are 'at the same time working towards improving the pupils' understanding of and skills in the theatre' (Jackson, 1993:44), thus fulfilling pedagogic and artistic objectives. Status exercises 'involve the conscious manipulation of our level of dominance' (Johnstone, 1999:219), aiding the participant to decode body language, use of voice, etc. My rationale for inclusion of these exercises is to allow the students to:

- interpret a character's status;
- apply their knowledge of status to the fictitious world in a whole-group exercise;
- participate in a discussion about status and stereotyping in our society.

There is a more detailed account of the status games in Section 3 of the book.

The facilitator's teaching tool is a deck of cards, minus the jokers. Each participant chooses a card and will play the game stereotypically at first, e.g. an ace might indicate a beggar on the street, and a ten might indicate a solicitor. The objective is to try to guess the status, i.e. card number, of the other participants depending on how they move in the room and how they treat other characters. The group dissolves into a discussion about their guesses, centring on their behaviour in the space.

In the second variation, the participants must guess their card numbers by interpreting reactions towards them. The characters begin to vocally engage with one another, with some 'side coaching' from the facilitator, e.g. 'how might this character say hello?' Side coaching is a technique advocated by American theatre practitioner Viola Spolin as a support for student actors/directors and workshop participants. This variation provides a stimulus for further discussion of stereotyping and gives the group the opportunity to reflect on the treatment of people in society, and how it feels to be treated in a positive or negative way. By engaging in drama activities the participants have the opportunity to explore theoretical aspects of their training 'through informed exercises while adapting a playfulness' (Raymond-Nolan, 2005). In this way the drama workshop can fulfil another objective, when it becomes an 'embodiment of experiential learning, where people will learn better by practice rather than by being asked to take in information passively' (Hahlo and Reynolds, 2000:xii).

It is useful to discuss the notion of status in relation to the world of drama and theatre, too, in continuing to further the participants' knowledge of the art form. For example, discussing the fall of Shakespeare's King Lear from a high to a low status, and inviting the participants to give other examples. The group may discuss the various statuses we use at different parts of the day: teacher, girlfriend/boyfriend, sister/brother, friend, etc., and how this impacts on our behaviour. The physical space we inhabit can also take on a high or low status—your first day in the college canteen will produce different feelings from being in your family sitting room.

Status game three: The Party

Armed with these discussions and reflections, we engage with a final variation. Again, the participants choose a card, but can decide what way they would like to play the card number, i.e. their chosen status. Thus, they are interpreting what the card number implied in previous games and discussions, and applying this knowledge to the fictitious world of the party. The facilitator plays the party host, as it is important that there is someone with good improvisation skills to keep the scene in motion. As Hahlo suggests, 'To make a workshop work, whoever leads it and whoever takes part must be prepared to play their part' (Hahlo and Reynolds, 2000:xii), and in the same way the facilitator expects the participants to play theirs. Participants enter the party as individuals and try to find out the various statuses at play in the room, but this time the conversation can give a lot away. The discussion afterward can be animated: participants discuss their guesses, how they came to this or that conclusion, what other characters said or did not say, and what this can mean in society.

Winding Down and Reflection

The final part of this workshop plan revolves around reflection and discussion: 'It is reflection on the experience that leads to a change in understanding' (Bolton, cited in Jackson, 1993:42). There will be points throughout each workshop where you can encourage vocal reflection, as sometimes the dramatic experience is a catalyst for deeper reflections within the moment. Bolton advocates the use of reflection with regard to the productive or unproductive nature of the experience (O'Neill and Lambert, 1990:144). The final part of the workshop is also an opportunity to help the facilitator and the participants wind down, and to prepare them to step off that bridge, ready to enter back into the real world: 'During an Arts workshop, people usually experience a different attention to the world ... Find a way to release participants back into the "normal" world' (Kuppers, 2007:111). This 'release' may be done in a variety of ways in a drama workshop—through discussion, through a calming exercise, with a reflective writing task in a reflective journal, etc. It is important to discuss with the participants the intended learning outcomes of the workshop and to mention what will be taking place in the next session.

Conclusion

In the drama workshop participants should experience activities tailored specifically to their personal and professional development, but that also serve an artistic purpose, giving them a familiarity with the art form. Roberta Raymond-Nolan describes the importance of the creative arts as follows: 'For the Social Care practitioner, the experience of performing ... can lead to empathy in future professional situations' (2005), and empathy is one of the key skills required of the caring professions. There are many avenues to be explored in whichever of the creative arts you choose to utilise, and as discussed at the outset of this chapter there are many options within each art form (e.g. community drama, TIE). However, 'The value of drama is that it invites people to make connections with their world to understand and to challenge it' (Fleming, 1994:19), and it is through active participation and reflection that we move towards a change in understanding.

Chapter Summary

▶ The creative arts promote collective learning.

▶ There are innovative tools in the creative arts that provide participants with the opportunity to learn about themselves.

▶ TIE's objective is to utilise the theatre as a learning medium to bring about 'social change'.

▶ The participants in a DIE process create, as well as participate in, their experience.

▶ Applied theatre responds to the stories and concerns of the community.

▶ Applied drama invites participants to 'move beyond what they already know' through active participation.

▶ The drama workshop should provide the participants with 'an opportunity to play, share ideas and exercises, and share the enjoyment of making a dramatic event together' (Hahlo and Reynolds, 2000:xvi).

▶ Reflection on participation in workshop practice is important in recognising the nature of our experiences and in bringing about change.

SEVEN

The Role and Value of Drama-in-Education for Students in the Caring Professions

Maria Kenneally

SNAPSHOT

▶ Drama-in-education.

▶ Understanding society.

▶ Personal and professional development.

▶ Example sessions.

Introduction

This chapter commences by investigating the role of drama in institutionalised settings and in the wider context of society. It then assesses its value with regard to personal growth, learning, cultural appreciation, community empowerment and socio-economic development.

Drama-in-Education

We live in a complex world. Our schools and institutions are microcosms of a world outside that is rife with cultural tensions, fear of difference and socio-economic deprivation. Very often we inherit personal beliefs that are deeply rooted. Drama is a module in the education of students in the caring professions of social care, early childhood care and youth work. Drama-in-education (DIE) encourages the questioning of opinions, beliefs and attitudes, which requires reflection on the part of the individual. Examining the self is an important part of the education of caring professionals. This chapter concludes by presenting a summary of three workshops, based on Augusto Boal's Theatre of the Oppressed, which were used with social care students.

Drama as a Tool to Understand Society

Caring professionals are required to consider service users' cultural, social and emotional development so that they feel safe and understood and, most important, valued. In the words of Edmond Holmes, drama enables participants 'to identify themselves, if only for a moment, with other human beings' (Holmes, 1911, cited in Bolton, 1998:278). It provides a place where differences between ethnic groups in society can be explored and better understood. It improves relationships through the creation of positive images.

Drama brings fresh ideas and new energy. Muscular exercises, movement, mime, dance, the use of music and artwork ensure that inhibitions are reduced. *Verbal* and *visual* communication is a key role of DIE. The games and image theatre techniques of Augusto Boal provide an opportunity for imaginative group work, where self-expression can take place free from the restrictions of differing verbal language abilities. This is particularly important for the many non-Irish national children and adults who arrive in Ireland and enter our schools and institutions with little or no English. They are now part of a system whose rules, regulations, procedures and practices may differ greatly from those of their home countries, and are also suddenly communicating in a foreign language. In this type of theatre the value of personal memories and experiences are highlighted, and these can be communicated more fluidly through means other than the spoken word. Augusto Boal argues that this non-verbal language is like a mirror and is a form of powerful, unspoken communication that allows participants to explore how they are seen by others. Through listening and observing quietly, participants have a better sense of self and as they acquire more self-esteem, they become more vocal and eager to talk.

The social role of DIE must also be discussed. It can determine the part that we play in moulding the communities in which we live. The use of thought-provoking material, such as photos, films, documentaries and real-life case studies, educates students about the realities of the outside world and gives them the knowledge and life skills to make a difference in it. Augusto Boal emphasises the role of DIE in empowering participants to challenge and overcome oppression in reality. He argues that 'all theatre is political' (1979:ix) and that it provides learners with the opportunity to better understand their rights and responsibilities in society. His games and Image Theatre explore self-awareness, group dynamics, injustices and social rituals and make a positive contribution to the development of the individual and the community.

Drama-in-education can also form new communities and social networks that involve participants, their families, community and voluntary organisations. Many drama pieces involve collaboration between theatre groups, homeless organisations, youth clubs and victims of violence. Belfast-based artistic director Paula McFetridge believes that location-specific theatre broadens the mind, and the dramas she has directed in prisons and religious institutions have increased awareness about the realities of life in these places. The skills acquired through DIE-based programmes have a clear role in teaching participants how to work with peers, appreciate difference and become actively involved in society. In addition, DIE increases the worth of our national economies through its investment in the development of people capable of dealing with career demands through creative thinking and sound people skills.

In conclusion, DIE creates spaces where more self-assured and informed young people and adults can imagine, reflect and care about others. Its value is seen in the building of communities where all forms of expression are valued and differences are celebrated. It has the potential to successfully tackle exclusion and underachievement. Where drama is incorporated into the social care context, relationships between practitioners and service users can be revitalised. It builds self-esteem and it promotes imaginative group activities.

The benefits of DIE are apparent in society, too. Boal spoke of a raised level of social consciousness that fosters greater willingness to accept responsibility for oneself and others. Greater self-confidence and self-determination extend into the family and the community. Faced with ever-changing cultural and economic challenges, participants are better equipped with the skills needed to make sense of the world. Their increased motivation and creative approaches to solving problems will ensure that they are assets to their team in the workplace.

Personal Development

The personal and professional development of caring professionals is an additional role of DIE. It encourages them to use more stimulating material and approaches in their work and it builds their confidence and enhances their creativity. Through experimentation with drama, social care practitioners more readily adopt a 'whole person' approach to working with service users and can see the benefits of creating relationships of collaboration, trust and belief.

This next section will outline three DIE sessions that were carried out with first-year social care students at third level as part of their module, 'Creative Studies'. The module had two aims. First, it required students to take part in an experiential drama process that would enhance their creative skills. Second, they were to assess the benefits of using creative arts in the community and healthcare sectors. This reflective practice was documented in a learner journal and discussed in class.

The focus for this first-year group was on the work of Augusto Boal, which can be used with actors and non-actors alike. Image Theatre allows the spectator of traditional theatre to become the spectator of this type of theatre, thus empowering the participants to appreciate their role in society and to communicate their inner thoughts and feelings.

Session 1: Games and exercises

This session gave students a greater appreciation of how the body moves and the importance of the senses. By their very nature the games are participatory and allow for creative group work. Energies are channelled into constructive rather than destructive behaviour, and a great sense of fulfilment is achieved through meaningful interaction with others.

Lesson aims:

- to introduce students to Boal's Theatre of the Oppressed;
- to encourage greater mobility and self-discovery through its games and exercises;
- to develop practical skill in using games and exercises to build relationships.

Lesson objectives

At the end of this lesson students will have a greater understanding of Boal's Theatre of the Oppressed, will have experienced a number of games and exercises, and will have reflected upon the benefits of physical activity for greater self-expression and more coherent group work.

Session outline

1   The aims of the session were outlined to the group.

2   Boal's 'Demon' exercise energised the class.

3   Students were introduced to the arsenal of the Oppressed through Boal's muscular series of exercises. In 'Colombian Hypnosis', students hypnotised each other and used sleeping muscles. In pairs, experiences of this exercise were shared.

4   The Walks series of exercises was explored. A line of five students faced their respective five partners across the room and in slow motion ran to meet halfway. Afterwards they discussed the difficulties encountered when slow-motion running.

5   A third series, the Blind series, allowed students to investigate senses and in particular the sense of sight. In pairs, pupils led each other blindfolded around the room. Participants all reported heightened senses of touch and hearing.

6   The final exercise was a group exercise. Each pupil in the group contributed a rhythmic movement and vocalised sound to create a machine that could accelerate and decelerate its rhythm and sound. These creations were performed.

7   The whole class reflected verbally on their experiences of these exercises and considered their possible uses with different service users.

Evaluation

This was a lively and energetic class, although some students were shy initially. At times there were outbursts of laughter, but pupils realised that concentration was necessary if they were to truly appreciate the experience. The group worked extremely well in pairs and on the whole bonds of trust were established. They were very keen to evaluate the benefits of activities and they reflected well, both individually and in groups, on the difficulties encountered. Excellent creativity was shown in the final exercise, 'The Machine of Rhythms', and great pride was taken in the group's ability to work together. The group showed sound understanding of the essence of Boal's exercises and the experience was made more real for having participated in them.

Session 2: The pre-text

Lesson aims:

- to explore how a relevant piece of material, or *pre-text,* can stimulate discussion about a social care issue;
- to encourage the use of body biographies to better build a profile of another;
- to develop confidence to discuss in a group, to show an appreciation of different cultural and personal acts.

Lesson objectives

At the end of this lesson students will have a greater understanding of the pre-text, and will discuss its use in planning a drama lesson with a group of service users.

Session outline

1   The aims of the session were outlined to the group.

2   A sub-titled extract of Pedro Almodóvar's film *Volver* was chosen as a pre-text and shown. This extract looked at the daily routine of Raimunda, the protagonist, who worked as a waitress in a Madrid restaurant by day and returned home at night to serve her chauvinist partner.

3   Impressions that emerged from the film were shared in a whole-class group. The most important action or words spoken by the characters were chosen.

4   In groups, students created a body biography of Raimunda.

5   All groups displayed their body biographies and discussed each other's offering.

6   Students were encouraged to explore the concept of Heathcote's Brotherhoods Code, focusing on the action of submerging one's hands in water.

7   Each group spoke about their Brotherhoods Code to the other groups.

8   Students debated the usefulness of these drama techniques used in class.

Evaluation

This lesson worked well. The use of a very dramatic visual pre-text gave rise to good discussion. The group embraced the character of Raimunda and they were eager to share their thoughts about her abusive relationship. There was much debate about the theme of machismo in differing cultures. Creating the body biographies allowed students to work in smaller groups and to consider the words and images that were most important to them.

Again, students discussed what they were writing. We examined the different body biographies on the wall and compared differences between them.

Students found Brotherhood Codes challenging and they looked at the deeper meaning of Raimunda submerging her hands in water to cool, cleanse and also obliterate the stain of her partner's blood. They were imaginative in their suggestions of other meanings for that act and it helped them to better understand Raimunda's mindset.

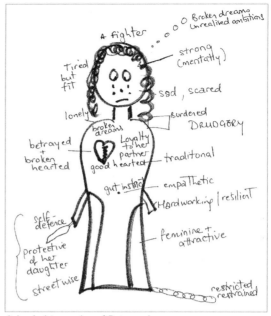

A body biography of Raimunda

Session 3: Image Theatre

Lesson aims:

- to develop understanding of Boal's Image Theatre;
- to work as a group and express more confidently through non-verbal communication;
- to interpret the images and messages of other groups.

Lesson objectives

At the end of this lesson students will have a greater understanding of Image Theatre, will have worked as a group to explore a social theme through Image Theatre and will have discussed their interpretations of other groups' images.

Session outline

1   The aims of the session were outlined to the group.

2   'The wooden sword of Paris', an integration game, was played. It animated the class and encouraged students to work collaboratively in groups.

3   The class was divided into five groups of four people. A still-image from *Volver* was projected on the overhead projector and discussed. In groups, the students were invited to share situations of similar oppressions, and they then chose one to explore through Image Theatre.

4   Each group created three images for their particular oppression: image of the reality, image of the ideal and the image of transition.

5   All groups performed their three images to the class. Some students were invited to dynamise their images.

6   All groups interpreted each others' images and reflected upon them.

7 Students mapped the objectives of the class to what they felt were their own accomplishments.

Evaluation

The overwhelming feeling in the classroom at the end of the session was one of achievement. For some pupils this was the first time ever that they had performed a piece of theatre. It developed their confidence and evaporated any initial fear of exposing themselves to peers. Students showed real understanding of the intricacies of Image Theatre and thoughtful treatment of the chosen oppressions. Image Theatre had been explored in a previous lecture, which resulted in more considered image formation. Some groups extended themselves to create more aesthetic body sculptures. All groups closely linked the experience of Image Theatre to the social care context, and debate afterwards was lively and relevant. An increased interest in Theatre of the Oppressed was expressed by the end of the class.

Refer to the Almodóvar film *Volver* as the visual support for your sessions, or choose a visually stimulating film that can evoke conversation and discussion. Before choosing a film, pay careful attention to the maturity, cultural identities and professional interests of your group.

Chapter Summary

▸ Drama is not simply acting but develops personal, group and social skills.

▸ As the sessions progressed, students became more knowledgeable about drama devices. Movement was one of the most successful elements of the sessions.

▸ Drama-in-education helps students to explore how the body works and to examine the senses. They agreed that drama games and exercises are both useful and important for work with service users.

EIGHT

Play is Drama and Drama is Play

Sue Callaghan

'Oh PLAYMATE, come out and play with me
And bring your dollies three.
Climb up my apple tree.'

(Words and music by Saxie Dowell; © 1940 by Santly-Joy-Select Inc.)

'Man does not cease to play because he grows old
Man grows old because he ceases to play.'

(George Bernard Shaw, 1856–1950)

> ### SNAPSHOT
> ▶ What is play? Theories and functions.
> ▶ The importance of play in a child's development.
> ▶ What is creative drama?
> ▶ The similarities between creative drama and socio-dramatic play.

Introduction

Caring professionals often experience the situation of having to join in children's play. It is therefore important for the worker to discover his/her own *'playfulness'*. This chapter brings us on an exploration of what play is, and how play and drama tie in with the everyday experiences of children and young people.

Playfulness

It is time to rediscover the playfulness in ourselves. A playful adult is more creative and has less trouble with problem-solving (Jennings, 2005). In crèches and playschools there should be 'free' play time with access to a socio-dramatic play space containing a dressing-up box, domestic role activities, such as kitchen/household furniture and appliances, and props for different trades and professions.

The role of the worker in play should be one of support and facilitation. If you are asked to join in a child's activity, do not take the lead but allow the child to retain ownership of the play. Play can be enhanced by suggestions and the introduction of new characters or materials. Other functions are to ensure safety, to manage and monitor noise levels so that play can take place, to ensure that no one is excluded and no one is intimidated and to provide choices between a range of activities (Wood and Attfield, 2008), but above all it is important to make it fun—to be playful.

A background in drama or theatre is not necessary to introduce creative drama into social care situations. Name games, movement games and trust games are all easy to facilitate and incorporate into homework clubs, youth groups, residential centres for those with special needs and centres for the elderly.

Task

Which of these actions can be defined as 'play'?
- *A young boy painting his bike.*
- *A baby dropping a rattle repeatedly.*
- *Two girls setting up a pretend dinner.*
- *A child stacking blocks.*
- *Children constructing elaborate sand structures.*

Is painting a bike work or play? Just what are the characteristics of play? This is a conundrum that has plagued eminent scientists for decades. We can tell what play is not, it's not work, but what is it?

Play has been described by those whose job is to study play as a child's work. It is a universal phenomenon. Children in all cultures play, though different cultures attach alternative values to children's play. Children from Alaska, Sierra Leone, China and Ireland all play games that are roughly similar: tag and chasing games, playing house or shop, for example. Play is an important part of our personal and social history. Dolls, toy carts and horses have been found in archaeological digs from the Orkney Islands to India.

Theories of Play

Early theorists sought to explain the existence of play and the need for play. Classical theories date from the late nineteenth and early twentieth centuries and attempt to explain and define the functions of play.

Classical theories are:

- Surplus energy theory: children have excess energy and if that energy is not required for self-preservation, it is put towards play.
- Relaxation theory: play exists to relax and restore energy and has no cognitive function.
- Recapitulation theory: the function of play is to 'rid the organism of primitive and unnecessary instinctual skills carried over by heredity' (Parhan, 1997:6). Children use play to help them learn how to pass through whole stages of the development of the human race (Garvey, 1977; Stagnitti, 2009).

Modern theories of child play arose from the development of cognitive and brain sciences that took place from 1950 onwards. Two modern theories of play are the cognitive development theory and the socio-cultural theory.

Cognitive development describes play as the force behind learning. Jean Piaget (1928) focused on cognitive development through the process of assimilation. Though play the child assimilates information that develops into mind maps in the brain. Just like a tower of bricks, play builds up information and experiences that facilitate learning. Piaget describes three types of play that facilitate cognitive development. Through play the child develops mental schemas or patterns that represent his/her concept of the world. These schemas grow richer and more accurate through experience as the child develops (Stagnitti, 2009).

1   Sensory motor: the child learns by moving, by exploring with the senses, by being an active participant in the world. For example, a baby puts a block in its mouth and learns about important things such as shape, taste, what is food and what is not. A three-year-old child with arms outstretched flies around the room as an airplane. By so doing she learns about physical space and the relationship between herself and objects.

2   Socio-dramatic play: in co-operation with others, the child learns by experimenting with adult lifestyles. They play out traits they have observed until the traits form meaningful patterns of behaviour. For example, two girls with a little brother tagging along. 'Right,' says girl one, 'we are going to play house. You're the baby and you are the Daddy. Daddy goes to work.' Girls one and two go off and little brother has to find something else to do as 'work'.

3   Play with rules: Piaget felt that this type of play replaced socio-dramatic play as the explicit rules are socially constructed. Examples of play with rules include musical chairs, chess, and What Time is it, Mr Wolf? (Fowler, 1980; Stagnitti, 2009).

Socio-cultural theories see play as a cultural phenomenon. Play influences culture and culture influences play. Children learn by playing with other children and through interaction with other family members.

Lev Vygotsky (1896–1934) was a pioneer in the field of developmental psychology. He worked in Soviet Russia and his work has gained prominence in educational circles both in

Russia and in the West. He is one of the leading exponents of the socio-cultural theory of play development (Daniels *et al.*, 2007). Vygotsky believes that personal and social development cannot be separated, that communities, families, education and culture all shape the child's world. The child's understandings of the workings of the world are influenced and developed from the attitudes and values of the others with whom they interact (Jennings, 2009). They practise social roles and develop self-identity; they are in essence making a voyage of discovery, reaching out to the world and trying to make sense of what is found there (Stagnitti, 2009).

Task

Take some time to think about your childhood and when you enjoyed playing. Did you have any special games? As an adult, what parts of your life are still playful?

From your personal experience, how do you define play? What are the characteristics of your play as a child? Can that be a definition?

Various experts, such as Catherine Garvey, William Fowler and Karen Stagnitti, have come up with the following characteristics of play. Does the list agree with your personal thoughts and experiences?

- *Play is pleasurable.*
- *It has no extrinsic goals.*
- *It is voluntary on the behalf of the player.*
- *It is often accompanied by sounds of mirth.*
- *It is controlled by the player.*
- *It transcends and reflects reality.*
- *It incorporates motor, sensory and cognitive skills.*

(Stagnitti, 2009; Fowler, 1980; Garvey, 1977)

Embodiment-Projection-Role

The current work by Sue Jennings looks at the dramatic development of play of the child and states that dramatic play forms 'the basis for the growth of identity and independence, strengthens and further develops the imagination, facilitates problem solving and conflict resolution, and gives the child the experience and skills to be part of the social world' (Jennings, 2008: np).

Embodiment-Projection-Role (EPR) is a value-free paradigm that charts the 'dramatic development of children' (Jennings, 2008: np). Value-free means that it can be applied to most modern theories of play. EPR marks the changes that a child goes through while playing and forming the ability to play '*as if*'. The ability to play '*as if*' is important to a child's development in order for the child to move freely from an imaginary world to reality. It is also important for the child to be able to play in a '*safe place*' where monsters can be banished with a word or gesture.

Competence in EPR is important for the child's journey towards maturity for the following reasons:

- it forms a basis for the growth of identity and independence;
- it establishes the *'dramatised body'*, that is the body that can create;
- it enables a child to move appropriately between *'everyday reality'* and *'dramatic reality'*;
- it facilitates problem-solving and conflict resolution;
- it gives a child the experience and skills to be part of the social world. (Jennings, 2009)

Embodiment techniques encompass gross and fine movement of the body, sensory movement using the five senses (*touch, taste, smell, sound and sight*), rough and tumble play, stories with sound and movement, and imaginative movement (*monsters, animals, space aliens*) (Sherborne, 2001; Jennings, 1998; 1999).

Example

Shake your whole body out. Shake your head, torso, arms and legs. Shake your feet. Start walking around the room. Try to feel the floor through your shoes. Take your shoes off and walk. What is the difference in the feel of the floor?

The second stage in EPR is the projection stage. In this stage the child moves from sensory play to a more patterned and dramatised play. Materials that were used in embodiment play are now used with more purpose creatively. The tower of blocks now becomes a skyscraper and stories are developed around it and the stories become more involved, more dramatic.

Example: puppets

The child uses materials to make a puppet and then projects a personality on to the puppet. This can also happen with ready-made puppets. The child can project their experiences into the puppet, but the puppet is removed from direct experience. The puppet can say things that a child cannot or will not. The puppet is removed from reality into 'as if' play.

> **Task**
> *Make a sock puppet. As you are making it think of what kind of personality it would have. What is its name? Where does it live? How old is it?*
> *Do not be surprised if your original thought at the start becomes something totally different at the end. As the material is shaped and moulded, the form and character changes.*

When doing this exercise, my sock puppet started out as a fairy but ended up a dinosaur. As I began to shape the head, it became thicker and more dinosaur-like. The fairy Donna became the dinosaur Donna and she had to deal with wanting to be small and dainty and in reality being large and strong.

The final stage is the pure role stage. In the role stage the child has built on the earlier foundations of embodiment and projection and can now step out of the real world into a world of his/her creation. He/she can become a character in a familiar story, can take on the role of an 'other' and therefore learn about him/herself (Schaefer *et al.*, 2000).

> **Task**
>
> *Choose a favourite story and read it aloud. Choose significant moments and divide the story into scenes. Develop character roles and think about how that person moves and talks and acts. Role-play the characters in a scene, come out of role and reflect on your experience.*

Lack of Play Opportunities and the Implications for Development

The reasons for a child's lack of play experience can be neurological, developmental, environmental or biological. But no matter what the reason, the lack impacts on self-development, learning ability, development of language, symbolic reasoning and development of creativity and imagination (Pearson, 1996). Peter Slade (1954) states:

> 'Play Opportunity … means development and gain. Lack of play may mean a permanent lost part of ourselves. It is this unknown, uncreated part of ourselves, this missing link, which may be a cause of difficulty and uncertainty in later years. [Challenged*] children often respond to further opportunities for play, for this and other reasons. They build or rebuild a Self by Play, doing when they can what should have been done before.'
>
> (Slad, cited in Pearson, 1996:98)
>
> (* The original reads *'backward children'*, a term no longer used.)

The results of a longitudinal study on play and language by Louise Jellie found that over four years the quality of a child's pretend play accounted for up to 20 per cent of language ability in early primary school (Stagnitti and Jellie, 2006). Play is very important for a child's emotional health. Vygotsky states that 'in play it is as though he were a head taller than himself' (Vygotsky, 1978:102).

With children who have experienced difficult life experiences, such as physical or developmental delays, pretend play can offer an outlet to safely relive the negative experience. They play out fears and experiences in the safe and secure make-believe place. In her research, Catherine Garvey (1977) observed children acting out family roles. She observed that playing 'house' has rules that have to be followed. These rules are gender-specific. If a child is playing 'house', there is usually a 'mommy' (girl) and, if a boy is present, a 'daddy'. A boy can never be a 'mommy', but can be 'baby'. If a number of girls are playing, there can be 'mommy' 'baby', 'auntie' and sometimes 'grandmother'. The 'baby' role is often not played by a child but delegated to a doll or stuffed animal. So when the 'mommy' is scolding the 'baby', she is acting out and mastering the emotions of the last time she was scolded by her real mommy (Garvey, 1982; Singer *et al.*, 2006).

Social Play and Drama

The literature on play often focuses on the child as an individual. However, we are born into social groups and will interact with various groups for all our lives. When playing in social groups we rehearse social roles and responsibilities. This does not stop with the ending of childhood, but continues with each new social situation that we encounter.

Of course, caring professionals must be aware of the importance of play. But when faced with a room full of seven-year-olds in an after-school group who can't find the resources to play together, an alternative method is needed. That method can be the use of creative drama. Peter Slade first drew comparisons between play and drama. He states the 'root of Child Drama is play' (Slade 1972, as cited in McCaslin, 1981:221). He observed the following constructs in the social play of children: the taking of roles and improvising the situations of life, and the repetition or rehearsal of these situations until the participants made sense of the situation. Roles, improvisation and rehearsal are all part of the doing of drama (Baker, as cited in McCaslin, 1981).

> **Task**
> *Watch a group of children playing house. There is usually some kind of conflict; the 'baby' may be acting up, or the 'mommy' trying to make the dinner. Conflict is central to dramatic structure. Participants then improvise, using different voices for baby and adult (characterisation) and repetition or rehearsal of the situation until the conflict is resolved or the play ends.*

> **Task**
> *When you hear the word 'drama', do you think of formal theatre pieces such as Shakespeare, Stoppard or Keane, or do you think of the improvisational television programme* **Whose Line is it Anyway?**

Theatre and drama have been with us for a very long time. There is a direct line from the first caveman acting out the story of his hunt to the elaborate productions of the West End and Broadway. Through the work of Viola Spolin (1986) and Brian Way (1967), creative dramatics began to find its way into the educational system. Progress was slow until Peter Slade, in his book *Child Drama* (1954), emphasised the importance for children of drama and dramatic play without the extrinsic formal performance.

'There was no stage just space; no audience, no axe to grind, no money to be made, no grown-up to titter to disturb the acting, no showing off, no worries, no clapping, nothing done for propaganda, it was not a social event. It was all done for the right reason. We were absorbed in creating real Child Drama, because we loved it and because we felt (we actually experienced) that we were creating something wonderful and beautiful.'

(Slade, 1995, cited in Jennings and Stagnitti, 2007:10)

'Drama is as intangible as personality itself, and is concerned with developing people' (Way, 1967:7). Creative drama is a form of drama that uses imagination, life experiences and playfulness to create learning experiences that benefit the participant.

Creative drama is an improvisational, non-exhibitional, process-oriented form of drama, where participants are guided by a leader to imagine, enact, and reflect on experiences real and imagined. Creative drama takes the children's natural world, creative play, and develops it further using theatre techniques, to create learning experiences which are for the participants. D. Heathcote, one of the pioneers of creative drama in the classroom, states that 'engaging in drama helps us to explore feelings of an experience, and thus decreasing any anxiety we may have toward the experience and thereby increasing our control over it' (Heathcote, cited in Wagner, 1999:137).

'Non-exhibitional' means that there is no performance at the end of the session. 'Process-oriented' means that it is concerned with the internal learning experiences of the participant. The process that the individual goes through is the important factor, not the final product. The final goal is the experience of the participants. 'Let's pretend', just like in play, is the norm for creative drama. Participating in creative drama exercises can facilitate learning about emotions, develop imagination, improve problem-solving skills and build confidence.

'Drama not only helps us come to terms with our everyday life and facilitates exploration of our inner life, but it also enables us to transcend ourselves and go beyond our everyday limits and boundaries.'   (Jennings, 1986:4)

One critical aspect of creative drama is that there are no right or wrong answers or right or wrong ways of doing the exercises. Children and adults can benefit from experiences in creative drama. Creative drama benefits children and adults with special needs. It can be used as part of the educational curriculum in schools and in youth clubs.

The beneficial effects are:

- creativity is a key ingredient to all dramatic explorations;
- working creatively encourages self-esteem and positive self-expression;
- creative drama is a safe way of exploring feelings;
- creative drama can help in developing new coping skills and patterns;
- there is a reduced feeling of isolation;
- through catharsis, there is a cleansing.

(Way, 1967; McCaslin, 1981; Jennings, 1986; Slade, 1995; Cattanach, 1996.)

Creative drama and socio-dramatic play have the same objectives, which are are to:

- facilitate social growth;
- develop a sense of social self;
- learn to work with others;
- practise collaborate and co-operative skills;
- provide a safe medium to explore difficult situations.

Drama Techniques for Caring Professionals

It is important for the student or worker to establish a rapport with the group with whom he/she is working. Often the simplest games can be the most fun and help to build trust between the participants.

Examples

Name game

Say the name of a person in the circle, make eye contact and toss a soft ball to them; they in turn say another name and toss the ball. Make it more difficult by adding more soft balls to the circle. This is a great fun way to learn people's names.

Mirror game

This game is done in pairs. One partner is the leader; the other is a mirror and copies the movements of the leader. This can be done sitting down or standing up.

Move if you ...

This game is known by many names, such as mixed nuts, fruit bowl, train wreck, etc. The group sits in a circle and a person in the middle calls out 'move if you have *a specific attribute*'. Examples of the attribute may be wearing runners, jeans, scarves, glasses, or red colours, or have blue eyes, blonde or brown hair. All those having the attribute must move chairs or places in the circle. You cannot sit back down in the same place. The caller can then get a place, another person takes over the centre of the circle and the game continues. This is a simple game, but can help participants to learn colours, articles of clothing and facial features. It is also very energetic and causes lots of laughter.

Role-play

Role-play should be introduced only after you have built up a sense of trust with the group and they are working well together. Role-play is an excellent tool for helping to discover new ways of social interaction and helps to extend the frontiers of role repertoire.

Role-play starters

First lines

Take a list of lines such as:

> Your breakfast is getting cold …
> Listen, I've got a great idea …
> Guess where we are going on our holidays …
> Are you new here? …

Use the lines as the first line in the start of a role-play. Give the line to one participant, they deliver the line, the second participant responds and the role-play continues from there.

A planned role-play:

Set up a scenario, such as a birthday party. Mother/father and daughter/son go over arrangements for the party. Friends arrive; conflict develops and is eventually sorted out.

Going to the restaurant: participants take the roles of the restaurant staff and customers. They deal with situations that can arise in a restaurant, such as poor service, cold food, no seating.

In all of the above it is important to remember to be a facilitator, not a leader or director. The drama should come from the experience of the participants. Remember that the goal is not a theatrical production but the process that the participant goes through.

Chapter Summary

▸ Play is a child's work and without it a child's development is severely disadvantaged. It has been recognised as important for healthy child development. It is fun and enjoyable. It develops creativity, imagination, emotional strength and intellectual competence. Embodiment-projection-role is the dramatic development of the child; the ability to play 'as if'. It is a process rather than a goal and, as with play, 'let's pretend' is central to the experience.

▸ Creative drama and socio-dramatic play have similar goals: developing the social self, learning co-operation and working together, a safe medium to explore life situations.

▸ Child care and social care practitioners have stated that drama is 'a healthy forum to express yourself', that 'it allows participants to understand different expressions and emotions', that it 'builds self-confidence' and that it 'gives the young person a chance to display behaviour through a third person'.

▸ The caring professional has to be a facilitator and a playful adult. Be enthusiastic with the participants and, above all, HAVE FUN!

NINE

The Therapeutic Benefits of Storytelling for Children

Jennifer Fawcett

SNAPSHOT

▶ How to use storytelling.

▶ Storytelling is a key to the inner world.

▶ The practitioner as listener.

▶ The practice of storytelling.

Introduction

Storytelling offers an age-old way of communicating that can be beneficial in helping people to express themselves. It is a method of providing a voice for those who feel powerless and for whom direct discussion of innermost thoughts and feelings proves difficult. Whether the stories are personal or more general, their myths and metaphors often give rise to a new perspective on old problems, and allow their users to experience a less confrontational approach to talking through their issues. For the purposes of this chapter, the focus will be on using storytelling with children, but it is hoped that by reawakening our awareness of the human connection with story, it can be shown that storytelling offers something to all age groups. Many of the activities discussed are geared towards children, but could be adapted for teenagers or even adults. Understanding why the language of stories can be so powerful is key in adapting these techniques.

What do Stories Offer?

'The Bushmen of the Kalahari desert say that without a story of one's own, one hasn't got a life of one's own.'   (Gersie and King,1990:38)

At its most basic level, we can see that each of our lives functions as a story. We narrate our life experiences and seek to prove our individuality through showing how daily events are reflected through our own mind's eye. Gersie and King suggest that stories 'provide encouragement to continue the formulation of questions rather than to abandon the search. … Untethered by the constraints of reality, yet within a plausible structure, our story characters explore alternative actions until an answer and a way out is found' (1990:35). From the fairytales our parents read to us at bedtime when we were little to the films we watch and the books we read as adults, stories provide an essential function of being human.

From the point of view of working with children, storytelling has a dual purpose. On the face of it, stories have an educational value. Riley and Reedy (2007) highlight the role of books and stories in 'developing oracy' and show how 'stories provide a basis for stimulation, for discussion, for debate and for fantasy' (Riley and Reedy, 2007:71). Stories can be a very effective tool for teaching basic language skills: repeated enjoyment of stories can reinforce reading and writing skills. The social element of storytelling must not be neglected, as stories for children often deal with peer and family issues, and techniques such as puppetry and shared storytimes can help draw children together. Riley and Reedy also point out how children, given the chance to play quietly with a teacher or caregiver nearby who is prepared to just listen, will readily 'confide their stories' (2007:47).

Another vital educational use of stories is indicated in the case of children with autism or autistic spectrum disorders (ASD). These students are described as 'sharing a triad of impairments that affects their ability to understand and use non-verbal and verbal communication, understand social behaviour … and think and behave flexibly.' Students with Asperger syndrome 'find it difficult to interpret social signals and interact with others. They often excel at memorising facts and figures but exhibit difficulty thinking in … abstract ways' (Special Education Support Service, 2008:30–31). One of the key approaches suggested for these children are *social stories*. According to *Signposts*, these are 'designed to enable the student to cope with social situations which he/she finds difficult. They are visual, identify relevant cues, provide easily accessible accurate information for the student and describe expected behaviours' (2008:32). For examples of these stories, please see *My Social Stories Book* (2002), by Carol Gray and Abbie Leigh White.

The use of storytelling can be taken to another level, however, whereby stories, accompanied by the chance to reflect on them and make them one's own, become a therapeutic medium for helping children to work through the issues they face. This brings a notion of emotional development into play, as a complement to pure educational development. Riley suggests that emotional development 'hinges on the ability to make meaning of one's experience in an often bewildering world and it is often stories which capture the imagination and provide the vehicle for that process of meaning-making' (Riley and Reedy, 2007:59). Whether the children with whom you are working have emotional traumas, are in vulnerable social situations, have learning difficulties or specific physical challenges such as deafness or speech impediments, the therapeutic value of giving them a means to express themselves cannot be overemphasised.

How do we Use Storytelling?

This chapter has two different branches. The first is a more theoretical one, inviting the practitioner to think of him/herself as 'listener' and pointing out some of the challenges and rewards of considering one's role within the storytelling situation. Understanding that we cannot stand separately from the stories being told to us is vital in providing a therapeutic experience for the storyteller. The second branch deals with the practicalities of setting up a storytelling environment. From a starting point of showing how story 'works' through a specialised use of language and the resolutions that a therapeutic story can bring, it is hoped that the discussion of some basic techniques for getting started and some do's and don't's will make the process easier.

The Keys to the Inner World

> '[E]very child develops with some sense of "self" and identity and … a central part of this self is what might be called the "inner world": the internal psychological and emotional picture which we evolve of the world and the people in it. This inner world consists of a mixture of the conscious and the less-than-conscious: thoughts and feelings, fears and imaginings, understandings and misunderstandings, dreams and nightmares, images of people and places and assumptions about their meaning and importance.'
>
> (Ward, 1998:11–12)

Ward (1998) highlights some important concepts that can help us to understand the complexities of communicating with children. He utilises Winnicott's theory of *holding* and Bion's concept of *containment* to show how the child develops a sense of self and an understanding of his/her place in the world. From birth, an infant starts to experience the 'holding environment' that his/her parents provide for him/her, literally through the physical act of holding and comforting him/her, as well as through helping him/her to process the unmanageable emotions and sensations that pass over him/her and at times threaten to overwhelm him/her. This helps the child to begin to recognise his/her own feelings and to begin to think about them, as well as developing 'the capacity to symbolise and to play' (Ward, 1998:14). This is the start of the formation of the inner world, which is sustained and developed as the child progresses from a stage of complete dependence to a more autonomous way of being. A secure holding environment is therefore necessary to allow the child to develop the ability to imagine, play and think about his/her emotions and feelings.

This development is also supported by the process of 'containment', a concept first introduced by Bion (1962), cited in Ward (1998). Ward (1998) describes how, according to

Bion, 'it is through the process of containment that the infant's most unmanageable feelings and deepest anxieties are "projected" onto the parent so that, initially at least, the parent can feel them for him or her, before handing them back in a more manageable form, as if to say, "There: that's what you were worried about. I think you'll find you can cope with this now"' (Ward, 1998:15). Through this facilitative process, over time, the child will gain the skills to be able to deal with his/her own emotions more effectively.

Ward (1998) tries to show how the child can, through these two fundamental processes, begin to create an inner world. The inner world is informed by both the concrete, 'real' situations the child goes through every day and the interpretations and assumptions the child draws from these. Ward does point out that problems can arise for children when these interpretations come from misunderstandings, or when the child's version of events does not tally with what others tell him has happened (Ward, 1998:13). This results in these feelings becoming hidden in the inner world as the child feels it is 'impossible to reveal them to anyone else' (Ward, 1998:13). This happens very often, even to the most secure child, as children have a tendency to view themselves as the centre of their world and 'thus the *cause* of all events whether good or bad' (Ward, 1998:13.). Ward also puts forward the concept of a 'magic' inner world, where 'people and events can be changed, destroyed or denied as the child tries to insulate itself from knowing and feeling the pain of the situation' (Ward, 1998:13). This is particularly the case for children who have experienced some kind of trauma, such as neglect or abuse, or bereavement and loss. They would rather seek refuge in their magical inner world than face the real world in front of them.

Having even a simple understanding of some of these processes can show us that working with children and communicating with their inner world requires a great deal of empathy, timing and patience (Ward, 1998:14). It is here that the work of Ward and his collaborator, McMahon, comes to the fore as they advance through some vital points on being both supportive and supported as a practitioner.

McMahon (1998) has described how some practitioners realise that their qualifications are only part of the process of working with children. Rather than being seen as 'experts', they feel that, perhaps more important, they have developed an awareness of the qualities of 'humanity and equality', or that 'they have learned that each situation requires a desire and an effort to understand' (1998:120). This desire to be empathic, to reach forward and connect with children in a meaningful way, is central to the use of storytelling as a therapeutic method. We can use McMahon's discussion of helping children to both symbolise and conceptualise their experience, in a way that helps them to deal with it and move beyond it, to inform some of our understanding behind our role as listener in a storytelling situation.

McMahon describes the importance, when working with extremely vulnerable or traumatised children, of building a fund of primary or sensory experiences for the child to draw on. A practitioner can provide these experiences by drawing on a range of techniques from many different arenas, such as play, music, art, drama or, in this case, storytelling. Attention to detail within this practice is vital, ensuring there is a sense of continuity, as is witnessing how a child deals with the beginnings and endings of the experiences shared with him/her (McMahon, 1998:112). Careful and sensitive work in this area is very restorative for the child.

An extremely effective example of an activity that could cover all these areas is the Lifebook, as pioneered by Vera Fahlberg (1991). With the assistance of their care-givers, children collate photographs and drawings to illustrate the main events of their life to date, and can use accompanying happy/sad face cards or cards with feelings written on them to help them explain how each event affected them. This work can be extended by making 'eco-maps', which describe all the significant people and places that make up their world, and by making family trees. This work has been found to be especially valuable for children who have gone through many transitions and lived in many homes, as it allows them to track their path through life and find threads of continuity. Creating a life storybook can be a creative endeavour between the people involved. The idea of a 'book' can be explored as a fun construction. It could be a pop-up, a fold-out or a scroll … the possibilities are endless. The life story content can be expressed visually in a number of ways, such as collage, paintings, cartoon, photos, symbols, interesting text, songs or poems. The content can also be played with through narrative and visual themes. Telling a story from a book or from a personal experience will stir the imagination and connect with the self to find meaning. An exploration through art can bring these visuals into a concrete form for further consideration. This matches very well with what McMahon suggests with regards to dealing with endings and beginnings in the child's life.

Once a good fund of experience has been built up, a process of symbolisation can be encouraged or, as McMahon puts it, 'the child uses symbolisation as a way of storing the good experiences inside' (McMahon, 1998:116). It is by re-enacting and reliving these experiences in a symbolic way, whether through artistic expression or play, for example, that other not-so-good experiences begin to surface. As McMahon puts it: 'symbolic communication occurs when a child uses symbols to represent something *else*' (1998:117), and it is at this point that painful feelings can begin to arise. Here McMahon describes something that is the centre-point of just why storytelling holds such therapeutic power. She suggests that 'the use in play of symbolisation which is not initially interpreted back to the child but worked within the metaphor helps give the child enough distance to think about some painful experiences' (1998:117). Simply put, this means that the child is given the space to illustrate his/her feelings without being pressed to analyse them or asked to try to place them in the real world. The child is allowed to remain 'in the metaphor', i.e. to immerse him/herself in depicting the good experiences that the care worker has provided for him/her and expressing the more painful memories or thoughts that might arise after reflection on these.

It is only after the child has had sufficient time to move through these two stages that 'conceptualisation' can occur, whereby the child begins to be able to 'understand intellectually what has happened and to be able to put this into words' (1998:118). In relation to the above, conceptualisation can be seen to start occurring as 'symbolic communication is increasingly interpreted to the child rather than remaining in the metaphor' (1998:119). For the purposes of this chapter, I will concentrate on the first two stages of building primary experience and working on symbolic communication, as conceptualisation often requires a more specialised approach that could be classified as actual therapy. It is important at this juncture to distinguish between the therapeutic benefit of allowing children to tell their stories and moving the process on to a level of therapy, which would require the specialised skills of a practitioner such as a qualified counsellor or child psychologist. Refer to Chapter 1 for a more in-depth discussion of the distinction between the two. In this chapter it is important to note that the child is facilitated through story to raise feelings, experiences and thoughts, good or bad. It is the role of the worker to witness, but not to explore, this process. If bad experiences or feelings are raised, it is the role of the worker to seek additional support through counselling for the child, for example play therapy, art therapy or drama therapy.

Suffice to say, it is best to follow the child's lead and only transfer the metaphors and stories to real life once the child has indicated that the conversation could go down that route, or when he/she makes a direct comment that connects the inner world and the outer world. Sensitive treading is called for and an understanding that sometimes the story will impact on the child's perspective enough to set up changes in his/her outer life. A seed may have been planted, and that is enough to start with.

The Practitioner as Listener

Both Ward and McMahon specifically refer to the term 'professional use of self' or, as Ward describes it, 'being real with people' (1998:26). Professional use of self means 'using one's own personal resources (including one's own emotions as well as certain skills and techniques) to achieve real communication' (1998:26) or being genuine while drawing on professional skills which may appear more 'artificial' (1998:26). The key to achieving this is to first understand oneself and to realise that one can also learn about oneself from interactions and activities with co-workers and service users (1998:27). This may involve garnering support from peers and supervisors, as caregivers need a 'holding environment' as much as do service users. Being able to be supportive depends on how well one is supported, and it is important to realise that strong feelings and reactions might occur when dealing with service users, and it is not easy to go it alone.

This, then, forms the basis of a caveat that can be given when discussing the use of storytelling to communicate with children. One must know the limits and know when it is time to call in more help, and equally know that we may be deeply affected by the stories that are told to us. It is hoped that this chapter has shown in some way the underlying reasons why storytelling may be a powerful and effective tool for communicating with children in a symbolic way. I have tried to illustrate some of the complexities of this communication and the necessity of recognising the hidden elements of these interactions. It is only once we understand the 'thinking' behind the practical activities that their true usefulness can come into play.

The Practice of Storytelling

The next part of the chapter is concerned with the 'doing' aspect of storytelling. To navigate the practicalities of storytelling and to highlight some pitfalls that may be waiting along the way, we turn to the work of Margot Sunderland, *Using Story Telling as a Therapeutic Tool with Children* (2000).

Sunderland's central argument in her book is that 'everyday language is not the natural language of children. Their natural language of feeling is that of image and metaphor, as in stories and dreams' (2000:2). Therefore, if we try to get them to use everyday language, they will find it more difficult to reply and we will have a great deal of trouble in making them feel understood. Drawing on what was discussed in the section above, we can see that we need to find methods that allow children to use the full range of their imaginary powers to convey their emotions to us. Sunderland argues that storytelling is a highly effective method for doing so. She provides essential guidance on how children listen to a story that we tell them, how we can listen properly to stories that they tell us, how to respond empathically and the problems we might face when carrying out these activities. We will first discuss these in greater detail, and then provide some concrete steps in creating a storytelling environment and the resources needed to get in the frame of mind to facilitate the storytelling process.

How does a child listen to a story?

First, if the story is well chosen to suit the particular child, 'he will identify with the main character in the story [and] in so doing, he will go on the same journey as the character' (Sunderland, 2000:16). The child can therefore begin to feel as though he/she is not alone in suffering difficult experiences because the story character will be going through a parallel experience. By experimenting with the way the character deals with the problem, the child can explore different ways of approaching it, and eventually will be able to 'feel the character's joys and relief in coming through conflict and crisis to a place of resolution' (2000:17). It follows that we must carefully select scenarios that allow this process to take place. The most vital point to consider is that presenting issues indirectly through imaginative metaphors allows children a safe distance to regard their particular problem, and staying within these metaphors allows the true powers of the story to take effect.

How to think up your own story

Sunderland next provides us with a basic method for constructing a story. For convenience, I have broken this down into four steps, but a fuller reading of Sunderland's work will allow for greater depth.

Step 1 involves identifying the emotional problem besetting the child. Some of these themes could be things like feeling rejected, feelings of being the least special child, 'feelings of needing someone too much', 'always needing to be in control', feelings of loneliness, anxiety or broken-heartedness or 'feelings of wanting to hit out, hurt or destroy' (Sunderland, 2000:23–4). When thinking about what theme to choose, it is important to think about the issues facing the child, the way he/she is trying to cope with them, the kind of emotional themes that come up in his/her games and any acting-out behaviour he/she demonstrates.

Step 2 requires choosing 'the characters, a place, and a situation that can provide a metaphorical context for this problem or issue' (2000:22). Here it is perhaps useful to take some time to place yourself in the child's shoes and think about his/her situation, and use this reflection to create a story that symbolises this. Bear in mind that it can be a good idea to use characters and places that children love, such as characters from a TV programme or a favourite animal, and use your own imagination to create a rich environment in which the story can take place. Remember that it is better not to replicate the exact situation facing the child and just change the names, as they will see through this. By utilising what Sunderland describes as 'indirect expression', you will give the child the 'protection of disguise' (2000:25). You are aiming to create a different context from real life, yet one that still reflects the child's concerns.

Next, show the main character trying to solve his/her problem by using similar coping strategies that the child is using in real life and that are obviously not working (2000:22). As Sunderland puts it, 'Show the ultimate failure of that coping mechanism which results in the character reaching some kind of internal or external crisis in his life' (2000:23). The second part of this step involves depicting the path from crisis to solution. Take your time at this point, and don't resort to shortcuts or hurried solutions, which can make the story very unrealistic.

Sunderland describes the fourth part of the process as 'the shift [...where...] someone or something appears in the story that helps the character to change direction and move on to a better coping mechanism, or a far more creative way of dealing with the situation' (2000:23). This shift allows the main character to adopt a new way of behaving or to form a new picture of him/herself that shows him/her a new way of living in his/her world. It is this shift that can plant the seed of thought in the child's head about how he/she could apply the story to his/her own life.

To illustrate how these principles could work in practice, read the story below. Lawrence Cohen (2001:118) shares this very simple story to show how the mother achieved a 'symbolic distance' between the actual issue of the difficult time her son had at his first school, and the story of the small mouse lost at sea. This allowed her son to process his emotions much more readily than if he had been requested to talk directly about his feelings at the difficult school, and this in turn resulted in the child solving the problem for himself.

The story of the mouse at sea

A friend of mine, whose son had a very bad time at his first preschool, noticed that he hardly ever talked about it and never played school when he was at home, even though usually he was very verbal and very imaginative in his play. Even after he started a new school, which he loved, he never seemed to deal with the difficulties he had at the old one. His mother couldn't believe he didn't have any feelings about it, and she assumed he must have buried them.

Not wanting to force him to face these feelings (and, of course, you really can't force a child to talk or play about something if he doesn't choose to), but wanting to help him with these feelings somehow, she decided to tell a story. She made up a story about a little mouse who was in a very leaky boat on a storm-tossed sea, but then was picked up by a sturdy boat with a wonderful crew. She never mentioned that the leaky boat represented the first school and the sturdy boat represented the new school. At some level though, he made the connection. He wanted to hear this story a dozen times the first day she told it to him, and then spent the rest of the day acting out the story, adding numerous details that the mom could see were representations of what had happened in the old school. After this, he was even more enthusiastic about his new school, and he was much more confident about trying new things. Did he realize the story was about his school experiences? She didn't know for sure, but it didn't really matter.

(from Cohen, 2001:117–18)

Having discussed some key points about taking the role of storyteller, we can now move on and address the other side of the coin, whereby the child tells us a story of his/her own devising. Assuming the role of listener involves some clear and intuitive thinking, knowing how and when to respond effectively and avoiding some common pitfalls. As the story is not really under our control in this instance, we have to carefully maintain our position firmly within the metaphor and allow the child to create the story in an environment where he/she does not feel that he/she will be suddenly exposed and possibly shamed. Here again, we can follow Sunderland's recommendations. Sunderland also suggested the use of a sandbox as a visual medium for storytelling.

Margot Sunderland's sandbox

Requirements

A box about 57 cm x 72 cm x 7 cm, which has been painted blue on the bottom. This means that when it is filled with sand, you can move the sand around to reveal the blue bottom, which can represent water.

About twenty miniature figurines that children can use to 'illustrate' their story. It doesn't matter what these are, but it is important to try and include a few from each of the following categories:

- transport (train, ambulance, aeroplane, car, etc.);

- people (figures of cruelty or aggression as well as figures of love, mythical creatures, family members, superheroes etc. as well as people in professions such as nurse, teacher, doctor etc.);

- animals (farm/jungle etc.);

- monsters;

- buildings;

- furniture;

- objects from the outside world, both manmade and natural (fences, gates, trees, stones).

To get the children started, let them watch as you put your hands in the sand and move it around. Show them how to make areas of water and land. If you like, you can wet some of the sand so it can be moulded into caves, islands, castles, etc. Then let them get started on creating their landscape and putting the miniature figurines in the sand to start creating their story.

How to make a helpful response to a child's story

'The central task of any counsellor, teacher or social worker is to imagine themselves into the world of the child's story, and then to reflect on that world' (Sunderland, 2000:46).

Keeping this in mind, we can see that it is important to reflect an empathic response when we have been invited to share a child's story world. We can show that the story is emotionally resonating with us by 'making appropriate vocal sounds' (2000:46)—without getting in the way of the storytelling, of course! The main thing here is to make sure that the child's emotional intensity is acknowledged; a very neutral, low-key response may have the opposite of the desired effect and actually make the child feel embarrassed.

Another tempting pitfall to avoid is beginning to offer advice or judgment on the story as it unfolds. It is very easy to try and step in and lead the action and make the story 'nice' again. Sunderland gives the example of the listening adult saying to the child, 'No, don't leave the little peanut in the gutter—let's get it a nice home to go to' (2000:47). From personal experience, this can happen very quickly, as when a child describes a violent end to a defenceless animal, one's immediate response is to point out that it is very wrong to hurt animals. In reality, it would be better to hear the comment and not pass judgment on it and instead just sympathise with the feelings of anger or violence that gave rise to the story event. Equally, we must try not to talk the child out of these feelings or try to persuade them to feel another way about something. Sunderland is very helpful here in acknowledging the difficulties we might face in these situations, where our own emotional lives come into contact with these highly charged stories. (Perhaps we could describe this as a meeting of 'inner worlds', where memories, repressed events, past hurts and strong feelings may come into contact.) She describes this as a kind of deafness or blindness (2000:48): 'if you are defending yourself against feeling some of your own very painful emotions, such as despair, hopelessness, fear or anger, you may not be able to hear these feelings in a child's stories'.

This goes over some of the ground that was prepared earlier in the chapter by Ward and McMahon's discussion of the need to understand ourselves, but it is worth mentioning again because it can come as quite a shock to the listener in a real-time practical event, where they find themselves very upset by something they have heard. It is vital to remember to gather support for yourself in this situation.

Helping children get started

As discussed earlier in the chapter, McMahon (1998) suggested providing tactile, sensory activities to help build up children's primary experience. This approach is also central to effective storytelling, as the use of toys, puppets, felt-boards and so on are often necessary to help children get started on their stories. Another useful technique to use is play with playdough. This is especially useful for young children, but the soothing associations with its use can also mean that it is enjoyed by older children, too. Hadley (1997) suggests that there are 'two major categories of behaviour with the playdough: (1) creation of a primary symbolic figure or sculpture, and (2) creation of multiple figures and shapes that can be played with in much the same way as toys. However, unlike toys, these figures can be transformed, elaborated, destroyed and recreated' (1997:91). For this reason, it can be an extremely effectual aid to storytelling. See below for an example from practice.

The playdough baby

This activity can be carried out one-on-one with the child but it can also be beneficial to work in a small group. The practitioner should also participate!

Show the children how to mould a small baby out of playdough. This can be very simplistic, and in its most basic form could be a sausage-like baby wrapped in a thin blanket of playdough. The children could use a pencil to make eyes on the baby's face. However, the children should be allowed to make the baby any way they like. As they are working, you can tell them that they are making a model of themselves when they were babies, by saying something like 'that looks like Baby [child's name]!' Encourage the children to play with the babies. Generally they will enjoy taking care of their baby and cradling it in their hands. Equally, don't be surprised if the baby gets squashed!

This game was relayed to the author by a resource teacher who played it with a group of children from the Travelling community. At the end of the session, a child who was often upset by younger siblings breaking her belongings asked to keep her baby on the windowsill of the classroom so that the baby would be very safe and no one could break her. As can be seen from this example, making a playdough baby can be an extremely expressive activity, and one which is enjoyed very much by children.

A note on older children and adolescents

While the same techniques can be applied for older children and adolescents, they might be more inhibited and less liable to come up with a spontaneous story. Relying on standbys such as toys and puppets may be less effective because they could be seen as 'babyish'. The practitioner may have to encourage results in other ways, such as by getting the children to paint pictures and describe the images they have represented.

Ending a storytelling session

Just as important as setting the stage for storytelling is drawing the session to a close. While we may not wish to draw conclusions about the story's connection with reality as a means of ending the session, it is still important to try and summarise all that has happened with the child. Sunderland suggests that making this summary helps the child to 'draw all the strands together [...and...] think more clearly about what he has just enacted' (2000:79). By doing this, you show the child that you have really listened to him/her and you also give an opportunity for the child to reflect on the story, and in fact consider if there is anything that he/she would *change* about the story. Sunderland describes how this may result in the child saying 'yes' and carrying out some action, such as hugging one of the figures or shouting at another, all because 'something has shifted in the talking about, understanding and working through of the story' (2000:79). This echoes the earlier remarks of McMahon about specifically acknowledging the endings of events to help children deal with them. On a practical note, I would suggest that some kind of neutral or pleasurable activity is carried out after the storytelling session is over to help the child transition back to everyday life. This may be as simple as tidying up the toys together or colouring or playing with a chosen toy.

Conclusions: Endings as Beginnings?

When working with storytelling with children, the fundamental precepts will underpin almost every situation. The practitioner needs to exercise empathy and an ability to imagine themselves immersed in the story, and be able to speak to the child through the language of the metaphors of the story. This involves keeping an open mind with regard to meanings and images, and understanding that we all view different events and images in different ways. We are seeking to discover the child's understanding and perceptions in this case, and need to recognise that our own may conflict with them, and further that our own emotions and memories may cause us to have strong reactions to the process. By maintaining the metaphor, or by using methods of indirect expression, we can help the child to feel safe enough to tell his/her story and to gain a symbolic distance that allows him/her to tackle difficult feelings and experiences which threaten to overwhelm when faced head-on. By following the child's lead and letting him/her determine the course of the story, we give him/her control over the expression of his/her inner world, which in turn allows him/her to feel validated and understood.

Equally, when the child chooses to speak 'out of the metaphor' or reveals something about his/her 'real' world, we can sensitively follow that train of thought and help the child to reach his/her own conclusions about the next steps he/she could take. By letting the children themselves be the ones who decide when it is time to talk about the real world, we remove the risk of them clamming up or feeling shamed and exposed.

From an adult perspective, we can reflect on how therapeutic it might feel for us to read a novel dealing with an issue we currently face or to watch a film that truly expresses our feelings about a situation, and then use that understanding to realise that metaphors and stories have an enormous power to heal. The sense that our emotions are shared by another can allow us to transform our perspective, which can have an impact on our external reality. This acceptance and empathy is vital in any form of work or therapy with human beings, not least with children, who are often struggling to live in a very adult world.

Chapter Summary

▶ Storytelling is a creative method used in the caring professions.

▶ In order to facilitate a storytelling activity, the workers need the ability to empathise, to have an awareness of their own story and to have an ability to listen.

▶ Storytelling enables the worker to learn about the inner world of the child, as the child tells the worker his/her story.

▶ Storytelling can be used as a tool to help children learn alternative ways to deal with difficult situations and memories.

TEN

Music, Emotion and Self: 'Sharing the Beat and Singing the Journey'

Pádraigín Caesar

SNAPSHOT

▸ Music—physical and emotional effects.

▸ Active and passive.

▸ Music workshops.

▸ Reflection.

Introduction

Music, an apparently universal language, crosses all barriers, cultures, age groups and can appear to unite even the most opposite of peoples. More than this, it can often provide more than just aesthetically pleasing tones to the listener in that it also offers ample opportunities for expression of 'self'. Music is not exclusive, it is not solely for entertainment and pleasure purposes, but has in the past and present been used for a wide range of purposes because of its positive social and physiological outcomes.

From early childhood, and even in the womb, children are exposed to different types of sounds. Time and time again, research on

babies pre-birth has shown that from approximately twenty-one weeks of pregnancy babies react to the muffled sounds of their parents' voices, or the sudden loud tones of the outside world (Kagan and Lewis, 1965; Hutt *et al.*, 1968). As children, we are exposed to a myriad of rhythms, musical forms, instruments and movement patterns. It is these sometimes unrecognised musical events or experiences that often help us to perfect speech, develop memory and motor skills and provide a sense of spirituality that we might otherwise take for granted.

I frequently ask the question of new students in creative studies, 'How many of you interact with or play music?' and I invariably receive the same answers: 'I don't play or sing, but I enjoy music', or 'I would like to help people with music, but I do not know how to use it', or 'I used to play a musical instrument years ago', or, wait for it, 'I'm tone deaf so please don't ask me to sing or dance, but teach me how to use music in social care'. There is a common feeling of apprehension that descends upon the group, like some feeling of dread or uncertainty before an exam. I reassure them that by the end of the lessons they will be moving to a rhythm and working with music created by themselves as a group. I also inform them that they will perform these rhythms on musical, tuned and non-tuned percussive instruments, and furthermore that they will learn how to use progressive and positive exercises during the process.

In this chapter the use of music as a creative intervention process is examined and discussed, with particular reference to its emotional impact. Throughout this chapter the exacting use of rhythmic exercises and their benefits for the participant and social care provider are explored and their purpose explained.

Experiencing the Beat!

I am always amazed and gladdened by the look of surprise on the faces of my students as they move from fearing the unknown to embracing and interacting with music in their Creative Studies class. One of the easiest ways to expose a participant to music is to listen to it, to play it or to engage with it. Whatever the level of engagement, music affects us in two ways: physically and emotionally. It is therefore important to understand how the music might impact on oneself and others before using it as a tool for practice.

Music and emotion

Not everyone experiences music in the same way, nor do they express emotion in the same manner. Emotions are sometimes contrasted with *moods*. Some researchers regard emotions as transient or episodic, whereas moods are regarded as 'feeling states' that may last for an extended period of time, perhaps several hours. For many researchers the term 'emotion' includes both transient experiences and moods. Accordingly, understanding a participant's 'state of mind' is extremely important when approaching the use of certain music intervention exercises. Participants appear to differ in their susceptibility to various emotions and mood states. Some tend to be frequently morose or depressed, whereas others tend to be perpetually sanguine and optimistic. In short, participants may differ according to *temperament*. Possible sources for differences in temperament might include genetic factors, cultural environment or significant life experiences.

Emotions, on the other hand, are widely regarded as evolutionary adaptations. As addressed by Lazarus (1991), they evoke behaviour that improves an animal's chances of survival and procreation. Tomkins *et al.*(1969) understand emotions as 'motivational amplifiers' that can confer meaning on the events of our lives and add passion and conviction to our actions. Emotions have been derided in many cultures, including the West: they have tended to be regarded as 'irrational' states; people who behave 'emotionally' are poorly regarded; we praise 'dispassionate' reason. Yet research by Damasio and Damasio (1977) indicates that the impairment of normal emotional functioning is often disastrous for the person involved. Nesse (1999) also emphasises that normal emotional functioning is essential for 'rational' and adaptive behaviour. Sloboda and Juslin (2001) argue convincingly that the typical characteristics of emotions can be applied to music. Their theory implies that the study of emotional responses to music might be usefully supported by mainstream theories of emotion.

North and Hargreaves (1997) and Ritossa and Rickard (2004; see also Madsen, 1998) produced findings showing that the emotions evoked by pieces of music could be predicted by a combination of arousal, pleasantness and familiarity. Schubert (2004) also identified a connection between arousal evoked by music (particularly by way of dynamics, loudness/softness and tempo) and emotional responses. There is evidence that specific musical events do indeed lead to physiological reactions in listeners. For example, Khalfa, Peretz, Blondin and Manon (2002) found that skin conductivity response (SCR), a measure of physiological arousal, was greater when music elicited more arousing emotions, such as fear and happiness, than when it elicited less arousing emotions, such as sadness and peacefulness.

Music and associative cues

Music can evoke a specific memory, when a piece of music is an *association cue* for a place, person or experience. For example, one of the best-known manifestations of associative cues is the 'our song' phenomenon, in which a piece of music holds special significance to a couple because they associate it with their first date, first dance at their wedding or their life journey together. Quite simply, this emotional response has as much to do with the event at hand as it has to do with the music itself. Also, it is worthwhile to remember that a piece of music often becomes an associative cue because of its association with the event. For example, a 'sad' piece of music at a funeral may be considered such because of where it is being performed and its appropriateness and not necessarily because it is a sad or melancholy piece of music. The music may have an intrinsic structure that allows it to be used for such an occasion and it becomes extrinsically 'sad' as a result.

As music interventions are such an effective 'gateway' to the emotions, music can serve the participant in many and various ways. Music is often described as a 'universal language', but one must look at and examine other elements in the language in order to express it properly. It is not enough to press 'play' on the CD player and hope for the best.

Finally, Sloboda and Juslin (2001) addressed the specifics of how a participant's mood changed as a consequence of hearing music on a vast majority of occasions; how the everyday experience of music led to increases in participants' degree of pleasure and arousal. The study found that 35 per cent of everyday experiences of music involved a move from the present situation towards, for instance, reminiscence, daydreams and nostalgia. In other words, the music not only made the participants feel better, it also acted as a gateway that seemed to transport them away from everyday concerns.

Task

Ask yourself these questions before engaging in music activities with others.

*What is an emotion? How does music **evoke** emotions? Does music evoke emotions, or does it **represent** or depict emotions? How do emotions differ from moods, feelings, sentiments or temperaments? Why does some music make us feel 'sad'?*
    Why do people willingly listen to music that makes them feel sad? What makes us hate songs? What is the role of imagination, thought process or social situation in evoking or changing emotions? Do people experience emotions in the same way? Are the moods we experience from music linked to personality? Can we experience musical emotions in the absence of sounds? Are emotions primarily communicative devices? Do children experience emotional reactions to music in the same way as adults? Do men and women experience music differently? Can we experience more than one emotion at the same time? Are there certain life experiences that add to a person's understanding of music?

Your answers to these questions will help you to understand your relationship with music and what different emotions are raised depending on the pieces of music you are listening to.

Hevner (1936) studied the relationship between music and emotions by asking people to write down the adjectives that came into their minds while they listened to music. The experiments substantiated the theory that music inherently carries emotional meaning. In short, emotional and like–dislike responses to music may not be as unrelated as existing literature implies. Listening to music (*passive*) is only one part of the story, as participating in music (*active*) is also an important way of experiencing it. The *active* and *passive* rudiments of creative interventions are key elements in the study and practice of music in Creative Studies. The passive and active elements of music are essentially the nuts and bolts of music in Creative Studies.

What are the *Musical* Creative Interventions in Creative Studies?

Musical creative interventions

Active	**Passive**
Performing percussion/singing songs	Listening/reflecting
Participation	Visualising
Role-plays	Meditation
Making musical instruments	Lyric analysis
Dancing/moving	
Song writing	

When you are involved both actively and passively, all the sensory organs are engaged. Here the rhythmic and melodic workings of music may be used as specific stimuli to obtain particular motor and emotional responses, thus combining motor movement with stimulation of different sensory pathways, that is tactile and auditory (multiple sense) stimuli with well-affirmed emotional quality. When people listen to music they have a physical response, for example relaxing, and an emotional catharsis, for example self-discovery, awareness, increased self-esteem and increased positivism. Through the exploration of and engagement in these music activities, participants experience a personal journey through four key areas.

Outcomes of exploration and experience of musical creative interventions

1   The building of rapport and self-esteem between the participants.
2   The acceptance and understanding of emotions.
3   The expression of emotions, or the catharsis phase.
4   Acceptance of changed status.

These four key areas are inherently linked to the understanding of 'self'. For it is in understanding our 'self' that we grow and move positively through various, sometimes difficult situations. The recognition of 'self' through the use of music-based activities serves both those who would help, and the children, youth and families who are the focus of service delivery.

Facilitating a Music Workshop

You do not need an ability in music to facilitate an experiential music session. The aims of an experiential music workshop include having fun; expressing your creativity through music; learning to communicate through rhythm with other members of your group; and self-awareness. However, you do need to have an understanding of the basics involved in composing a piece of music, for example tempo, rhythm and pitch.

Tempo

Tempo in music refers to the speed of the beat and the flow of the piece of music (Schonbrun, 2006). Music is divided into *bars*, and the bar is a length of time. In music the *bar* contains a number of beats. The most common is four beats in one bar, which is called *common time*.

Rhythm

This refers to the length of time that you hold the note, and we experience rhythm though the 'beat'. When you are at a concert, you might clap along to the beat of the song, normally made by the drum or the bass guitar. Your claps will be in rhythm with the beat of the song.

When composing and improvising a piece of music in an experiential workshop, it is important to understand the impact of tempo and rhythm on the experience of music. For example, with regard to time-related factors, Bruner (1990) has argued that music in 2/4 (two beats in the bar) time is expressive of rigidity and control, whereas music in 3/4 time (three beats in the bar) is more relaxed and vacant; fast tempo expresses animation and happiness; staccato, detached and uneven rhythms display complex emotions, whereas even and smooth rhythms express simpler, unrestricted feelings; firm rhythms imply a serious mood while smooth-flowing rhythms suggest a more playful mood; staccato or detached, jumpy rhythms place more emphasis on a passage than a smooth note. In this sense, often how one speaks is how one feels.

Pitch

Pitch, or the highness and lowness of music, also provides cues to evoking a particular emotion. Bruner argued that the rising and falling of the pitch conveys a correspondingly growing or diminishing intensity; music in higher keys is generally viewed to be 'happier' than music in lower keys; music in the major mode expresses more animated and optimistic feelings than music in the minor mode; and complex harmonies are more agitated than simple harmonies, which are happier.

Texture

Finally, there are also textural considerations to be aware of when playing and performing different musical exercises; dynamic variance can suggest different things. For example, loudness can often suggest closeness or proximity, whereas softness can suggest distance or peacefulness; a *crescendo* or building up of sound can express an increase in force, whereas *diminuendo* or gradual reduction in sound can suggest a reduction in power. The following are examples of workshops that you can facilitate with individuals or a group. Read Chapter 2 on facilitation first and apply similar rules of safety and preparation as are outlined there.

Exercise 1: The listening/visualisation exercise

Resources needed: tape recorder/CD player or piano/keyboard.

Types of music used for this exercise: classical, pop, modern, rock, world music, or music used for meditation purposes.

Instruction: play calming music and invite the participants to visualise peaceful images with the aim of producing a state of mental relaxation. Describe a serene image, for example at the seaside or beside a river, or ask the participants to visit a place in their minds where they are at peace or relaxed. The imagined scenery might aid the participant in focusing on the exercise. When music is combined with imagery (cinematic experience) the effect on the mind and body can be immense. Different moods and emotions can be explored through the use of different music pieces, so do choose carefully. Classical pieces of music are often the easiest to access and can provide a good starting point.

Analysis: reflecting on the exercise that just took place, seek to ask some of the following questions:
- How did the participants feel as the music was playing?
- Were they distracted? If so, why? If not, why not?
- How did the music affect the participants?
- What were the emotions felt by the participants during the listening exercise?
- Did the feelings of self-awareness in the participants increase/decrease during this exercise?
- How did they feel before, during and after the event?

Whether the participants like your choice of music or not is not the point, but it can be useful to find out if there is any particular music which they dislike, as your aim is not to upset the participants. The point is, however, to link the music to experience and emotion while also creating a sense of calmness and fun. Let us not forget that the activities involved when performing or engaging in music-making and creative studies can act, for many, as a 'release valve', which is an effective tool to have for de-stressing or relieving anxieties of various kinds. Many participants speak of 'feeling relaxed' or 're-energised' after engaging in such activities. This can only have a positive affect for both participant and service provider.

Exercise 2: Feeling the beat!

Instruction:

1   Placing the musical instruments into the centre of the room or space provided, ask participants to form a circle around them.
2   Ask the participants to visually pick out an instrument, but do not let anyone touch the instruments. Calmly ask the participants to choose an instrument in order of where they are standing (clockwise or anti-clockwise).

Notice the participants' responses to certain instruments being removed from the floor. Notice the self-awareness of some of the participants. Notice the sounds, be it silence or lack of silence.

3   Once all the participants have instruments, remind them *not* to play them. Then, asking them to return the instruments to the centre of the circle, observe their reactions. Getting the participants to reflect on their emotions here is important. They might be feeling frustrated, confused, excited, nervous or calm. How are they feeling?
4   Finally, ask each participant to choose the instrument he/she really wants. Again, see the varied reactions to this exercise. Ask the participants to verbalise or write down how they are feeling about this task.
5   Once they have selected an instrument (preferably the one they wanted!), move on to Exercise 3.

Exercise 3: Sharing the beat!

1   Gather all the drums or percussive instruments into the centre of the space provided.
2   Participants form a circle around the instruments and again select an instrument, one at a time, in a clockwise or anti-clockwise fashion.
3   When all participants are holding an instrument, select a *starter*. This starter will create the first beat and the rest will follow, one by one.

It should be noted that this exercise can sometimes take time as the members of the group may vary in their ability to produce beats.

The aim of this exercise is to have fun and be creative in your rhythms. Remember that, no matter what the construction of the beats, they are neither right nor wrong.

4   Beats are created by striking the drum or percussive instrument with the hand, drumstick or mallet.
5   Instruct the group to play out what they feel or, in other words, to do what comes naturally to them when they have chosen their instrument.
6   Be prepared for some to feel very self-conscious; it is often helpful to play a piece of light music in the background.

Exercise 4: Follow the leader!

This exercise involves movement, both rhythmic and physical. It can be tailored to suit the space, participants or situation. The exercise is to be used by a group who have played percussive instruments for a short period of time (twelve weeks) as confidence and building of self-esteem are key to this being an effective and fun exercise.

1   Participants will require percussive instruments of their choice.
2   Clear a space so that participants can move around.
3   Create a circle and select one person to lead the group.
4   The selected leader provides the rhythm and direction for the group.
5   The group must 'follow the leader' and imitate in every sense, e.g. posture, dance, rhythm, expression and dynamics (loud and soft), in other words the leader's actions.
6   This exercise can be as long or short as time permits.

Reflection: ask the participants to write down their thoughts on this exercise. Use the following questions as a guideline.

(a) How did you feel when following the leader?
(b) What emotions did you feel and express?
(c) What concerns did you have?
(d) Did you step outside your comfort zone?
(e) Did you have fun/enjoyment?
(f) How do you feel now that the exercise is completed?
(g) What are the most challenging elements of this exercise?
(h) What would *you* do differently?

Exercise 5: Call and response

This is a modified version of the previous exercise. The leading percussionist plays a beat and the participants imitate the exact rhythm or phrase played.

1   Listening skills are heightened in this exercise.
2   The patience of both the listener and participants is tested here.

This is a great exercise to indirectly approach the notion of *waiting a turn*. In short, the listener must pay attention and share in the excitement of completing the exercise correctly. This exercise can prove to be challenging, especially when the participants become inspired!

Reflection

Reflective practice is a key element in the study and provision of music as one of the creative interventions. In his research, Ricks (1989) says we all see through our own personal lens, our own rose-tinted spectacles (or not so rosy, depending on the kind of day we are having). It is therefore essential to understand how the participant is developing through the music intervention process. A journal can help participants reflect on their journey through this music experience. The most important thing to remember is to have fun, knowing that music can be experienced by everyone, at any age, either passively or actively or both.

Chapter Summary

▶ The simplicity of the music exercises and activities makes music interventions accessible to all. They are not exclusive to those with a music background, music education or musical talent.

▶ The creative activities and processes discussed in this chapter can be used as intervention methods with children, people with disability, elderly people, youth groups, people with mental health issues and community groups.

▶ With music around us we can dance, sit and listen, engage and perform, write lyrics and reflect or compose both melody and rhythm.

▶ The research evidence and exercises in this chapter show that reactions to music have value to specific individuals in specific contexts, serving particular and practical goals in the social care arena.

▶ In time, I hope that music, alongside all the creative interventions, shall be recognised as being of great benefit and importance to both the study and practice of all caring professionals.

SECTION 2

Creativity in Practice

ELEVEN

To Play or Not to Play? Play in Residential Care

Mario R.J. Corbin

> **SNAPSHOT**
> ▶ Play in residential care.
> ▶ Play and attachment.
> ▶ Features of effective play environment.
> ▶ Play in social care TCI training.

'Play makes an important contribution to the social development of an infant. It allows the individual to gain personal knowledge of other group members; permits certain social skills to be practiced, such as fighting, without risk of injury; and helps the individual to establish long term friendships.'

Smith (2003:86)

Introduction

The thought of play may conjure up memories of childhood games with your brother(s) and/or sister(s), or with friends you went to school with and neighbours who lived nearby. It may bring you comfort and a sense of longing for times that seemed so simple compared to the hectic pace of life we lead as adults. Unfortunately, many young people do not have an easy start in life. Whatever the reasons may be, children often find their way into residential homes, unable or unwilling to play as a result of their past experiences. Often, the grim reality is that many children end up in residential units because of abuse or neglect or simply because they have become a danger

to others as well as to themselves. Whether it is a process of bad parenting or something more, these young people often lack guidance and understanding of the world into which they have been thrust.

Some children in residential homes may lack many of the social graces that allow them to communicate effectively in society. Understandably, mistrust of adults and even of their own peers can play a major role and oftentimes many participants lose out on those years that are vital to their development into emotionally stable and mature adults. As a result, something as seemingly simple as the act of playing can have a tremendous effect on their lives. There is more to playing than meets the eye, however, and this chapter will discuss in detail both the different kinds of play that exist and the way play helps develop the interpersonal skills needed to function within society and, indeed, get through the difficult process of residential care.

What Exactly is Play?

As adults we tend to forget, however unintentional on our parts, how important playing can be not only for ourselves but for those children and adolescents in care in residential units. Over time we can sometimes become guilty of believing that play is unproductive and even that it is counter-productive to obtaining the life goals set out for children. Psychiatrist and writer Mihaly Csikszentmihalyi describes playing as a *flow state*.

Involvement	Complete focus and concentration, either due to innate curiosity or as the result of training.
Delight	A sense of bliss and positive detachment from everyday reality.
Clarity	Great inner clarity and a built-in understanding about the state of affairs.
Confidence	An innate sense that the activity is doable and that your skills are adequate to the task. Additionally, you don't feel anxious or bored.

Serenity	A sense of peace and an absence of worries about self.
Timeliness	Thorough focus on the present and a lack of attention to the passing of time.
Motivation	Intrinsic understanding about what needs to be done and a desire to keep the moment of play moving.

(Helpguide, 2004)

Thus, beyond words, beyond any act of vocalisation comes socialisation. Play provides this outlet, giving participants an opportunity to test the waters, so to speak, and learn the social graces and etiquette that is expected of them in their residential unit. By our very nature we are designed to play: it is an inborn ability that is hard-wired into our genetic code. As Csikszentmihalyi (cited in Helpguide, 2004) surmises, play is part of how humans have transmitted cultural norms and appropriate behaviour from one generation to the next. Play is instinctive and fundamental to our existence and is one of the unique evolutionary mechanisms that have enabled us to develop socially. The act of playing helps us to survive by connecting us to other human beings whilst simultaneously providing a source of mental and physical stimulation.

It is important to distinguish between different types of play when talking about play amongst children and adolescents. The social interaction between children is vital to the structuring and maintenance of social ties as well as aiding the process of learning what the rules of culture are. By simply adhering to and understanding the need and function of playing, children become productive members of their community. Play will become increasingly important in our future as we will need to be more inventive, creative and flexible to handle the tasks, flow and rhythm of life in this century and beyond.

Play for Attachment

Play is essential for successful attachment bonding between infants and those who care for them. Interactive play—playing together for the fun of it—brings about self-regulation in the infant and sets the stage for self-awareness, self-confidence and trust in self and others. Aggression, anxiety, mixed signals or indifference from parents, social care practitioners and teachers can stop the development of optimism, hope and playfulness in children, which in turn can lead to depression, fear and disillusionment in adulthood. Play and playing together for the fun of it is a powerful resource for creating emotional well-being. In residential units, for instance, the benefits of play can be found via the participants' ability to develop social skills with other participants, as well as with social care practitioners who are entrusted with their care. Thus, developing skills of communicating trust and pleasure allows participants to refine their innate concepts of verbal and non-verbal language.

Furthermore, notions such as safety and danger, freedom and boundaries, empathy, compassion and, inevitably, the capacity for intimacy all make up the emotional intelligence necessary for participants in residential units to develop relationships with their peers and with their families. It also eases their understanding of what they think they know of the world around them into what the reality of the situation is, empowering them to re-integrate back into society as productive members. Personal strengths, the ability to learn, health, perseverance and even joy and happiness have been intrinsically linked to the act of playing. Playing in itself can help children in residential care to avoid such feelings as loneliness, isolation, anxiety and depression. When we play vigorously, we trigger a mix of endorphins that lifts our spirits and distracts us from pain, fear and other burdens. And when we play we are reminded that we are not alone. Participants who avoid or have never learned to play properly may become lost within their inner world of uncertainty that often accompanies any period of time spent in residential units away from parents, extended families and friends.

What you may not realise is that playing can also act as a means of overcoming difficulties experienced in the past by participants. When participants play interactively together for the fun of it, they are reinforcing positive mental and physical wellness. Studies show that an emotionally insecure participant can replace insecurities and negative behaviours with positive assumptions and actions by interacting with peers and social care practitioners or care-givers who are secure and self-confident within themselves. Healthy, caring and emotionally empowering relationships inevitably heal and create emotional resilience. Thus, play provides a safe and therapeutic environment in which both participant and social care practitioner can develop a trusting relationship within a relatively short time (Helpguide, 2004).

'When I was young, I would visit my friend's house and play outside in their backyard. Each of us had a horse that lived there, invisible to all except us. We would spend hours grooming, feeding, and training our horses. Then we would gallop around the backyard for hours. When my friend's mother would occasionally step out the back door, we would instantly stop our play because it was too personal to share.'
(An Adult Remembering her Childhood, cited in Scarlett *et al.*, 2005:162).

Features of Effective Play Environments

Regardless of whatever culture one comes from, play is a fundamental element in the development of children's overall ability to cope with stress. It is important to note here, however, that the types of play available to young people are often limited. There are many reasons for this, including age appropriateness, availability of financial funds to provide and/or maintain certain activities and suitable activities that promote appropriate behaviour among and between participants. It is not uncommon, for instance, to find in any given residential unit today a PlayStation, Xbox or Nintendo Wii. Arguably, game consoles and computer games have changed the way participants in residential units play, both individually and together. According to Scarlett *et al.* (2005:118), these games are played because of: '(a) their graphics and realism; (b) their levels or graded challenges; and (c) their ways of encouraging interaction.' The video game has inevitably begun to replace children's imagination in creating nearly lifelike environments for them to explore. It is the ultimate escape from an otherwise painful reality. It promotes interaction not with peers or social care staff, but with an artificial reality that allows them to manipulate, control and even blow up an imaginary world to which they can relate their own existence.

Game consoles and computer games may provide young people with a temporary release from their anxiety, fears and anger and may provide children with a way to challenge authority in a fictional reality. However, they lack the ability to help young people interact in real world situations. It also relieves social care staff of their duty to help residents interact effectively not only with staff but with other young people within the residential unit. Particularly as most games available today require no less than one hour to complete a basic challenge, it can be argued that the structure of residents' schedules during a single calendar day may cause conflict when it comes to using and/or ending video game sessions. Nevertheless, game consoles and computer games are still used as, if nothing else, a relief from constant contact and a means of reward for appropriate behaviour. Thus, it can be argued that young people only behave well in order to obtain the privilege of playing games on computers or games consoles. Caution must be taken when dealing with such rewards as young people will inevitably learn how to *play the game* without in fact learning how to effectively communicate and work together. The best learning environments in residential units are those that provide participants with good-quality playtime. According to Scarlett *et al.* (2005), four dimensions for a good-quality play programme include a protected time and space, age appropriate and culturally sensitive play materials, a carefully balanced adult presence and involvement, and the presence and involvement of peers, family and the community at large.

In residential environments young people are subjected to an array of activities during the day that are highly structured and enforced by sanctions and rewards. For example, sanctions can include a loss of time spent on games consoles or, in the case of a reward, an extra ten minutes' playtime on a games console. In their daily routine participants must also go to school, complete school assignments, have breakfast or dinner, meet with their key worker and so forth. There is little time left at the end of it all for participants to simply spend quality time alone or with other participants. Thus, a protected time and space is essential in allowing residents to play an activity uninterrupted, preferably something other than a games console or computer game. Participants must be able to feel safe and secure in this play environment. This includes using their imagination to make crafts, draw or play a sport with other participants. Whatever is decided by participants, the choices should be restricted to age-appropriate and culturally sensitive play materials. According to Scarlett *et al.* (2005:221), 'this is a welcoming and operational playroom that includes a variety of materials that are familiar to the participants or that hold special meanings for them'. It is not uncommon for young people to bring with them when being placed in residential care something of great importance to them from home. This could be a specific toy. It allows young people to put aside feelings of anxiety and stress in a more constructive and productive way than by simply escaping via a video game.

This is not to say that participants are left completely unattended. On the contrary, a carefully balanced adult presence and occasional involvement is essential in ensuring that a sense of security exists for young people in the residential home. Social care practitioners are there to be supportive, consistent and trustworthy. They are also present to ensure that order is maintained. Their presence is also valuable for young people new to the residential unit as it allows them to move about with more ease and calm than would be possible if they were left to fend for themselves among the other residents. However, as Scarlett *et al.* (2005: 224) illustrated, there are debates about how much participation is necessary between social care practitioners and young people during playtime. For instance: 'Facilitating a child's play involves continuously adjusting the mode of interaction with the child on the basis of each particular child's needs, in a specific context, and at a certain time' (Linder, 1990, cited in Scarlett *et al.*, 2005:224).

As social care practitioners, it is important to access the wealth of information that can be found within the social care team. Individual placement programmes (IPPs) for each child are available and regular discussions between social care practitioners and key workers are vital for understanding all the nuances that exist around each particular young person. Therefore, social care practitioners need to be able to differentiate between inappropriate behaviour and coping mechanisms and, especially, when to intervene. Furthermore, it is equally important that, as care providers, staff accept invitations to participate in certain play activities, where appropriate, as participation is an excellent opportunity for both parties to grow to trust each other and maintain lines of communication and understanding.

According to Scarlett *et al.* (2005:226), social care practitioners 'work with each child both in an individual and in a social context'. The presence and involvement of peers and, when possible, family and the community at large allows young people to integrate successfully into the residential unit. Through role-playing and imaginative play, participants learn how to communicate with loved ones in a safe and instructional environment. They learn to express thoughts, ideas and feelings in a productive manner that builds a bridge of understanding between them and their loved ones. It also helps to alleviate the stereotypes that are associated with their predicament in life by interacting and getting involved with community events. Traditionally, residential units have been looked at with disdain and worry by neighbours, but through active participation and co-operation between social care practitioners and residents of a given community, these difficulties can be overcome. Education is power and it is no less important to help residents of a neighbourhood understand the ethos of a particular residential unit than it is to educate young people on the importance of reintegrating into their own families and neighbourhoods. This also gives families an opportunity to better understand the emotional and physical needs of their children and adolescents in care whilst also doing what is necessary to ensure that they can in future maintain the progress made by their children whilst in residential care.

Exploring the Use of Play in Residential Care

'I have come to a frightening conclusion. I am the decisive element in the juvenile [treatment] centers. It is my personal approach that creates the climate. It is my daily mood that makes the weather. As a teacher [counsellor], I possess tremendous power to make youth's life miserable or joyous. I can humiliate, humor, hurt or heal. In all situations it is my response that decides whether a crisis will be escalated, and the youth humanised or dehumanised.' (Haim G. Ginnott, cited in Brown, 2005:27)

Residential units for children are designed to meet a variety of needs and purposes. Residents range from eight to seventeen years of age and often come from broken homes where a variety of difficulties may have existed. The range of difficulties are too broad to be discussed here, but suffice to say that many young people in residential care lack the skills and confidence necessary to cope with the often strenuous relationships they have with parents, extended family and friends. With no decision-making power at their disposal, residents find themselves thrust into a bureaucratic system among strangers, policies and procedures, all of which are foreign and frightening. Residents, regardless of their home environment, find ways that work for them to cope and manage the day-to-day life they lead. By being removed from their home environment and placed into a clinical environment, such as a residential unit, residents are being stripped of any coping mechanism that they may have developed over time.

The act of playing in itself suddenly disappears within these stressful environments. Residential units are designed to protect and keep from harm, and the roles of both young people and social care practitioners are clearly defined. Social care practitioners are governed by policies and procedures set out by the State and by the institution that employs them. A strict set of rules applies regarding how and in what way social carers can speak with, interact with and provide support to participants. Thus, the residential environment holds many stressors for both residents and social care practitioners. A balance must be sought, one that will allow both parties involved to interact with each other and reap the benefits and rewards of working together. For residents, this process is invaluable because it allows them to regain a sense of self-identity as they explore their own behaviours and attitudes and work together in conjunction with social care practitioners and other professionals to reintegrate into their lives. For the social care practitioner, their knowledge and skills are tested constantly but, unlike the young person, social care practitioners do not have the luxury of communicating ineffectively (arguing, fighting or even walking away) as the stability of the residential unit and indeed the health and wellness of the participant rests on the shoulders of the social care team.

Thus, the success or otherwise of residential units in developing a young person's ability to acquire the skills and knowledge necessary to overcome the difficulties he/she is facing depends on the professionalism of those involved with their everyday care. The use of play as an activity is a key way of training present and future social care practitioners in a variety of residential care environments. Residential units, including secure units, in North America and in both the Republic of Ireland and the United Kingdom employ the use of therapeutic crisis intervention (TCI) as a means of working with and in extreme circumstances, restraining participants who have become a risk to themselves and those around them. However, it should be noted that the latter is a last resort.

Play as Part of Social Care Skills Training

Therapeutic crisis intervention (TCI) trains social care practitioners to 'prevent crises from occurring, de-escalating potential crises, managing acute physical behaviour, reducing potential and actual injury to children and staff and teaching young people adaptive coping skills' (Brown, 2005: 26–7). With the aim of reducing the need to rely on high-risk interventions, TCI provides a framework for care professionals to nurture and maintain a safe and therapeutic environment for young people and staff alike.

The onus of responsibility for ensuring that young persons are provided with this secure environment therefore lies squarely on the shoulders of the social care team. However, the skills required are not innate and it is through continuous training and practical experience that social care practitioners can hope to undertake their duties with the energy and enthusiasm required. As discussed, residential care units are stressful environments and such stress is, to an extent, unavoidable. However, staff training in TCI is but one way that they can help teach participants important skills-sets to cope with their new environment. It is also through the process of TCI training that staff reacquire the need for play to help instruct them on the various attributes of this crisis prevention and intervention model. TCI training usually runs over the course of five working days, and it incorporates several elements of play, including role-playing, play-fighting and the use of imaginative play.

Instructions

Equipment: large area preferably with soft ground, i.e. grass.
Time: 20–30 minutes
Brief description: in pairs of similar size, one becomes the Faller and one the Catcher. Teach methods for spotting, falling and catching. Start small and build to bigger falls, then swap. Debrief: what made you feel more or less trusting?

- Create a careful, concentrating, respectful tone. Watch out for bravado; focus on trust and care.
- Sequence appropriately, e.g. after icebreakers, name games and initial get-to-know-you activities, but often before or as part of team building activities.
- If possible, use Trust Lean as part of a progression of trust-related activities, e.g. from Willow in the Wind to Trust Lean to Running Free to Slice N Dice.
- Ask participants to find a partner of similar height and weight; same-sex pairs are not essential, but often occur.
- One person is the Faller and one the Catcher.
- Faller must adopt the falling posture:

- standing upright
- feet together
- hands across chest, resting on shoulders
- tight butt cheeks and keep body stiff (to avoid buckling)
- Catcher is taught 'spotting'.
  - one leg in front of the other
  - arms extended
  - 'give' with the weight, taking it mostly through the legs.
- Start with small falls, then build.
- Establish clear communication calls (like climbing calls), e.g.,
  - Faller: 'I am ready to fall. Are you ready to catch me?'
  - Catcher: 'I am ready to catch you. Fall away.'
  - Faller: 'Falling.'
  - Catcher: 'OK'
- After about 5–10 minutes, swap Catchers and Fallers.
- Can progress to Trust Falls and Dives from chairs, tables, etc. with whole group catching.
- Debrief.
  - Ask partners to share with each other:
    - What made you feel trusting? (e.g. clear communication, positive encouragement, etc.)
    - What made you feel less trusting (e.g. laughing/joking, lack of communication, etc.)
    - Invite people to contribute to a group discussion about what things their partner did to make them feel more or less trusting.

(Wilderdom Store, nd)

Trust lean activity in TCI training

All three forms of play occur during the process of acquiring the skills necessary to conduct TCI, where staff alternate between roles (resident, social care practitioner and observer) in an artificial environment. Restraining techniques, communication exercises and problem-solving activities are all employed to help staff learn to work together and begin to depend on one another as a team. The training is designed to promote understanding and an empathetic attitude towards both colleagues and young residents in social care environments. Once social care teams learn to work together effectively, they are in a better position to alleviate any fears and anxieties that residents experience in their new environments. Cases where social care staff have failed to learn to work effectively together can sometimes result in greater stress and violence in residential units among young persons and, sometimes, towards staff. A successful residential unit depends entirely upon the social care team working together. This includes managerial support and supervision when required to allow staff to express themselves among their peers. Activities in residential units vary greatly and it is vital to recognise that play is an essential aspect of health and well-being for young persons and social care practitioners alike.

Let's Play

'Rather than a distraction in our lives, play should be an essential part'

Cook (2009:110)

Human beings are naturally inquisitive, curious animals who depend upon a social network made up of immediate family, extended family, friends and the wider community in order to gain the appropriate norms and values of their given culture. Thus, we need to ensure that children and adolescents alike have access to:

- a protected time and space;
- age-appropriate and culturally sensitive play materials;
- a carefully balanced presence and involvement of adults, peers, family and the community at large.

These are some of the many ways in which social care teams can contribute to the quality of life for young people entrusted to their care. Furthermore, as adults, social care practitioners themselves can learn effectively through acts of playing, as has been discussed in relation to TCI training. According to the California-based National Institute for Play (cited in Cook, 2009:110), the ability to play, explore and push boundaries can help social care practitioners to solve problems. It is through this exploration of play that both participants and social care professionals can learn to understand how and why events have unfolded in the way that they have for each participant in residential care.

The act of playing is more than a frivolous activity and to embrace play requires an 'emotional letting go—whether it's laughing, horsing around with friends, flirting or teasing. These are moments when the intellect—and that judgmental inner voice—are quiet, moments that become crucial for forging bonds of trust' (Cook, 2009:111).

Chapter Summary

▶ Play can help young people in residential care to form appropriate attachments with adults.

▶ Play can help young people deal with difficult issues and realities.

▶ Not all play is created equal—time spent in front of games console is not the same as dedicated play time, set aside for age-appropriate, sensitively supervised, interactive play.

▶ Play teaches both staff and participants alike the discipline necessary to interact with one another in a constructive and meaningful manner.

▶ Play is used as a learning tool in staff TCI training.

▶ Play is an effective tool in providing young people with safe and therapeutic environments and their families with peace of mind as the steps necessary to reunite young people with their families are taken one at a time.

TWELVE

Creativity in Early Childhood: An Introduction from a Parent's Perspective

Una O'Grady

SNAPSHOT

▶ Evolution of early childhood practice and education.

▶ Creativity in early childhood practice and education.

▶ Creativity in the classroom.

▶ How to encourage more creativity at home.

Introduction

I am writing this chapter not as an academic but as a mother of two children and from the practical perspective of having worked as a teacher's assistant. I have always enjoyed working with children and have been fascinated by the influences that various disciplines have upon their development. This chapter will include a very brief overview of how early childhood practice has evolved and the influence it has had in the classroom. I have also included practical advice on how to use creativity in the classroom and at home.

Evolution of Early Childhood Practice and Education

When looking at early childhood practice and education, it can be useful to discuss its evolution as this will lead to a greater understanding of modern early childhood care. When talking about early childhood care and education, it is best to be clear on what this term really means. Noirin Hayes (1995:2–3), a leading Irish figure on early childhood practice, describes it as 'both the care and educational element of a wide range of services delivered to young children. It includes creche and nursery services, Montessori and infant classes in the primary school.' This term of reference helps to focus us upon the area I wish to examine and discuss. Early childhood development has for a long time been an area of extensive discussion and study. There are numerous names synonymous with developmental psychology and I could not possibly do justice to this area of research in one chapter, so instead I shall focus on those I am most familiar with and who I feel have played an important role in how we look at early childhood learning today. With that in mind, I will discuss in very brief terms the ideas set forth in relation to pre-school and infant learning by Jean Piaget and L.S. Vygostky.

Jean Piaget was a Swiss psychologist who revolutionised the way we understand children's thinking (Birch, 1997). His work was influenced by what he observed in his own children, which made him believe that children's ability to think and reason moved in a series of stages. His theory was universal in that it applied to all children throughout all cultures and he believed that the order of these stages was fixed, with all children having to pass through each stage before moving on to the next. He did not believe children were empty vessels waiting to be filled, but rather he classed them as enquiring scientists (Staples New and Cochran, 2007). He argued that children developed schemas or internal representations of specific mental or physical actions as a way of understanding their world (Birch, 1997).

Piaget said that when introduced to new information, children use either assimilation, a process whereby a new object or idea is understood in terms of concepts they already possess, or, when the children realise that their existing schemas do not fit, would modify their existing schema, thereby expanding their view of the world (Staples New and Cochran, 2007). This formed the basis of learning and Piaget called the stage where children are faced with new information 'disequilibrium'. This was the most important stage for Piaget, the stage where teaching skills were key and encouraged children to discover information for themselves through asking questions. Piaget felt that children move through four stages of cognitive development: sensorimotor stage (0–2 years), pre-operational stage (2–7 years), concrete operational stage (7–11 years) and formal operational stage (11–15 years) (Staples New and Cochran, 2007). As children pass through each of these stages they develop different abilities, from realising the permanence of objects in the early stage through to logical problem-solving and abstract thinking in the final stage.

Vygostky was a Russian psychologist who was relatively unknown until his work was translated into English in the 1960s (Birch, 1997). Like Piaget, he too saw children as curious problem-solvers and not as passive recipients. He differs from Piaget, however, in that he gave a greater role to social influences on children's cognitive process. He described how an adult guides the child through development, placing great emphasis on learning from others in the children's environment, especially the family and adults, who provide the framework in which children learn (Staples New and Cochran, 2007). The adult gradually withdraws as children develop and became more able. Vygotsky stressed the social framework within which children learn and the importance of a wide variety of social settings. For Vygotsky, children were active learners who were both curious and problem-solvers. He advocated the help of '*experts*', giving the children help and prompts, then gradually withdrawing as the children's competence grew (Staples New and Cochran, 2007). Piaget and Vygotsky have had a great influence on our understanding of how children learn and therefore on the practice and development of early childhood education, especially in the nursery and primary school areas (Birch, 1997).

Another very influential person in pre-school education was Dr Maria Montessori (Flanagan, 2006). In his book, *The Greatest Educators Ever*, Flanagan (2006:152–60) discusses the work of Dr Montessori and her influence on early education. Montessori qualified as a medical doctor and went on to work in the University of Rome's psychiatric clinic, later becoming a professor of anthropology. In 1907 a project was started to supervise children of pre-school age of working parents, and Montessori was appointed director. She called it the '*Casa dei Bambini*' or the 'Children's House' (Flanagan, 2006). By working so closely with these children she made some amazing discoveries about how children learn. She discovered that young children were capable of intense periods of concentration, of self-discipline and making informed choices and that they preferred quiet and order and purposeful play. She came to the conclusion that education must be child-centred rather than curriculum-led. She believed in using what she termed self-correcting materials, such as a jigsaw (Staples New and Cochran, 2007). If it is done incorrectly, the jigsaw cannot be completed, which leads the child not only to persevere in the activity but to get it right. Montessori used buttons and laces as a way of helping the children to learn useful life skills, like dressing themselves.

Dr Montessori perhaps won widest respect for her success in teaching 'the three R's': reading, writing and arithmetic (Flanagan, 2006). She developed a system of learning the shapes of letters, usually cut out of sandpaper, which the children learned through tactile experience rather than visual analysis. The children used phonics in learning to recognise letters and by repeating the sounds of letters and running them into each other they quickly learned to master words. She also advocated the use of proportional furniture in the classroom as this gave the children control over their environment, which in turn led to increased freedom. Dr Maria Montessori still has an influence today, not just in Montessori classes but also in our primary schools: child-sized furniture is widely used in infant classes as well as in most pre-schools; phonics are used to help children learn their letters; and children are encouraged to find a degree of freedom in learning to do things for themselves.

Creativity in Early Childhood Education and Practice

As a parent I have noticed the important part that art has played in both my children's lives. Like most parents I can remember my young children coming home from pre-school and infants with a picture or piece of art held proudly in their hands as they beamed with pleasure at their achievement. Creativity in early learning should not be underestimated, as the benefits are so numerous. Not only do children gain an enormous boost to their self-esteem, but it is actually teaching them skills they will use for the rest of their lives. All pre-schools and primary schools are aware of the value of art as a teaching medium, which is clearly set out in the primary school curriculum (1999) in the section titled 'Visual Art'. It advocates the use of the visual arts as a teaching tool and says:

'A purposeful arts education at primary level is life-enhancing and is invaluable in stimulating creative thinking and in promoting capability and adaptability. It emphasises the creative process and so ensures that the child's work is personal and has quality. Attempts at artistic expression are valued, self-esteem is enhanced, spontaneity and risk-taking are encouraged and difference is celebrated. It is this affirming aspect of the creative arts that makes participation such a positive experience.'

(Department of Education and Science, 1999:2)

In 2009 the National Council for Curriculum and Assessment (NCCA) released its publication, *Aistear: the Early Childhood Curriculum Framework*, which can be used by a range of practitioners or anyone involved in the education of children up to six years of age, and which includes some very useful lesson plans for different age groups, with activities listed plus their benefits to each area of development for children. It is available to anyone running a crèche or pre-school programme, but parents looking after their children at home will equally benefit from its advice.

There are numerous books available to study the benefits of creativity in early childhood development, but I will focus on one I found to be invaluable. *Creative Activities for Young Children* (Mayesky, 2009) gives a comprehensive view of the benefits of creativity plus a breakdown of activities for children of different ages. Dr Mayesky's overview of how creativity helps children to learn has excellent information, so I will give a quick rundown of its main points (2009:183–206).

Art allows children to explore the world around them and to develop skills they will use for the rest of their life (Mayesky, 2009). It helps them to express themselves by giving them a medium through which to articulate their ideas, which they might otherwise be unable to do. It gives children the opportunity to work with their peers in a co-operative setting and to learn new ideas from the other children. It also improves their social skills simply by having to interact with the other children and learning how to share and work within a group. Using new media opens up a whole new vocabulary to children and helps them find words to describe the world around them and to be able to discern similarities and differences in objects they come in contact with. It opens them up to describing things in terms of hard and soft, wet, squishy, etc. and also in terms of colour and shape, and helps them to begin to group things according to these qualities, which is of great advantage later when they come to do maths.

Motor skills improve in both the gross and fine motor areas as children gain control of their movements with repeated use of different tools and materials (Staples New and Cochran, 2007) and gradually advance to using tools that require fine motor skills, such as scissors and pencils. These fine motor skills will be used when the child starts to learn to write (Flanagan, 2006). Hand–eye co-ordination is also improved when using paint and brushes, for example, as the child uses its eyes to pick the colour and its hands to do the painting. This skill can help improve children's ability to learn to read as they have the skills required to hold the book with both hands while their eyes read from left to right.

Language skills are enhanced as children learn words to describe what they see and feel around them, while encouraging them to explain what is happening in their picture helps them to begin to tell stories through art, which in turn helps to feed their imaginations (Mayesky, 2004).

The main points derived from Dr Mayesky's book are set out below in Table 12.1.

Area of Development	Creative Activities Used	Benefits to Learning
Large muscle development	Painting with brush, group murals, clay modeling and crayon rubbings.	Helps to develop the larger motor skills and gain control over their bodies.
Small muscle development	Tearing and crushing paper, clay modelling, drawing with pencils.	Develops fine motor skills, which can help in learning to write.
Hand–eye co-ordination	Painting with brush, clay modelling and finger-painting.	Can help child to learn to read (holds the book with two hands while eyes read left to right).
Sensorimotor development	By throwing, banging, blowing, pushing, mixing, tasting and smelling objects.	Child observes the changes that occur in objects and becomes better able to see relationships between objects and to classify them.

Table 12.1: The benefits of creative play, as set out in *Creative Activities for Young Children* (Mayesky, 2009).

> *Tip!*
> **When working with children, try using one of the above activities and see what effect it has on the children. See if you notice any improvement in the area listed and if so how this benefits the children's learning in other areas.**

Creativity in the Classroom

When I worked as a teacher's assistant I helped with a class of senior infants, and part of my job was to supervise the children while they participated in art and creative projects. One of the most enjoyable aspects of this was seeing how the children interacted while taking part in these activities and how much enjoyment it brought to them. It was a great chance to see how some children naturally worked collaboratively while others preferred to work alone, and to see in practice the theories of how art can affect the learning process. It was wonderful to see children blossom when they felt they had done a good job and to feel more confident when approaching the next project. They were able to compare their work with each other and, with encouragement, were able to see how other children can view a similar topic from a different perspective. It opened them up to seeing that there are points of view other than their own and to accept new ideas. It also helped them with learning to share, whether it was sharing paints, crayons or brushes, and this in turn gave them a more socially responsible outlook.

As a teacher's assistant I personally loved this aspect of the job because it gave me a chance to interact with the children on a one-to-one basis or in groups of four. Each child had a unique perspective on the world and it was wonderful to see how, with just a few encouraging words to those who were more timid, the children flourished and became more self-assured and confident. The wonderful thing about creativity in the classroom is that the children learn about various aspects of education without even realising it.

There are numerous creative activities for use in the classroom, each with its own benefit to the children. I will list some of the activities that were used in the classroom I worked in and I will refer to other options that can also be used.

Tip!

A handy tip I picked up working with the children was to get them to bring in an old shirt. This was used as a smock, put on back to front, which saved on washing uniforms for the parents. One of my favourite activities was a collaborative one called the Hand Tree.

Activity 1: The Hand Tree

For this activity you will need a large piece of card or stiff paper (you may need to stick four sheets together), paints, glue sticks, safety scissors, smaller sheets of white paper and brushes, crayons, etc.

You start this activity by drawing the outline of a large tree on the sheet of card/stiff paper. It needs to be big enough to hold the same amount of leaves as there are children in the class. You then get the children to help with colouring of the trunk of the tree, which they can do in teams of four. When this is done, get the children to trace the outline of their hands on to the white paper and either assist with the cutting out or get them to do it using safety scissors. When they have cut out their hand shapes, they are free to decorate them as they wish, putting their names and ages on the reverse side. When all the children have finished their hands, help them to stick them in place on the tree as leaves. I found the children loved this activity as they worked both as a group and individually and were able to talk about and compare each others' hands. It was a great activity to use as an informal way for the children to get to know one and other and to break the ice. The children observed how each of them had decorated their hands and discussed these differences, which again opened them up to new ideas and ways of looking at things. It also fostered a sense of community in the class when the tree was displayed on the wall in the classroom and they could look at it and remember the fun they had making it.

Each season offers the opportunity for creative activities that help supplement the learning in the classroom. Creating their own Hallowe'en masks was great fun in the classroom, with each child having the chance to make a mask totally unique to them.

Activity 2: Masks

For this activity I used ordinary paper plates, some elastic string, a stapler, scissors and a multitude of decorative bits and pieces, including feather, beads, glitter, paint, string, wool, cotton wool, pipe-cleaners and stickers.

Each child can decide if they wish to decorate the plate as is or draw an outline of a shape they want to cut out of the plate. Some wanted a spider shape, others a pumpkin or a bat. You can help them to cut out eye-holes, mouth-hole or nose-hole, if needed. Once this is done, they are free to decorate it as they wish. The spider mask used black pipe-cleaners attached to the sides as legs. Use a stapler to attach the elastic string on both sides of the mask. This is a great activity for firing the imagination and the children soon realised that the more imaginative they were, the better the mask they ended up with. They also had the great pleasure of taking them home and wearing them, telling any admirers that they had made the masks themselves.

For other seasonal ideas try some of these:

Activity 3: Christmas decorations

Making decorations for the Christmas tree out of paper plates. You can help them make puddings, decorated on top with cotton wool as cream, or stars made from lollipop sticks, which are then painted gold or silver and decorated with glitter. Santa can be made from old toilet-roll holders, which they paint as Santa and decorate with cotton wool; use a Styrofoam ball as his head. The more advanced in age, the more sophisticated the decoration can be, with older children making hand-made cards or decorative gift boxes out of recycled boxes. They could bring an old small glass and paint it using glass paints to make a unique votive candle-holder.

The selection of activities that can be used in the classroom is vast, and I have given only a very brief idea of what is out there. It must be remembered that creativity in the classroom covers more than just art and crafts. I have simply discussed art activities as a means to begin thinking about creativity and how it can be applied in practical usage. Each teacher or pre-school will have a programme they wish to use where music, drama, role-play and many other forms of creativity will come into focus. I worked with the children in the senior infant class in preparing for the school play, which required making props to use during a song, ensuring that they each had a costume for the play and helping them to remember the words to the songs they were singing. It was great to see first-hand how much they got out of this experience and how, given the right tools, children can grow and develop and learn even as they are having fun.

How to Encourage Creativity at Home

Both my children are quite creative in their own way and both have loved different activities at various stages in their development. I would say that the only thing limiting creativity at home, besides the obvious problem of time, is your imagination. My daughter especially loves art in all its forms and is never happier than when she is sitting down with something to make or do. All children benefit from getting creative, even if this can only happen at the weekend. It is amazing how creative you can get with time and budget constraints. Obviously it will depend on the age of the children and the amount of time available to you. If you are a working parent, children will be using creativity in their school/pre-school, but you can still supplement this with at-home activities. If you are a stay-at-home parent, you will have more time to get creative, even if this means leaving a chore until after the children are in bed!

At any age, creativity helps children to see and notice the world around them. For the very young this can mean bringing in toys especially designed for tactile play. Anything that engages children's imagination is good. Use of building blocks, jigsaws and stacking cups all help children through repetitive play. The child is learning how the objects relate to each other and hand–eye co-ordination is improved. As children develop, giving them a piece of paper and a crayon and allowing them to make whatever mark they wish is a freeing exercise. This can lead on to the use of paints and other materials once they have developed the motor skills to use them.

Creativity does not have to be confined to using paint and brushes; there are numerous ways to get creative at home. A simple walk can be transformed into a nature walk by bringing a bag to collect anything that catches the children's eye. Leaves of different shapes and colours, or acorns, conkers and pine cones are there to be collected. In spring wild flowers can be gathered and once home can be examined, discussed and identified. If you have the time, bring along some paper and crayons and get them to make bark and leaf rubbings. They can set up a nature table if you have the space or simply use a scrapbook to record their leaves, flowers and rubbings. You can make them aware of the changing seasons by getting them to organise what they collect according to the season in the scrapbook, and in no time they are learning as they have fun.

The Hand Tree exercise described above can be adapted for at-home play. It can be used as a way of making a family tree, with children making a hand for each member of their family and sticking them in to show the relation of each member to the other. It is a great way for children to become familiar with how their own family is shaped and also works as an opening for you to discuss the different types of family unit children will see around them. It helps them to think about what is different about their family, if anything, from other families they come into contact with and to be open to new ideas. It is also a great opportunity for children to discuss with their extended family what their family was like when they were growing up and to talk about the similarities or differences they find. It gives children a chance to see how they fit within the family unit and to see themselves as one part of a larger unit.

Another activity that I used at home to great advantage involved making up a sheet of card with smaller pieces of card to stick on which had the months of the year and the days of the week written on them. I used different-coloured card for each day of the week. I also made up cards with different pictures of the weather on them. So each day my son would stick on the day of the week it was and put up as many cards as needed to show the weather for that day. This simple activity enabled my son at a very young age to be able to tell what day it was and to open up his vocabulary. His teacher in pre-school commented that she could always rely upon him to tell her what day it was, even if she didn't ask! It was another way of getting him ready for the world and teaching him to notice what was going on around him. He always knew and appreciated what a weekend was and would know on a Friday evening that he did not have to be up as early the next day.

As my children have grown, so too has their interest in creativity. My daughter's interest is in all things to make and do, while my son is much more of a how-does-it-work and engineering type of person. By having creative projects to work on, all children can learn about themselves as they learn about the world around them, helping them to become questioning and inquisitive individuals. When faced with problems that need to be solved, they have already been given the tools they need and are able to approach them with an open mind and to think creatively about finding a solution.

Chapter Summary

▸ The theorists Piaget and Vygostky are relevant to understanding the importance of play and creativity in the education of young children.

▸ Maria Montessori redesigned the educational setting for young children to include smaller furniture and achievable tasks to stimulate learning through creative activities.

▸ Creative play has an important role in the educational development of young children.

▸ Parents can foster creativity at home, and this practice supports the child's overall learning experience.

THIRTEEN

Working with Siblings of Children with Special Needs

Lucy Hyland, Sheila Kissane, Joanne Seymour

SNAPSHOT

▶ The experience of being a sibling.

▶ Having a sibling with a disability and the supports available.

▶ Sibshops: what they are and how to facilitate them.

▶ What young people have to say about Sibshops.

Introduction

Between March 2006 and April 2006 twelve children who have siblings with special needs attended a series of five workshops in Kilkenny. During May and June 2006 another twelve children attended a further series of workshops. These workshops are called 'Sibshops' (Meyer and Vadasy, 2007) and are designed specifically for children who are growing up with a brother or sister with special needs. This chapter is an account of our experience as facilitators of Sibshops. Creative activities are central to the aims and objective of a Sibshop, and this chapter provides examples of creative activities that can be adapted for any group work with young children.

The chapter will first review literature on the experience of siblings of children with special needs and on the benefits of support groups for siblings. It will then describe what Sibshops are and how they try to address the needs of siblings. It will outline some of the activities that took place during the workshops in Kilkenny, including feedback from the siblings who participated and from their parents. The chapter will conclude with an evaluation of the outcomes of the Kilkenny Sibshops and some practical considerations that need to be taken into account when planning and running Sibshops.

Literature on the Experience of Siblings

Significance of sibling relationships

Sibling relationships are usually the longest and most enduring of any family relationship. They last a lifetime and have a significant effect on personality development (Strohm, 2002). They provide opportunities to develop identity, to practise conflict resolution and to openly express a range of emotions, including love, anger, rivalry and loyalty. Strohm (2002) and Trachtenberg and Batshaw (1997) point out that when one sibling has a disability, the relationship between siblings can be changed significantly. Research findings indicate that there are both positive and negative aspects to the experience of growing up with a brother or sister with special needs.

Positive aspects of being a sibling of a child with special needs

According to Taunt and Hastings (2002), some of the positive effects include increased sensitivity on the part of siblings and increased closeness and support within families. Some siblings have been found to show increased compassion, tolerance, appreciation of their own health, more acceptance of difference, awareness of the consequences of prejudice and a deeper knowledge of disabilities (Eisenberg and Baker, 1998). Siblings often exhibit a sense of responsibility beyond their chronological age (Dale, 1996; Seligman and Darling, 1997). Growing up with a brother or sister with special needs has led many siblings to choose a career in the caring professions (Marks *et al.*, 2005).

Challenging aspects of being a sibling of a child with special needs

Lack of time and attention

A child with special needs in a family will require more parental time and attention. Parents worry about the effect a child's disability has on their other children (Baldwin and Carlisle, 1999). Children must adjust to a brother or sister who, due to their condition, may require a large portion of family time, psychological support, attention and money. Siblings may become understandably resentful when their need for attention is overshadowed by that of their brother or sister. As explained by Osman (2001) and Ives and Munro (2002), each child in a family typically craves all the resources available from parents and anyone vying for these resources is seen as competition.

Need for information

It is crucial for children to understand their sibling's condition. Siblings need their parents to communicate and explain thoroughly about their brother or sister with special needs (Osman, 2001). Siblings need to have open and honest conversations with parents and with each other about disabilities in order to understand and manage the issues that arise (Dawson, 2005). Seligman and Darling (1997) state that limited or misunderstood information can confuse siblings. They may feel responsible for causing the condition, wonder if it is contagious and question what implications the child with a disability has on their future (Ives and Munro, 2002; Marsh, 2001; Osman, 2001; Strohm, 2001).

Greater responsibility and isolation

Another important aspect is the responsibility siblings often have for their brother or sister with special needs. Due to the fact they may be more able-bodied, parents may give siblings more responsibilities and rely on them more heavily to ease the workload for the family (Osman, 2001). Children can often find themselves with added housework or excessive care-giving. This can result in feelings of resentment, anger and guilt (Seligman and Darling, 1997).

Siblings may feel that they are the 'only ones' and they may not have the opportunity to meet other families who have children with similar conditions. The presence of a child with a disability in a family can inhibit social outings (Strock-Lynskey and Keller, 2007). The amount of pre-planning required for outings may act as a deterrent to attending events as a family.

Fear for the future

A fear for the future can be a great concern to siblings of children with special needs. Research (Seltzer, 1985) shows that, of all relatives, it is the siblings of people with disabilities who tend to take over the primary support role when parents are no longer able to carry out that role. Only 12 per cent of a sample of older 'care-giving' mothers in the United States reported that they had failed to make plans for their son or daughter with special needs (Egan and Walsh, 2001). By contrast, 40 per cent and 62 per cent in the Republic of Ireland and in Northern Ireland, respectively, had no plans for future 'care-giving' (Walsh *et al.*, 1993). This comparison between the Irish and American experiences suggests there are cultural differences around discussing the future care-giving plans for children with special needs.

Supports Available for Siblings

Support and information are of paramount importance for siblings throughout their lives (Porter, 2000). Strohm (2001) states that support can prevent siblings developing emotional problems as a result of their experiences. She says that if children are supported, they are more likely to be able to contribute to the quality of life of the person with special needs. Research carried out by Navior and Prescott (2004) shows that support groups for siblings can help resolve frustrations, enable greater self-expression and encourage increased interaction with brothers and sisters with special needs. The research also concluded that being around others who knew what they felt, without having to go into lengthy explanations, was a positive experience.

What are Sibshops?

Sibshops can be best described as 'opportunities for brothers and sisters of children with special needs to obtain peer support and education within a recreational context' (Meyer and Vadasy, 2007:1). The Sibshop model uses a group-work approach. It intersperses information and discussion exercises with a range of fun activities. The workshops integrate a variety of creative approaches to dealing with difficult topics in a positive and child-friendly manner. The emphasis is on having fun with other siblings.

Sibshops may have therapeutic benefits, but they are not therapy groups and children do not need to be presenting with 'issues' in order to attend. The Sibshop model acknowledges that most brothers and sisters are doing well, despite the challenges they face in having a child with a disability in their family (Meyer and Vadasy, 2007).

Aims of Sibshops

Sibshops aim to provide brothers and sisters of children with special needs with the following opportunities:

- to meet other siblings in a relaxed, recreational setting;
- to discuss common joys and concerns;
- to learn how others handle difficult situations;
- to learn more about their brothers' or sisters' conditions.

(Meyer and Vadasy, 2007)

Another aim of Sibshops is to provide parents and other professionals with opportunities to learn about the concerns frequently experienced by siblings.

The challenge for facilitators of Sibshops is to achieve the aims set out above in a manner that is age-appropriate and appealing to children. The Sibshop model is flexible in that the talents and skills of the facilitators, whether they are in music, art, drama, dance, creative writing, sport or cooking, can all be utilised. The programme of activities can also be adapted to the interests or needs of the particular group of children and to the resources available in the locality.

Kilkenny Sibshops

These Sibshops were co-ordinated by Parent to Parent, a parents' group in Kilkenny, and funded with a grant from the Health Service Executive. Information advertising the Sibshops was sent to all the local service providers and voluntary agencies that cater for people with special needs. Recruitment of children was made easier by the fact that many of the families were already known to the facilitators through their work as social workers in local disability services.

Three facilitators ran the workshops, two of whom are siblings of adults with special needs. Two of the facilitators attended a training workshop given by Don Meyer in Cork in December 2005. Information required for setting up and running Sibshops was provided during the training and is also contained in *Sibshops: Workshops for Siblings of Children with Special Needs* (2007), by Don Meyer and Patricia Vadasy.

What follows is a description of a sample of the activities that typically took place between 6.00 p.m and 8.00 p.m on Friday evenings in a school hall in Kilkenny. Full instructions for all the activities described below can be found in Meyer and Vadasy (2007). As mentioned, there were three facilitators with a group of twelve siblings, aged between seven and fourteen years, and the emphasis was on having fun. As discussed in the introduction, with some modifications these activities can be applied to group work with young people.

Visual schedules, or session plans, were displayed at the start of the evening and indicated clearly the planned programme for the duration of the workshop. These schedules helped to put a structure on the progression of activities and to inform the children of what to expect next. Having the schedules displayed worked well, particularly with the younger children, but the plan could easily be changed to accommodate different suggestions from the children.

'Trickle in' activities were set up before the children arrived. These consisted of art materials for making name-tags, cards or decorating individual folders, which could be taken home at the end of the series of workshops. It was important that children who were unsure about attending for the first time had an immediate activity that they could get involved in while waiting for everyone to arrive.

Introductions. Many of the siblings were not known to each other or to the facilitators. The children were asked to introduce themselves and to briefly describe their brother or sister with special needs. After the introductions, a fun activity always took place.

Knots quickly became one of our favourite games. This involves a group of participants tying themselves up in knots and trying to unravel the knot without breaking their hold on the other participants' hands. It does not have a particular disability focus, but is a good activity for getting people to know each other by requiring them to hold hands and work together to figure out how to untangle the knots.

Information-giving activities: Autism, Asperger syndrome, Down syndrome, cerebral palsy and global physical and intellectual disabilities were some of the conditions that the siblings' brothers and sisters were living with. The benefit of having siblings of children with such a range of conditions in the group was that the siblings got a broader understanding of the different types of disability. The disadvantage was that it was not possible to deal with any single condition in detail. Even when children had the same disability but with a different level of severity in terms of intellectual ability, mobility, communication or health, the issues that arose for their siblings were not the same.

Some of the siblings had brothers and sisters in residential care and their experience as siblings was different from siblings who lived with their brother or sister with special needs. Different situations therefore needed to be taken into account during discussion activities. According to the children, they enjoyed learning about all the disabilities and the common bond of being a sibling was enough for them to feel supported by one other. We found it difficult to source material that was suitable for the age group we were working with. We showed brief excerpts from videos by the Down Syndrome Association, Irish Autism Society and Enable Ireland, Kilkenny. These helped to stimulate discussion and to raise questions. We gave each child a copy of descriptions of different disabilities taken from *Views from our Shoes* (Meyer (ed.), 1997). We also gave each child a booklet entitled *Brothers and Sisters: Linking Children who have a Brother or Sister with a Learning Disability*, by Yvonne McCarthy and Nuala NcDonnell, which is available from Brothers of Charity, Southern Services, Cork.

The experience of many siblings is that they spend their time in waiting rooms while therapy appointments are taking place and that they are not informed about or involved in what is happening. We invited a physiotherapist and a speech and language therapist to come to workshops on different evenings. The siblings got a chance to use some of the equipment and to practise some of the exercises that their brothers and sisters with special needs routinely do as part of their therapy. An adapted form of charades was used to show how communication is possible without speech.

Party games: after each sit-down activity, there was usually a more high-energy activity. We played musical chairs, dodge ball, chain tig, relay races, set up obstacle courses and played whatever games the children suggested. We purposely tried to play games that were non-competitive and that everyone could enjoy, regardless of their level of sporting ability. We also tried to include games that the siblings could play at home with their brothers or sisters with special needs.

Strengths and weaknesses exercises: these exercises ask children to identify things that they are good at and things that they are not so good at. It then asks them to identify what their sibling with special needs is good at and what they find difficult. The idea is to convey that all of us have strengths and weaknesses and to encourage children not just to focus on the weakness of their brothers and sisters with special needs but to also acknowledge their talents. Some of the 'talents' listed were not, strictly speaking, positives, for example, 'she is very good at pulling hair', 'she is good at screaming', 'she is good at biting'. Facilitators needed to help identify more positive strengths.

Sightless sculptor: this is another exercise that can be used to illustrate the different talents that people with disabilities may have. The introduction to this activity involves asking the siblings whether a person with a disability can be an artist. The response is obviously in the affirmative. The activity entails people being divided into teams of three. One person is blindfolded (the sightless sculptor), the second person (the model) then strikes a dramatic pose and the third person (the blob of clay) gets moulded by the hands of the sightless sculptor into the same shape as the model. The participants need to be comfortable with being touched and may need to be divided according to gender.

Break: taking a break allows children to socialise informally with each other and with the facilitators. Having snacks and drinks available was an important part of the workshops.

Things I like to do: this exercise entails filling out a worksheet that lists things the siblings like to do with their friends and different family members. Again the idea is to focus on the positive activities they enjoy doing with their brother or sister with special needs.

Dealing with difficult situations: we used a variety of creative approaches to address how difficult situations might be handled. We used published letters and stories (Meyer, 1997; Meyer and Vadasy, 2007) to raise issues typically experienced when growing up with a brother or sister with special needs.

Aunty Blabby is an agony aunt whom Don Meyer introduced us to. Siblings write to her for advice on how to handle difficult situations. We encouraged the children to read the letters and to write a response suggesting how the situations described might be handled. These are two examples of letters we read and of the responses the children composed:

Dear Aunt Blabby,
I am beginning to feel like Cinderella. My parents make me take care of my little sister who has Down Syndrome. I never get to go out with my friends. What can I do?

Response: 'Dear Cinderella,
You should talk to your parents and tell them how you are feeling. They might not have noticed you are feeling this way.

Dear Aunt Blabby,
When I tell my friends about my little sister, they don't understand what a great sister she is. All they see is her wheelchair and her floppy arms. Am I the only one with this problem? What can I do?

Response: Dear Big Sister,
No, you are not the only one. Maybe ask your friends to come over and get to know your sister.

The letters needed to be adapted to use terminology that Irish children (as opposed to American children) would be familiar with. The responses the children composed and the discussions that ensued gave the siblings ideas on how others handled difficult situations.

Storytelling: we read stories written by siblings whose life experiences were similar to those of our siblings. We encouraged our group to write their own stories. This is what one child wrote:

> My sister is eight and has autism. Most of the time I like her but sometimes I don't, like she never plays with me and is always grumpy. Whenever we go on holidays we have to do what she wants. She always gets her own way. It's not fair! But I like giving her hugs.

Rather than just reading the letters and the stories, sometimes the children turned them into role-plays and acted them out. This is yet another example of how a creative approach, drama in this case, was used to help the children deal with difficult topics.

Sound off: this is a worksheet that asks the siblings to write about things that annoy them and that they would like to shout about. This activity is usually done in twos and then brought back to the bigger group for discussion. Again this exercise gives the siblings opportunities to say things that they might find difficult to say at home and to find out if others are bothered by the same issues.

Walking in my sister's or brother's footsteps: on a long roll of paper, we drew each child's footprints. We asked the children to write in the footprints what they felt it would be like, on a daily basis, to be their brother or sister with special needs. The words they wrote showed that they had clear insight and understanding of how their brother or sister might feel every day. These are some of their words: 'confused', 'frustrated', 'not understanding', 'angry', 'upset', 'funny', 'cute', 'loving'.

Party games: the siblings were invariably ready for more high-energy games at this stage. This was usually the last game before sum up and home time.

Sum up: we gathered the group to summarise the evening's activities, to see how everyone was feeling before going home and to gather suggestions for the next workshop.

Contact with parents: before the Sibshops began, parents received an information leaflet and completed an application form for each child. Parents were given an outline of all sessions and a description of some of the activities so that they could understand what their children were referring to when they came home. At each session, siblings were encouraged to talk to their parents when they went home and to ask them questions about their brother or sister.

All family members were invited to the last session. This session provided a social and fun outlet for all the family. Parents got an opportunity to meet other parents and to discuss common concerns that arise for siblings. It gave the siblings an opportunity to introduce their brother or sister with special needs to their new friends and, at the end, everyone joined in what had become known as 'Sibshop games'. The children enjoyed playing the games with their parents. In subsequent feedback, the parents were very positive about the opportunity afforded them to meet other parents. Additional facilitators were needed to cope with the extra numbers.

Children's Opinions on Sibshops

At the end of each series of workshops we asked the children to fill in questionnaires to let us know how they felt about the Sibshops.

When asked what they liked most, the responses were: 'all of it', 'the games', 'chain tig', 'meeting others', 'sweets', 'breaktime', 'indoor soccer', 'gym mats', 'the parachute'.

When asked what they liked least, the responses were: 'nothing', 'talking', 'I wish there were more weeks'.

When asked about the ways in which Sibshops had helped them, the responses were as follows:

'It was a help to talk about it and it was great to meet others with a brother/sister with special needs.'
'I got away from the house.'
'I can tell people about her.'
'Knowing what to do.'
'Helped to learn about other types of disabilities.'
'It was helpful in the way that you can understand your brother/sister's special needs.'
'You get to know new people.'
'I learned more about my brother.'
'Got me away from my brother and sister.'
'I know I am not alone.'

All of the children stated that they enjoyed attending the Sibshops. There was close to full attendance at every workshop.

Feedback from Parents

Parents were also asked to fill in a questionnaire on the last night. We needed to find out if the time, location and frequency of Sibshops were suitable for parents. The responses were all positive. One parent wrote that five sessions was not enough and that her son had only started to open up towards the end. The parents said that all the children spoke to them about what happened at Sibshops. The parents stated that their children enjoyed the Sibshops and that they always (after the first night) wanted to attend. The parents felt that their children enjoyed the games most and that they did not appear upset after any of the sessions.

In relation to how the children had benefited, comments included:

'Both appear to be volunteering more to play with their sister.'

'It gave him the opportunity to open up to his peer group.'

'He realises that there are other children with a brother and sister with a disability experiencing the same feelings and frustrations.'

'They learned that there are so many disabilities and that all children deserve an education.'

'They got to talk to other children that have the same thing to deal with.'

'I notice she is more gentle with her brother.'

'She learned that she is not the only little girl with a brother or sister that is special.'

'He's inclined to think he's the only one ... so that myth is blown.'

'He has made friends with other sibs.'

All of the parents stated that they were very glad that their children had taken part in the Sibshops. A number of parents suggested that the group meet biannually to preserve the bond they had formed and to check in with the children about any new issues that might arise.

Evaluation of Sibshops

The review of literature identified the key challenges for siblings of children with special needs as:

- a lack of time and attention from their parents;
- feeling isolated;
- a need for information;
- being concerned about their present and future responsibilities;

Sibshops are specifically aimed at meeting these needs. As already stated, they aim to help siblings:

- meet other siblings in a recreational setting;
- discuss common joys and concerns;
- learn how others handle difficult situations;
- learn more about their brother's or sister's special needs.

(Meyer and Vadasy, 2007)

From the feedback already quoted, it is apparent that the children who attended the Kilkenny Sibshops benefited from attending groups that were designed specifically to address their needs. According to their own testimonies, everyone had fun, enjoyed meeting other siblings, benefited from sharing stories about common experiences and from discussing ways of handling difficult situations and learned more about different disabilities.

Parents reported that their children asked them more questions about their brother or sister with special needs. Attending Sibshops raised topics for discussion at home that might not otherwise have surfaced. According to some parents, there was increased interaction between the siblings and their children with special needs while the Sibshops were taking place.

A clear indicator of 'success' is the almost 100 per cent attendance record at Sibshops in Kilkenny. The only negative aspect mentioned by both children and parents was that there were not enough sessions. The request for more Sibshops is yet another indication of how much the children enjoyed them and how beneficial their parents felt they were. These conclusions are similar to those of an evaluation of Sibshops conducted in Cork (D'Arcy *et al.*, 2005). In the Cork study, 81 per cent of child participants expressed a wish to meet siblings again. The children reported enjoying the Sibshop activities and the attendance rates across Sibshops were consistent. Parents in Cork also reported a dramatic increase in their child's conversation about their special needs sibling. The overall conclusion of the Cork study was that the majority of children enjoyed and benefited from Sibshops. These findings replicate our assessment of outcomes of the Kilkenny Sibshops.

Practical Considerations

The time involved in planning and in administration was greater than anticipated. Meetings were held before each session, schedules were prepared, materials were sourced and, occasionally, contact needed to be made with parents. American worksheets also had to be adapted for use by Irish children. Sibshops can be costly to run. The costs we incurred included hire of the hall, insurance, payment of facilitators and guests, materials and food. Each child paid a nominal enrolment fee. (Costs may be lessened if the co-ordinating agency already has the necessary resources.)

Group composition: it is important that the age span of the children in the group is not too great and that the proportion of boys and girls is fairly evenly balanced. There were some challenges in mixing the boys and the girls, as would be expected given their age. These challenges were overcome by playing a variety of games that everyone, regardless of their athletic ability, could enjoy participating in.

We had a number of siblings from the same families, partly due to the children's reluctance to attend alone. We were also conscious that it was easier for parents if all their children could be included in the same sessions. In hindsight, individual siblings may have benefited more had they attended separate Sibshops. Our reservation is that siblings may have been inhibited from openly discussing their concerns by the presence of their siblings.

Chapter Summary

▸ Sibshops are a focused way of integrating a variety of creative approaches to working with groups of children who are growing up with a brother or sister with special needs.

▸ The Sibshop model can be used with siblings at various stages in their lives.

▸ It can be adapted for use with younger children, with teenagers and with adults.

▸ The Sibshop approach provides a tried and tested model for working with siblings. We would encourage people in the caring professions to consider the needs of siblings when working with families.

▸ Participating in Sibshops in Kilkenny was definitely a very worthwhile and enjoyable experience for the children, for their families and for the facilitators.

FOURTEEN

The Importance of Creativity for Young People from Disadvantaged Backgrounds

Bradóg Regional Youth Service

Pauline Brennan

SNAPSHOT

▸ Background of Bradóg Regional Youth Service.

▸ What is creativity?

▸ Creative studies and its relationship with youth work.

▸ How creative studies can be used in youth work.

▸ How creativity enhances non-formal education.

▸ How the creativity process benefits young people.

Introduction

The purpose of this chapter is to convey to the reader the importance of using creativity in youth work, using the particular example of Bradóg Regional Youth Service. When working within the youth sector a care worker's eyes are opened to various scenarios. The young people we work with are often stigmatised with the name of being from a socially disadvantaged area.

But beyond this belief and from first-hand experience, these young people are those who are socially excluded. They are brought up in a society from which they are excluded as a result of many enviromental and emotional factors, largely attributed (in Bradóg's case) to inner-city living. Creative activities play an important role in the service provision of Bradóg, and this chapter aims to demonstrate how this is done. The chapter concludes with some advice for students aiming to work in youth services in the future.

Background to Bradóg Regional Youth Service

The service provides programmes and activities specific to each young person's needs. It is located in Dublin's north west inner city. The core staff comprises four full-time youth workers who carry out these programmes and work with young people in creative ways to accomplish goals in the young people's lives. There is also an outreach team, which comprises two outreach workers, who work on the street to engage the most at-risk young people through different street interaction methods.

The team is led by an active project leader who works on the ground and also by a manager who manages the staff, volunteers and students. The project leader is responsible for scheduling weekly work and also for implementing the programmes.

The regional manager oversees the whole project and his job is to network on a high level with relevant agencies, promoting Bradóg's profile and keeping staff updated with any relevant information that will enhance the service they provide. The regional manager also has the difficult task of aquiring the funding necessary for the future running of Bradóg. The administrative manager's role is to take care of Bradóg's finances, including wages, funding responsibilities and any other financial arrangements.

Youth services provide an extremely important service in different communities and it is because of this that we try to impact on the lives of those young people who are socially excluded. As a youth service, we use different creative methods to engage young people in our care.

What is Creativity?

There are many theoritical answers to this question, but how do we define creativity? According to some, creativity relates to writng, carpentry, music or art (Gardner, as cited in Lynch & Harris, 2001), while for others creativity is central to all human experiences and activities. Whatever the definition, creativity defines something that is unique to the person and there is no right or wrong way to personal creativity. In the youth sector, creativity is used as a means of communication between youth workers who act as advocates on behalf of the young people. Young people inform youth workers of their needs in the community. This type of work is done through a creative process.

Creative Studies and its Relationship with Youth Work

When working in a youth work setting it is very difficult to apply a theoretical view to practical youth work. So how do we define creativity in a youth work setting? As there is no definitive answer to the theory of creative studies, creativity in the youth work sector is displayed through its relationship with youth work practice.

Creativity in youth work is the freest form of self-expression. It gives socially excluded young people an opportunity to express themselves openly and without judgment. The way this is included within the youth work practice is through creative programme work. Creative programme work that is specific to a young person's needs should allow plenty of opportunity for creative thinking and experiences. This can be achieved by providing activities based on young people's ideas and interests.

A young person's creative activity can enhance youth workers' knowledge of that young person's thoughts and feelings. The act of self-expression allows a young person to develop their creative style and make whatever activity they are doing their own. This is important for a youth worker to encourage because these creative experiences can help young people to deal and cope with their feelings. Any creative act is a process of self-expression. Research has shown that the cultivation of creativity is a key component of programmes and strategies to produce positive outcomes for young people (Todd and Shinzato, 1999).

How Creative Studies can be Used in Youth Work

There are many ways of utilising creative studies in youth work practice. Creativity is a means to an end, therefore youth workers have the freedom to work with no set boundaries. Creative experiences come in many different forms, such as play, art, music, outdoor trips, media creations and anything that allows a young person to express him/herself. The key is that whatever project you work on with young people must be of interest to them: this will inspire and motivate them. In turn, this offers opportunities to the young people to develop skills, take ownership, gain a sense of community and realise their creative potential. This is of particular importance to socially excluded young people because it allows them to become socially engaged and increases confidence and self-esteem.

There are many ways in which we can engage in creative activities in youth work practice:

- 'Provide a special, private area for young people to work creatively.
- Supply materials (costumes, instruments, etc.) for creative activity.
- Display creative work, but avoid excessive evaluation.
- 'Allow children to be unique and express their individuality.'

(Feldman and Piirto, 2001:207–8)

The youth services provide a safe environment for young people to drop in and take part in non-formal activities and mix with their peers. There are many activities that challenge the young people in a creative capacity and the young people are unaware of this. These drop-in centres allow young people to flourish and gain self-esteem. They encourage non-formal chats with youth workers through which other needs of the young people can be identified and addressed through different types of creativity in programme work.

Another example is a music programme called Singer/Songwriter, which involves young people writing lyrics, composing music and singing their original song in front of a live audience. This is a form of creativity in youth work that can be carried out at any level. At Bradóg, this programme allowed groups of young people to take ownership of a song. This increased their confidence and self-esteem and subsequently gave this group of socially excluded young people an opportunity to gain a sense of community ownership. This was a very important stepping stone in this group of young people's lives as it allowed them to aspire and dream of bigger and better things. It has further fuelled their imaginations and allowed them to believe that the world is their oyster.

Youth arts are also carried out through the creative process. At Bradóg this has included various forms of youth art media, such as stilt-walking, costume design, samba drumming and performance.

These experiences provided multicultural and creative community experiences for all the young people involved. The more varied the experiences young people have in their lives, the wider the range of creative expression. This particular programme allowed the young people to explore expressive materials. They gained new skills and confidence from the creative process of each activity. The process is key to the success of developing and enabling young people to express themselves.

Another creative process that is used in our youth service on a regular basis is a media process. Media technology is a new and developing concept in the world of youth work and it allows young people to become involved and informed about new technologies through various media programmes. This in turn allows young people to express themselves creatively through different characters in fiction films and to creatively portray their communities through documentary-style short films. In Bradóg, each youth worker has basic media training and uses this as a tool to promote creativity among young people who attend the service.

There are many different media styles used in the media process, from basic to more advanced. This training gives young people the opportunity to engage in a creative process that both enhances their social and personal skills and allows them the opportunity to keep up to date with more advanced technologies that are becoming prominent in society. The process gives young people the chance to use various media equipment and computer technologies to plan, create and execute a final product, which always fosters a sense of achievement.

An example of this creative media process is the Valentines Project, which the youth service carries out every year. This is a media project in which six different groups of young people make short movies on the theme of love. The young people can interpret the theme in whatever way they want. The only criterion that must be adhered to is that each movie is no longer than forty seconds. When the films are completed, they are aired in a Valentine's Day booth, which is heart-shaped, in a public space in Dublin. The public are welcomed into the booth to view the movies and then asked to give their opinions and views on what they have seen. The young people are involved in the whole process: they interview the public; use the camera to record the interviews; and interact with the public. Valentine's Day is a public event that is celebrated by the general public and Bradóg uses media as a tool to allow the young people to portray their feelings on that day and share their work with the general public.

This project has proved very successful each year because it engages young people who are socially excluded and affords them an opportunity to creatively interact with people outside their comfort zone. In turn, the young people gain self-confidence and find new, creative ways to explore and convey their feelings.

How Creativity Enhances Non-formal Education

Non-formal education is a key component of youth work practice. It is the way in which youth workers operate and promote their services to make them attractive to young people. Creativity is a main component of the non-formal system used by youth workers. In order for non-formal education to be successful, young people have to learn by having fun in a non-formal setting, through interactive games that are made appealing by a creative process.

The creative process is a key component to making non-formal education a success. The process is very important as this where young people's creativity is developed. The possibilities for a creative process in non-formal education are endless. Young people can be creative through a whole range of non-formal activities, such as art, music, clay, paper, photography and so on: there is no end to the list. The creative process allows young people to learn in a non-formal way.

For example, young people can use a creative process, such as paper folding. In this process they have to count corners and measure paper to size. This activity uses a creative process and throughout the process young people are gaining mathematical competencies and learning new skills in a informal environment. The end product isn't the important stage of non-formal education. The process is the vital stage as this is where the young people gain their skills and self-esteem.

Throughout this process it is important to give young people enough time to explore materials and to explore their own individual ideas. This also includes time to allow the young people to plan, prepare, design, construct and implement their ideas.

The following case study is a project that received external funding and was carried out by the young people and a youth worker. It is known as the Ignite Arts project.

Case Study: Ignite Arts Project

Background

The case study is based on a group of thirteen young people from the various catchment areas of Bradóg Regional Youth Service. The group is of mixed gender, with members aged between thirteen and eighteen years. Over the last few years these young people have shown an interest in taking part in and designing art projects. The Ignite project was a 'next stage' programme from the Kindle project. Half of the group were members of the Kindle project, those who wanted to further develop their artistic skills, and half were other members who had previously taken part in different youth events. This was a collaborative project between youth worker and artist, who jointly mentored and supported the young people in coming up with an idea for a public artwork/event.

Issues

The group comes mainly from Dublin City Council flat complexes. Among the members there are some behavioural issues that have led them to be excluded from groups/other clubs in the area. Some of the young people come from family backgrounds where family members have been in trouble with the law, local council or misuse of alcohol/drugs. There is also a risk of teen pregnancy and poor health choices. Some have lack of confidence and low self-esteem.

Intervention

The Ignite arts project is a programme set up to engage the young people in a substantial arts experience. It differed from previous arts programmes they had taken part in in that the aim of this project was to challenge/enhance the skills levels of the older group both artistically and in peer leadership/transferring of skills to the younger group, who had a small part in fabrication and taking part in events.

The project aim was to devise concepts, draft designs and fabricate costumes/structures/artworks that relate to the given project. It also aimed to give the group project/event management skills, to come up with an idea/concept, design the project, make a work plan and apply for funding, to advertise the event, then to gain permission from the local authority to present it to the public.

This project/event was called ROLF (Roll On the Floor Laughing) and was an interactive public art project. The group invites members of the public to come and write their funniest moments on four large, three-dimensional letters on April Fool's Day. This process took over four months to complete. They worked closely with the artist and the youth worker every Wednesday for two to four hours, from December to April, and these facilitators supported and guided them in the decisions they made and the steps they needed to complete to create this event. The group also filmed the event with the support of the Bradóg film club, which some of the young people attend.

Outcomes

The group started off well together over the first few weeks. They came up with the design and the plan for what they wanted to achieve very quickly. The entire group felt they had played a part in this process and were very happy and pleased with their idea. We then time-lined the work plan. The young people were very aware of the tasks that needed to be done. The youth workers were very impressed by the group's knowledge, their team work and the support the older members gave to the younger and new participants to this group, especially by how the older young people included the younger ones in the decision-making.

When the group started their work plan, however, some difficulties arose as some of the older ones didn't stick to the process they had agreed in picking the venue for the event. After trying different methods with the young people, the youth worker and artist needed to step in and take control of the group and bring them back on track. They did some team-building exercises/discussions and divided them into working groups for each session as the youth worker felt that not all of the group had the necessary management skills and feared that the project would be jeopardised.

After this issue some of the group felt differently about the project and about continuing with it. The youth worker gave these young people extra one-to-one sessions to work out their issues and encourage them to stay with the project. Four young people dropped out due to other club/school commitments. The project got back on track and the working group format worked very well. The youth worker teamed the groups together, with a younger and older member in each group, and gave them tasks that would suit their interests and skill level.

Nine young people completed the event and all enjoyed taking part in the project and would be interested to be part of something like this again. This project also provided an opportunity to learn skills in event management and an understanding of how other projects come about and the work involved in them. The young people involved made new friendships and built up some peer leadership skills, which came into practice when some of the group worked in the summer programme. It also required team work, dedication and commitment in order to complete this task.

Some of the group would be able to do a project like this again and have put forward a suggestion for another programme that will hopefully be successful in its application for funding. The rest of the group needs extra time and support to develop these skills. During the project some young people were referred to the outreach team for extra support around behavioural issues.

Empowering the young people to design their own project encourages feelings of ownership of the project. It will help the youth worker to acknowledge the uniqueness of the young people's ideas and allow the youth worker to take a scaffolding approach to specific young people.

How the Creative Process Benefits Young People and Youth Workers, with a Note for Students

The creative process enables young people to create change in their own lives and their community. It gives youth workers an opportunity to allow young people to feel more socially included in their neighbourhoods. The creative process has been described over the last few pages, but how do we put this into practice? It is inevitable that we are creative within our work, but how do we implement this creative process purposefully? Each year in Bradóg we give placements to a number of students from various colleges. Students come into the youth service with expectations, which may be different from the reality, about the work involved in the youth service.

Social care students undergo a formal educational process and learn about the relevant theories for youth work, which they then try to apply to practice within the youth service. This is why a practical placement is a vital part of the course. It allows the students to learn through a non-formal setting and to become involved in the grounded, practical work. As youth workers we mentor students and allow them to shadow youth workers in order to gain an insight into how youth work is carried out. The creative process is a prime example of this. As the non-formal process unfolds, the student can identify that the process and the practical work being carried out are the key components to non-formal learning. By observing this work the student can also have an opportunity to identify emotions, gestures and attitudes and in turn apply theories to the behaviours of young people. The process of integrating theory into practice is also a creative process as it is revealed through creative activity and abstract thinking.

> 'The key question isn't "What fosters creativity?" But it is why in God's name isn't everyone creative? Where was the human potential lost? How was it crippled? I think therefore a good question might be not why do people create? But why do people not create or innovate? We have got to abandon that sense of amazement in the face of creativity, as if it were a miracle if anybody created anything.'   (Maslow, 1980–89)

The creative process is very important in the youth work process, but as youth workers it is up to us to create and allow young people the opportunity to benefit from the creative process. Young people who are socially excluded can gain great opportunities from the creative process. Through creativity, opportunities are afforded to young people to learn through a visual process, rather than a formal academic process.

Chapter Summary

▶ The importance of creativity and how we define creativity.

▶ The practical way in which creative studies is used in youth work.

- ▸ Ways in which we use creative studies through example.

- ▸ Creative studies and examples of ways it is perceived as a non-formal activity.

- ▸ The importance of creativity and how it benefits young people.

- ▸ A note for students on the practical side of creative studies and the theoretical side of the creative process and combining the two in their work experience.

- ▸ In conclusion, as it has been defined above, creative studies takes many different forms and works well as a tool when working with young people who are socially excluded. This type of work can be envisaged through both practical examples and theoretical ideologies.

FIFTEEN

Asperger Syndrome and Social Skills Education through Creative Drama

Carmel O'Sullivan, Una McNulty, Lesley Conroy, Anthony Walsh and Des McKernan

SNAPSHOT

▶ Autistic Spectrum disorders.

▶ The triad of impairments.

▶ Definition of Asperger syndrome.

▶ Educational support for Asperger syndrome.

▶ Making sense of the world of Asperger syndrome through drama.

▶ Results.

▶ The practice.

Introduction

It is widely accepted that although individuals with Asperger syndrome (AS) have average or above average intelligence, they lack social and communication skills as well as the ability to empathise and identify with others. It has been suggested that the root of the problem lies in their inability to read emotions in others and to understand how others feel in order to respond appropriately and interact. Individuals with AS are therefore often perceived as being socially inept and can be bullied and isolated as a result. This chapter will outline the origin of the terms autism and autistic spectrum disorder, identifying the

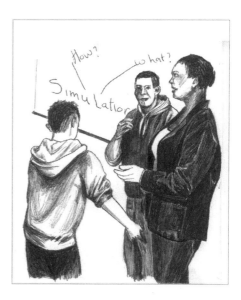

connections between autism and Asperger syndrome. It will summarise the major educational programmes currently in use and discuss how creative practices can be used by those in the caring professions. The results of a recently completed, large-scale research project that used a creative drama approach to social skills education will be presented. Finally, creative drama processes, with an emphasis on how the art form can be specifically communicative in a social and educational context, is examined, and a sample programme of work is presented to demonstrate the use of the approach in helping individuals with AS to improve their social, communication and imagination skills.

Autistic Spectrum Disorders

The word *autism* is derived from the Greek word *autòs*, meaning a 'withdrawal to the self' (Frith, 2003), and is used to describe a disorder that causes considerably limited interaction with the environment. Autism is not a new phenomenon and throughout history people appear to have lived with what we know today as an Autistic spectrum disorder (ASD). Some of the earliest published descriptions of behaviour that resembles autism dates back to the eighteenth century (Wing, 1996). In 1911 Bleuler coined the word autism, believing that the symptoms of autism were in fact a fundamental disorder associated with the condition of schizophrenia, in which patients isolated themselves and were self-absorbed (Frith, 2003). It was not until the 1940s that the subject of childhood autism gained attention. Leo Kanner (1943), working in the USA, and Hans Asperger (1944), working independently in Vienna, published very similar accounts of case studies of young boys who had in common a fundamental disturbance resulting in severe difficulties with social integration (Schreibman, 2005). Although the work of Kanner (1943) became associated with autism and subsequently became very well known, AS research remained virtually unheard of for many years and his original paper was not translated into English until 1991 (Frith, 1991). The term Asperger's syndrome was coined by the UK psychologist Lorna Wing to replace Asperger's original label of 'autistic psychopathy', and it was only after her influential paper (Wing, 1981) was published that international attention was drawn to the condition, and a growing number of researchers started exploring the relationship between the two conditions (Frith, 1991; Prior, 2003; Hippler and Klicpera, 2003).

There has been considerable discussion as to whether AS and autism are two different conditions with distinct neurobiology and aetiology or variants of a single disorder (Howlin, 1998; Happe, 1994; Gillberg, 2002; Rinehart, 2006; Baird *et al.*, 2006). The most recent accounts of the two major classification systems for mental disorders (American Psychiatric Association (APA) Diagnostic and Statistical Manual (DSM IV), 1994; and World Health Organisation (WHO) diagnostic manual, known as the *International Classification of Diseases* (ICD-10), 1993) present distinct criteria for autism and AS, indicating normal language and cognitive development in AS as the major differentiating criteria between the two syndromes. The validity of the diagnostic criteria to distinguish the two conditions is questioned (Freeman *et al.*, 2002; Leekam *et al.*, 2000), and the view of an autistic continuum or spectrum is alternatively proposed (Wing and Gould, 1979; Wing, 1996; Gould, 1998; Prior,

2003). Autism is not viewed as a single mental condition but rather as a spectrum of autistic disorders, with different forms of autism taking different positions on the spectrum (DES Task Force on Autism, 2001; Jones, 2002; Sicile-Kira, 2003; Biklen, 2005; Heflin and Alaimo, 2007).

The Triad of Impairments

Autism and AS are both recognised neuro-developmental disorders that are principally defined in behavioural terms and, like all conditions along the autistic spectrum, they share features described as the 'triad of social impairments' (Wing and Gould, 1979). Three broad aspects of development are affected: social interaction, communication and imagination (DES Task Force on Autism, 2001). Impairment in social interaction includes failure to develop age-appropriate peer relationships, lack of social and emotional reciprocity, and social awareness but inappropriateness in reciprocal interaction. Impairment in communication indicates both verbal (pedantic, literal, stilted, flat and repetitive speech, idiosyncratic choice of words and phrases, literal understanding of speech) and non-verbal difficulties (impairment in the use and understanding of non-verbal behaviours, eye contact, facial expression, body posture, gestures). Impairment in imagination can be described by a limited range of imaginative activities, possibly copied and pursued rigidly and repetitively, an inability to develop creative pretend play appropriate to developmental age, narrow interests and preoccupations, restricted and repetitive routine, stereotyped patterns of behaviour, inflexibility and obsession with complex topics (Rotatori *et al.*, 2001).

In addition to Wing and Gould's (1979) original triad of impairments, further defining features of an ASD were added later, such as limited planning ability (Wing, 1996) and difficulty coping with more than one activity/dimension simultaneously (Jordan and Powell, 1995). In the mid-1980s and 1990s the theory of mind (TOM), or '*mind blindness*' as it is often called, encapsulated the difficulty that individuals with an ASD have in conceptualising how people imagine others' beliefs, i.e. the ability to perceive and understand the world from another person's perspective (Baron-Cohen *et al.*, 1985; Baron-Cohen, 1995; Bogdashina, 2005). Another important feature relates to difficulties in seeing 'the larger picture'. The central coherence deficit involves attention to detail rather than seeing a problem as a whole (Cumine *et al.*, 1998). More recently, researchers have been looking for links between cognitive deficits and social impairment (Schultz, 2005; Baron-Cohen, 2006). Cognitive deficits may act in isolation or may combine to form a more encompassing difficulty, such as executive dysfunction (Russell, 1997; Hill, 2004). Executive functioning is described by Luria (1966) as the ability to maintain an appropriate problem-solving set for the attainment of a future goal. Ozonoff (1995) proposed this particular deficit as the central deficit in autism. Executive dysfunction describes the inability to make advanced-level planning decisions and relates to the control of behaviour.

In summary, when considering ASDs, it appears that 'General behavioural problems, ritualistic and stereotyped interests and motor delay difficulties, are the first concerns for AS, whilst language delay and social difficulties are the main concerns for autism' (Howlin, 1998).

Definition of Asperger Syndrome

Asperger syndrome is a pervasive developmental disorder at the high functioning end of the autistic spectrum. Individuals with AS generally have average, or occasionally above average, IQ. However, they have difficulty with social interaction, communication and flexible thinking, and may experience difficulties with transitions or changes, generally preferring sameness. They often have obsessive routines and may be preoccupied with a particular subject of interest. They have a great deal of difficulty reading non-verbal cues (body language) and very often experience difficulty in determining proper body space. Often overly sensitive to sounds, tastes, smells and sights, a person with AS may prefer soft clothing or particular foods and can be bothered by sounds or lights that no one else seems to hear or see (Hippler and Klicpera, 2003; Attwood, 2007). It is important to note that a person with AS may perceive the world quite differently in certain aspects and thus many behaviours that seem odd or unusual are due to neurological differences and not the result of intentional rudeness or bad behaviour.

Individuals with AS often have an uneven pattern of abilities and can achieve excellence in one particular area while having serious difficulties in many others. Because of their high degree of functionality and their naiveté, those with AS are often viewed as eccentric or odd and can easily become victims of teasing and bullying. While language development, on the surface, seems normal, they can often have deficits in pragmatics and prosody. Vocabularies may be extraordinarily rich and some children sound like 'little professors'. However, people with AS can be extremely literal and have difficulty using language in a social context (Fitzgerald, 2004).

Educational Support and Intervention

Students with AS may have unique abilities, but because of their difficulties their progression through the normal education system and acquisition of an adequate education can present many challenges (Jordan, 2005; Owen-DeSchryver et al., 2008). Hans Asperger, who recognised how severely these difficulties affected their daily lives, commented that 'they made their parents' lives miserable and drove their teachers to despair' (Cumine et al., 1998). However, he also recognised that, given appropriate supports, they could make a huge contribution to society. Often it is the single-mindedness and determination to persist with a task when most would have given up long before that characterises the condition.

It is acknowledged that there is currently no known treatment that has any effect on the basic impairments underlying AS, but difficulties can be diminished by appropriate management and education (see Bogdashina, 2004 and 2005; Gray, 1994 and 2000; Jackson, 2002; Attwood, 1997 and 2007). It is important that appropriate supports and procedures are put in place to allow children and young people with the condition to achieve their full potential. There are a number of approaches and programmes used by teachers and social care professionals to support students throughout their education and these can include the following:

- Son-Rise/Options Institute (see Jones, 2002);
- Developmental, Individual Difference, Relationship model (DIR, also known as Floor Time, see Greenspan & Wieder, 2006);
- TEACCH (Treatment and Education of Autistic and Communication Handicapped Children, see Mesibov *et al.*, 2004);
- Lovaas programme (Discrete Trial Training, see Tarbox and Najdowski, 2008);
- DLT (Daily Life Therapy, see Jones, 2002);
- Social Stories (see Gray, 1994, 2000 and Gray and White, 2002);
- Video Self-Modeling (see Darden-Brunson *et al.*, 2008);
- PECS (Picture Exchange Communication System, see Dunlap *et al.*, 2008);
- PROGRESS curriculum (Program for Remediating and Expanding Social Skills, see Krasny *et al.*, 2003);
- Mind Reading (a computer-based interactive systematic guide to emotions for adults with AS, see Golan and Baron-Cohen, 2006);
- SODA strategy (Stop, Observe, Deliberate, and Act, see Bock, 2001, as cited in Elder *et al.*, 2006).

Despite an increased emphasis on the importance of resources and expertise being made available to all schools (DES Task Force on Autism, 2001) and social care settings, Elder *et al.* (2006) note that there is little research detailing the efficacy of social skills training specifically for individuals diagnosed with AS.

Research conducted to date has shown mixed results, identifying that social skills training using some of the methods listed above can be very effective, but similarly noting that generalisation is a common problem. Gutstein and Whitney (2002) add that the gains may not be maintained over time, and when skills are taught in isolated sessions, in a rote learning fashion and without a natural social context, there can be difficulties with generalisation. Thus, people may learn a skill in the context of the training, but are then unable to transfer it to other situations. It is arguable that social skills should therefore be taught 'in context', using authentic resources where possible, and in a variety of situations in order to promote their use in a range of real-life social situations, thereby improving the possibilities of generalisation. There should be co-operation between the school/social care/educational unit and the parents/carers at home to ensure that skills are being reinforced in various situations and that teaching is consistent. Elder *et al.* (2006) suggest that programmes that allow parents to participate in social skills groups either with their child or in separate but simultaneous groups should be encouraged and developed.

Drama-in-Education as a Creative Intervention

Despite a desire to have friends (Biklen, 2005), children with AS have major difficulties with social interaction. It is generally agreed that all students with AS should have access to social, emotional and communication training programmes in all educational and social care settings as a core part of the curriculum (Klin and Volkmar, 1996). The 'hidden curriculum' of social skills, which most children pick up intuitively, has to be taught to children with AS. The literature in the field suggests that naturalistic and experiential teaching and learning methods, which provide a context for the exploration and acquisition of social skills, may prove useful here and that learning through fun activities is also a very powerful method to explore social skills (Attwood, 2007).

It was against such a background that a collaborative research project involving the School of Education, Trinity College Dublin and Aspire (the Asperger Syndrome Association of Ireland) was initiated in 2004. The prime motivation for this research came from the realisation that although it is widely recognised that young people with AS lack skills in the domains of social skills, communication and imagination, there is little research on *how* to help people develop these abilities as most literature in the field focuses on the outcome rather than on the process, and also on methods to enable them to achieve social skills by imitating the 'correct' (acceptable) behaviours rather than helping them to decode the images they see and understand the meanings below the surface. To date, most teaching and learning methods for people with an ASD are advocated in virtual isolation of any social, emotional or logical context. Limited research has been done in this area, however, and the literature focuses mainly on understanding the disorder and how to act upon it, i.e. treat the symptoms. Scant reference to the beneficial effects of the arts is made, despite their relevance to the condition. Little reference to music or the visual arts is found and references to the dramatic arts usually refer to it in its most limited forms: drama as simulation, drama and theatre games and role-playing (Peter, 1994; Attwood, 2007). It is interesting that a nurse, Viktorine Zak, at the Vienna Children's Hospital where Hans Asperger worked, developed drama programmes for children with AS as far back as the 1940s. She used drama activities to teach the children social skills (Asperger, 1944; as cited in Attwood, 2007).

This research project therefore aimed to investigate whether the sustained use of an integrated creative arts approach with specific focus on the use of drama-in-education could lead to a more successful social, personal, emotional and cognitive education of young people with AS. It sought to bring about a greater understanding of what it means to live with AS and the implications for the person's life. The overall aim of the research project was to devise and critically evaluate a creative intervention strategy that would appeal to the participants and lead them to become more confident, socially motivated, self-fulfilled individuals who could interact successfully with their peers and others. The research sought to explore the full use of educational dramatic conventions for the benefit of individuals with AS, and to determine its efficacy as a constructive medium to help people with AS make sense of the world and interact more effectively with other people, adapting to different situations as the need arose. Drama in this study is seen as a creative method to provide a safe environment for the individual to try out and test their social skills, and an important distinction between simulation, a method commonly used for teaching social skills, and drama-in-education is employed. Simulation is about imitating other people's behaviour without necessarily understanding the logic behind it, which can be particularly frustrating and mentally exhausting for an individual with AS. Drama-in-education, however, offers an existential experience, enabling personal, social and emotional growth whilst providing opportunities for enhanced communication, understanding and decision-making processes. Role-play and simulation have a valuable place in social skills training (see Conn, 2007; Sheratt and Peter, 2002), but the overriding aim in drama-in-education is always to achieve *understanding* through the arts. Even the simplest form of drama must use the art form to illuminate some truth about the world, otherwise dramatic activity simply remains at the level of reiterating facts or practising limited vocational skills (Bolton, 1992).

Making Sense of the World through Drama

In the wider field of drama and theatre arts there is a degree of confusion about the word 'drama' and its definition when applied to education and social care practices. It is therefore important to clarify the two extremes of practice on the drama/theatre continuum. On the one hand, there is a category of practice commonly called theatre arts, which includes the study and staging of both scripted and devised plays. At the other end of the continuum is what is often referred to as drama for learning or drama-in-education (DIE). In DIE the emphasis is not on performance or a public 'showing' of participants' work but rather on a range of creative and active learning strategies that capture the intrinsic motivation of learners through 'as if' scenarios and contexts, which engages them through well-structured, meaningful learning episodes. The emphasis is on internal coherence within the work and mystery, dilemma, tension and problem-posing/solving are used as strategies to entice participants to engage fully with the learning context. In effect, DIE provides a fictional but well-structured framework from which to explore any content or situation in life. Thus, it is not about 'acting out' pre-determined scenes or performing social scripts, it is learning through play for increased social awareness, communication and understanding (see Bolton, 1998; Johnson and O'Neill, 1991; O'Neill, 1995; Wagner, 1999; Fleming, 2003; Morgan and Saxton, 1989; O'Sullivan and Williams, 1998).

Creative and effective education is fundamental to human development and therefore relevant to all aspects of learning (NCCA [O'Sullivan *et al.*], 2002). However, what has emerged in many social skills training programmes designed specifically for people on the autistic spectrum has been the use of 'drama as imitation' or mimicry, theatre games and exercises, and simple role-playing activities (see Peter, 1994; Conn, 2007; and Sheratt and Peter, 2002). Little, if any, emphasis has been placed on the more important role of drama in this context as a means of making sense of the world we live in, or the use of drama to bring about change in a person's social and emotional growth.

Results of the Creative Arts Research Project

This project revealed that a particular use of dramatic activity substantially enabled participants with AS to develop social and communication skills using activities that they enjoy and could control. Results from this study (2004–2009) indicate statistically significant results in all categories assessed. Over fifty young people with AS between the ages of six and twenty-one participated in the study, which was conducted by the authors of this chapter and which involved attendance at one DIE workshop per week (typically between seventy and a hundred minutes in duration, depending on age). The participants were rated when they first joined the drama group in terms of thirty-three different abilities and skills, for example self-confidence, empathy, turn-taking, ability to make eye contact, level of competitiveness, etc. and were then rated in terms of improvements either when they finished or at the end of the most recent term. Analysis of the data revealed that on every single measure the participants were observed for, the difference before and after was statistically significant, with all of the effect sizes being either medium or large.

One of the key outcomes of this project is the successful response to the research question relating to the value of imitation versus understanding, i.e. whether people with AS should be educated to 'imitate' neuro-typicals in order to be socially accepted, or whether the focus should be a greater emphasis on achieving understanding and building trust as the cornerstones of developing relationships. Many social skills intervention programmes have emphasised the need to train children to play or learn certain skills, and yet give limited opportunities for children to learn spontaneously through self-discovery, meaningful interaction and choice. The outcomes of this project concur with O'Neil (1998), a writer with autism who argues that 'normalising' people on the autistic spectrum, pushing them into behaving in a way that is alien to their true nature, is not just ineffective but wrong. The research demonstrates that while role-play and simulation have a valuable place in social skills training, the most successful outcomes were achieved when the emphasis was placed on logically understanding the situation under study and then using the DIE approaches to illuminate some truth about the world, which subsequently led to emotional engagement and empathy. When the order was reversed and the world was presented 'as is', as an unchangeable entity in which the participants had to 'play the game' according to pre-set rules and 'do the right thing', the activities remained simply at the level of practising socially acceptable norms and behaviours (such as greeting new people and initiating conversations), and these skills were rarely demonstrated of participants' own volition in subsequent sessions. Imitation and simple role-playing, when practised in isolation and without an appropriate social context, did not offer a solution to participants' difficulties with social interaction or the development of their imagination, as these methods bore little resemblance to actual, real-life situations, which often have unquantifiable and unpredictable challenges. When performed out of context (i.e. they did not form part of a bigger story that was being worked on at the time), they remained at the level of mere enactments of rehearsed situations and did not require intellectual or emotional understanding or response.

In contrast, the new approach, using a DIE methodology, offered a safe environment for practising social and communication skills in contextualised, fictional situations, and the data supports a degree of transferability of skills into other social, educational and familial contexts. Understanding, not imitation, was therefore demonstrated as the key to 'fitting in'. In effect, DIE provided an effective and enjoyable framework from which to explore any content or situation in life, and was not about 'acting out' scenes or performing short social scripts or sketches. Instead it involved the intellectual, creative, imaginative and collective stimulation of participants as they grappled with age-appropriate problems/images/language/concepts/themes, etc. in order to arrive at a deeper and more reflective understanding of the content/situation under consideration. Making such techniques available to the participants in this study enabled them to explore new experiences, decreasing their anxiety by increasing their control over those experiences. Significant improvement was recorded in participants' emotional well-being, their social and communication skills, their ability to interact and empathise with others, and their levels of interest and enjoyment in attending the weekly sessions over a number of years. This supports the authors' insistence on the use of social skills *education* through the arts, as opposed to social skills *training*.

Social Skills Education through Drama—The Practice

This creative educational approach involves participants in fictionally created contexts that are based on problem-posing and problem-solving methodology. Imaginative and engaging characters are presented to the participants in various dilemmas. The intention of this approach to learning is to engage the participant in an exploration of another character(s)' life, and to involve him/her in following that journey and working collaboratively to resolve various difficult and challenging situations as they arise. Generic and transferable skills development should be planned for through this approach, and thus the units should focus on encouraging and developing such things as imagination, turn-taking, maintaining eye contact, listening and responding appropriately to others, collaborating, working in pairs and small groups, visual literacy, reading and interpreting non-verbal body language and tone of voice, making presentations, changing routines, and sharing space, etc.

The sessions should maintain an important objective distance from the participants' own lived reality, but experiences can be gently resonated back to the individual through periods of planned reflection in each session (i.e. it is not advisable to deal directly with a person's own real-life situation as the basis for a drama session, but references, as appropriate, can be made to enable the participant to make, understand and appreciate such connections, where they exist). It is important to note that this work is creative drama as applied in educational and social care settings, and not drama therapy as may occur in clinical and other settings.

Throughout the session participants should be facilitated both as 'artists' (participants who are involved in creating the drama scenes with the social care professional and their peers) and also as 'spect-actors' (responding to and interpreting dramatic scenes and situations created and presented by the facilitator or other participants in the group) (Boal, 1979). The emphasis in these strategies is on moving from particular examples presented and explored through the medium of drama to generalised and universal levels of meaning in participants' own lives and in wider society, in order to make sense of the world and then act within and upon it. Stories were used to enable the participant to aid this process, for example 'The Vale of Tears in the Silent Kingdom', 'Mr Boring is Hiding in Jollywood' and 'The Story of Amy'.

Title of unit	The Vale of Tears in the Silent Kingdom
Summary	The Queen from the story of Alice in Wonderland has lost her voice. It has been taken by the magic mirror that once belonged to the wicked Queen in the story of 'Snow White and the Seven Dwarves'. The children respond to the plea by the town crier to claim the reward and find the stolen voice. It involves them going on many adventures into the Silent Kingdom and meeting/negotiating/outwitting/speaking with/ignoring, etc. some very interesting characters who live in that land. One of the first challenges is to successfully transverse Tantrum Valley, which lies at the opening to the Silent Kingdom. The children have to outwit goblin-like creatures who try to force the children to have tantrums so that they can take their voices and escape the dreaded valley themselves forever.
Aims	(i) To increase understanding about the causes of tantrum behaviour and its effects on others, and to investigate concrete ways within a fictional narrative to manage and control such behaviour. (ii) To provide opportunities to consolidate and extend language skills explored in earlier units. (iii) To present children with imaginative and engaging fictional characters and to encourage children to interact creatively with these characters whilst trying to address and resolve dilemmas and difficulties as presented. (iv) To develop individual and collective problem-posing and problem-solving skills. (v) To enjoy the experience of working collaboratively with one's peers in a fictional, make-believe world.
Skills	How to recognise the onset of a tantrum and deal effectively with the consequent emotions in order to control and manage the resultant behaviour. Problem posing and problem solving. Oral language skills, such as interrogation, interpretation, negotiation. Listening skills. Differentiation between sound and stillness. Dramatic presentation skills.

Title of unit	Mr Boring is Hiding in Jollywood
Summary	A character (Mr Boring) has gone off-script in the world of film and entertainment and is threatening to transform the lively Jollywood into a quiet and boring place. The Tasmanian Devil, who is working for Mr Boring, is intimidating and frightening the other stars (the Mad Hatter, Miss Piggy, Mad Dog McGrath, Miss Elastica, the Incredibles, etc.). We have been asked to enter that world and interact with the stars in order to pick up clues as to Mr Boring's whereabouts. Each interaction with a different star demands a new set of skills and understandings as these characters are very demanding and have various mannerisms that have to be negotiated and mediated, if possible. For example, Mad Dog McGrath goes crazy if he doesn't win! Miss Piggy is so direct that she passes what could be interpreted as insensitive remarks about others and their appearance. Mad Hatter won't make eye contact with you and insists on doing everything according to his own routine. The children have to assume a fictional identity in order to enter Jollywood and resolve the ensuing dilemmas.
Aims	(i) To practise the skills required to prepare a short performance piece that is filmed and reviewed. (ii) To observe and study the mannerisms of fictional characters. (iii) To negotiate and interact with difficult and unique individuals in the safety of the drama world. (iv) To reflect on the mannerisms of others. (v) To provide opportunities for learning to change through resonating the experiences gently back into their own lives.
Skills	Interacting in pairs and small groups. Negotiating and decision-making. Identifying strengths and weaknesses in yourself and others. Listening to others. Team building. Problem solving. Interview skills. Competitiveness and dealing with losing. Meeting characters who are self-absorbed. Performing skills.

Title of unit	The Story of Amy
Summary	The young people are presented with an extended case study of a young girl who has stopped talking and communicating with others. In attempting to review the case, they examine the evidence as presented from a number of different perspectives and meet a number of interested parties involved in the case as it unfolds.
Aims	(i) To enhance participants' visual literacy skills. (ii) To build a case from various pieces of evidence. (iii) To examine a situation from a number of different perspectives. (iv) To collaborate on a project and share ideas, resources and information. (v) To develop empathy and understanding for others.
Skills	How others form impressions of us and how to make impressions on others. Seeing things from different perspectives. Representing the case of others. Looking at the whole picture. Visual literacy. Picking up clues from observing body language and oral communication.

Table 15.1: How participants learn social skills through DIE.

Chapter Summary

▸ Autism is not viewed as a mental condition but rather as a spectrum of autistic disorders, with different forms of autism appearing at different positions on the spectrum.

▸ Asperger syndrome (AS) is a pervasive developmental disorder at the high functioning end of the autistic spectrum.

▸ Children with AS need educational programmes that promote social skills development.

▸ Drama-in-education is an effective learning tool for people with AS.

▸ Fifty young people participated in a collaborative project between Trinity College Dublin and Aspire (the Asperger Syndrome Association of Ireland) between 2004 and 2009.

THIS PROJECT REVEALED THAT A PARTICULAR USE OF DRAMATIC ACTIVITY SUBSTANTIALLY ENABLED PARTICIPANTS WITH AS TO DEVELOP SOCIAL AND COMMUNICATION SKILLS USING ACTIVITIES THAT THEY ENJOY AND COULD CONTROL.

SIXTEEN

The Creative Arts in Services to People with a Physical Disability

Sinead Foskin and Fiona McSweeney

SNAPSHOT

▶ Disability, social policy and the arts.

▶ Importance of arts in disability services.

▶ How the arts change the learning experience.

▶ The Irish Wheelchair Association and how it operates.

▶ Role of the assigned staff member.

▶ Programme outcomes.

Introduction

The entitlements of people with disabilities as full citizens can only be met where the specific requirements of people with disabilities are prioritised by society (Arts Council, 2005). Equality of access is at the heart of full citizenship. This chapter commences by defining the role of social policy and the arts towards people with a disability.

Disability, Social Policy and the Arts

The mid-1970s marked the beginning of a period of profound societal change for people with disabilities in Ireland and the United Kingdom. These social changes helped to generate a shift in emphasis from institutional to community care (Brown and Smith, 1994), in tandem with a shift from a medical model of service delivery and a focus on welfare and protection to a social model of inclusion, equality, citizenship, rights and partnership (O'Brien, 1987). It was proposed that services were to be delivered to disabled people in the same way as the rest of the population at a local level, using community facilities. Disability therefore became a social justice or equality issue rather than a medical one.

The lack of investment resulting from the economic recession of the 1980s and the absence of specific disability legislation meant that barriers, both structural and attitudinal, such as the inaccessibility of buildings, continued to present people with disabilities with obstacles to full participation on equal terms. Since the 1990s the government has recognised that poverty and social exclusion can be responded to more innovatively through the collaboration of statutory agencies and local community and voluntary groups. With the Local Development Social Inclusion Programme (1994–1999), the various social partnership programmes, from the Programme for Economic and Social Progress (1991) to Towards 2016: Ten Year Framework Social Partnership Agreement (2006–2015), have invested significant resources to bring about social and economic change at a local level and to enable local communities and groups to address specific areas of disadvantage. People with disabilities are recognised as a key target group in all of these programmes. One of the key objectives of the National Development Plans (NDP) 2000–2006 and 2007–2013 was to target social exclusion by allocating specific funding to address educational disadvantage and to enhance local and community development.

The 1990s in general are viewed as a turning point in relation to social policy-making and people with disabilities. The government set up the Commission for the Status of People with Disabilities, and the *Strategy for Equality* was published in November 1996. One of the major findings of this report was a 'failure to provide comprehensive education for people with disabilities resulting in them being denied access to employment and training opportunities comparable to those without disabilities' (Commission on the Status of People with Disabilities, 1996:np). This report made recommendations on the rights of people with disabilities, stating that 'The Arts are very important for creativity and self expression and help people to achieve [their] personal objectives' (*ibid.*).

The 1990s also saw considerable developments in standards of training for people with disabilities. This was as a result of the Employment Equality Acts 1998–2004 and the Equal Status Act 2000. The *Towards Equal Citizenship Report* (1999) also stated that people with disabilities who had been excluded from arts education should be offered compensatory education through adult education programmes, such as those funded by the VEC. The 2000 White Paper on Education recognised that there was a need to introduce and support *lifelong learning* for people with disabilities and it recommended that providers of adult and second chance education should ensure that arts education be made available to people with disabilities.

To summarise, the Education Act 1998 did not legislate for specific changes to the educational system for people with disabilities, but as a result of other social policy changes in the 1990s and the Equal Status Act 2000, for the first time in the State there was a legislative framework for the inclusion of people with disabilities in all aspects of life, including education. Accordingly, as social policy developed in Ireland throughout the 1990s, more people with disabilities began to progress though the adult education system. The availability and variety of adult education programmes also increased substantially from the 1990s with the development of the VEC Community Education programme, the Back to Education Initiative and the availability of funding for particular educational programmes targeting disadvantage through the NDP's Community Development Programme and the Leader programme in rural areas. However, the *Living in Ireland Survey* (Eurostat, 2001) reported that half of those who confirmed they had a long-term illness or disability had no mainstream educational achievements, as opposed to a figure of one-fifth of non-disabled adults.

The Arts Plans 1999–2006 recognised that there was a clear need to develop further policies in relation to people with disabilities. These plans advocated that access to community arts needed to be recognised as a valuable means of addressing exclusion of vulnerable groups, such as people with disabilities.

Importance of Arts in Disability Services

Traditionally, arts educators have tried to strengthen the role of the arts in education by arguing that the arts can be used to strengthen and improve the basic core skills of reading, writing and arithmetic as well as the understanding of scientific concepts (Winner and Hetland, 2000). The danger in this reasoning is that if the arts are given this role in our education system because people believe they influence academic improvement, then the arts may lose their position to that of academic improvement. The core argument that the arts are good for people with disabilities, the *arts for art's sake* argument, must stand to maintain the centrality of the arts in Irish education.

Fiske (2000) stated that the arts provide an authentic learning experience, engaging hearts, minds and bodies, and that when taught effectively the arts provide meaningful learning experiences for the person. Furthermore, he suggested that arts education provides unparalleled opportunity, enabling people to reach for and attain higher levels of achievement in their lives.

There are four acknowledged claims for the arts:

- promote a sense of personal competence and achievement;
- self-expression and communication;
- social development;
- promote self-confidence and self-esteem (Lacey and Ouvry, 1998).

These are desirable aims and very good reasons for offering the arts to people with disabilities. The arts are a vital means of communication for many people with disabilities and the arts serve as catalysts for change in learning and growth (Fiske, 2000).

How the Arts Change the Learning Experience

Steve Seidel (2000) stated that learning is deepest when students have the capacity to represent what they have learned, and the multiple disciplines of the arts provide these different modes of representation. There is a strong argument that the arts provide diverse opportunities for learning and expand development beyond the linguistic intelligences and mathematical/logical intelligences usually provided through traditional education programmes. Veenema, Hetland and Chalfen (1997) state that the arts are beneficial for:

- teaching for understanding;
- promoting lateral thinking skills;
- rational thinking;
- experiential learning.

Furthermore, the arts have a wide spectrum of appeal among people with disabilities as opposed to other educational or academic programmes because in the arts self-expression is paramount. The arts engage a wide spectrum of individual interest and provide more opportunities for people to demonstrate understanding. Veenema *et al.* (1997) argue that the arts encourage higher-level thinking. This thinking deposition produces better-educated human beings (Fowler, 1994). Furthermore, evidence from brain sciences and evolutionary psychology suggests that the arts play an important role in brain development and maintenance (Sylwester, 1998). From fine-tuning muscular systems to integrating logic and emotion, the arts have an important biological value. The arts is a system of meaning in that it is a language through which people can express their fears, their hunger, their struggles, their anxieties and their hopes.

Arts explore the emotional, intuitive and rational aspects of life that other subjects do not. The arts are a means of expressing feelings and experiences and can help release frustration: 'Arts can be the glue that holds society together' (Fowler, 1988:63). One example of the arts being used by people with disabilities is the activities of the Irish Wheelchair Association.

The Irish Wheelchair Association and How it Operates

The Irish Wheelchair Association (IWA) is a voluntary organisation that was founded in 1960 by a small group of wheelchair-users who wanted to do something about their exclusion from all aspects of life. Today it has a membership base of 20,000 people with limited mobility. The IWA uses a community development approach in its work that is based on the following principles:

- delivering person-centred services;

- collaborative inter-agency working;

- facilitating and supporting advocacy development;

- facilitating community inclusion.

While the organisation delivers a wide range of services, both in home and in community, the cornerstone of delivery lies in the promotion of choice and the creation of opportunities for individuals to identify and address the areas of their life that are of priority to them.

IWA supports and empowers each person's capacity for growth through a range of options that allow them to define their own requirements within the service. On engaging with the service, the person is supported and empowered through opportunities to explore the issues that affect their quality of life, their immediate wishes, concerns and priorities.

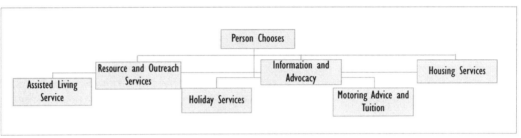

IWA Services

IWA Resource and Outreach Centres are person-centred, community-based services that provide access to various IWA services and partner agencies. The service operates in fifty-seven locations across Ireland. The scope of the programmes and facilities available in each location is flexible, so that each centre can be tailored to the requirements of people living in that community. Resource and outreach services have a strong focus on creating links and partnerships with other local community and disability services.

Through its network of Resource and Outreach Centres, IWA offers a range of programmes, which can be broken down into five areas:

- social and recreational programmes;

- developmental programmes;

- training and education programmes;

- therapeutic programmes;

- supports for individual community activities.

IWA is concerned with the issues that affect people's quality of life. The requirement is that the service expands to meet people's requirements and explores the wider community to meet people's priorities and to enable them to enjoy an enhanced quality of life lived within their local communities.

The organisation, through an assigned staff member, will work in partnership with the wheelchair-user to identify steps to address their needs and locate natural supports in the community (friends, family, community groups, etc.) with whom the person can work in order to achieve their goals. These priorities become identified goals and are recorded in a 'Individual Service Plan,' which is reviewed and redefined every six months in partnership with the person.

Expressed goals are met through a range of group programmes, or individual actions that will require individual support in pursuit of personal outcomes, or a combination of both. The service explores the external community to identify opportunities for integration and collaboration and the quality of service is measured in terms of how well the inputs and processes of the service facilitate the requirements of the person, as defined by themselves.

Case Study

KF is a fifty-year-old man who had a stroke in 2005. He lives with his wife and children and has not been able to return to work due to the physical and cognitive effects of the stroke. KF applied to IWA for services in 2008 and spent most of the intervening period prior to his application at home, not participating in community life. The service manager of IWA met KF in his own home and through a conversation KF identified that his concerns and priorities were to interact with other people and to engage in activities that would improve his fine motor movements. It is agreed that the service that can best address these priorities is the Resource and Outreach Centre. On commencement of service he is linked with an assigned staff member assistant, who will support him to achieve his priorities. The pathway to services is the same for all who engage with the IWA.

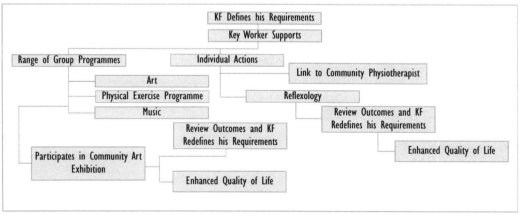

Pathway for engaging in resource and outreach services

Role of the assigned staff member

The role of the assigned staff member in IWA is twofold. Their responsibility is to explore the internal and external environment in partnership with the person and to explore options and agree steps that will address the person's immediate priorities.

In partnership with the person, the assigned staff member and the service co-ordinator explore the range of programmes, activities and services available through the Resource and Outreach Centre. The requirements expressed by people are the basis for the development of a range of new programmes. In this instance KF and others have expressed interest in participating in a group creative arts programme. The role of the staff member in that programme is to:

- facilitate and inform;
- support;
- empower;
- advocate.

Creative arts programmes are of primary importance in that the outcome for the person can be a social, developmental, educational and therapeutic experience. Primarily, the programme supports the participants in acquiring new skills and experiences, and working in a group context provides opportunities to enhance interpersonal skills. A creative arts programme could be an easy entry activity for KF as he hasn't accessed any services in the past. Arts programmes have a particular relevance for participants who experience difficulties with written and verbal communications. All IWA programmes attempt to create links and opportunities in the local community and the programme will afford participants opportunities to explore the creative art facilities and events in their local community. The programme will culminate with an exhibition of work in the local town hall.

IWA would actively link with the arts community in the area and seek supports to enable the programme to be appropriate and relevant to the target group. Key contacts would be the local authority arts officer, artists and art groups or arts festival organisers.

Programme outcomes

Personal outcomes

These are the outcomes that each person aims to achieve by participation in their chosen activity. In the case of KF, his personal outcomes could include the development of new, art-related skills and the experience of participating in a structured programme of further education based on their interests and abilities.

The programme can assist KF and others to identify their own strengths and weaknesses. Low self-esteem due to social exclusion can be channelled to generate change and positive thinking and can be enhanced through the acquisition of new skills. Visual arts can assist

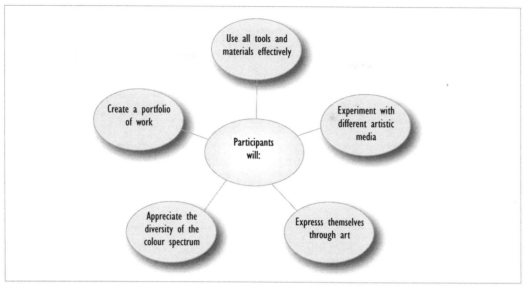

Specific programme objectives

participants to work through their issues and express their feelings, which can be recorded through visual images and can demonstrate the progression of the individual through the programme. KF and other participants may experience a better quality of life and acquire the ability to transfer the skills learned on the programme to different contexts and situations. These skills include communications, social and vocational skills, self-motivation and working with others in a group setting.

Interpersonal outcomes
Participation in a creative arts programme offers KF and other participants opportunities to develop confidence in communicating their needs and priorities by working as a group member, speaking at group meetings, working with others, assuming leadership responsibilities and affirming their rights and the rights of others. The interpersonal skills acquired on the programme could enhance the capacity of KF and others to engage with a wider range of community activities, vocational or educational programmes.

Community inclusion outcomes
Participation in a community-based art exhibition represents an opportunity to demonstrate achievement and to participate as a citizen in a mainstream context. An art exhibition invites people to be part of the real world, rather than passive observers. It can enable people to invent a broader understanding of new dimensions and create their own vision of the community. These are human experiences and perceptions that would be difficult to acquire any other way due to the social isolation that many people experience on a daily basis. Fowler

(1994) stated that the arts can enhance the capacity of the person to participate fully in his/her community. As the visual arts convey the spirit/personality of those who created them, they can help students and others to acquire cultural/intercultural understandings. The community-based art exhibition can promote cross-cultural understanding between non-disabled and disabled people. This is central to creating a sense of community. Cross-cultural understanding promotes the following:

- openness to those who are different;
- identification and understanding of own and others' feelings;
- empathy with different cultural groups;
- humanity and empathy.

In addition, the planning, preparation and mounting of an art exhibition involves a wide diversity of skills and community networking opportunities for those participating. The group needs to agree the theme of the exhibition, source and book a venue, agree and invite the local dignitary who will open the exhibition, develop promotional material and circulate it to invited guests. Members of the group can promote the exhibition through the local media, radio, newspapers, community diaries, etc. Furthermore, KF and other participants may decide to continue their arts education in a mainstream context and will be offered supports to access such services by their assigned staff member.

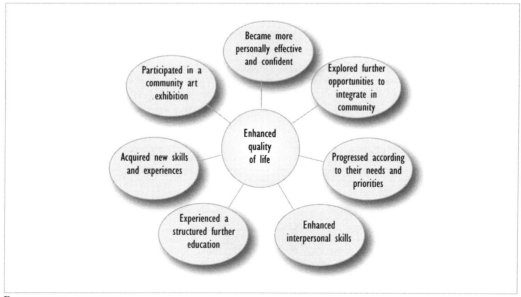

Programme outcomes

After the exhibition the group become partners in a programme evaluation. Evaluations ideally establish:

- programme/project relevance, effectiveness;
- efficiency in the light of specified objectives;
- programme/project impact and sustainability;
- level of usage and satisfaction with services.

The participants may decide to enhance their creative arts skills and choose to engage in further programmes where alternative progression options may be available, such as FETAC accreditation or participation in a mainstream creative arts programme for which IWA may be required to offer minimal supports to participants.

Future decision-making, group and individual project planning and development can be enhanced when guided by evaluation of previous projects, etc.

Chapter Summary

▶ There has been a shift in social policy since the late 1970s in relation to the provision of services to people with disabilities from a medical model of welfare and protection to a social model of inclusion, equality and citizenship.

▶ Lack of investment in services and lack of specific rights-based legislation from the 1970s to the 1990s has meant that many people with disabilities are still at risk of poverty and social exclusion.

▶ The *Strategy for Equality* (1996) represented a comprehensive study of the experiences of people with disabilities in Ireland and identified areas for investment and development.

▶ Government has responded through programmes that support initiatives to address disadvantage at a local level, with community groups as partners in the process through the various social partnership programmes 1994–2015 and through the National Development Plan. People with disabilities are a key target group.

▶ The White Paper on Education (2000) recognised the need for lifelong learning and second chance education.

▶ There has been an increase in the availability of adult education programmes at local community level through VEC programmes, and community development programmes to address educational disadvantage. The arts are considered a powerful means to improve general education and are popular lifelong learning activities.

▶ The arts promote a sense of personal competence and achievement regardless of prior education or learning experiences.

▸ The arts facilitate self-expression, communication and social development and promote self-confidence and self-esteem.

▸ The arts can be a tool to develop rational and lateral thinking skills and to deliver experiential learning to those who have not had access to mainstream education.

▸ The Irish Wheelchair Association (IWA) is one of the largest providers of services to people with physical disabilities in Ireland. It operates to a community development model of service delivery, which consults with service users as partners in service delivery and collaborates with other agencies to support service users' priorities. Other key principles are facilitating and supporting advocacy development and facilitating inclusion of service users in their local communities in accordance with their expressed requirements and priorities.

▸ The IWA's resource and outreach services operate in fifty-seven locations throughout Ireland, offering individual support services, community bridging programmes and developmental training programmes that enhance the quality of life of people who access the services.

▸ People's expressed priorities lead them to a range of group programmes and/or individual actions in pursuit of personal outcomes.

▸ Role of assigned staff member is to facilitate and inform, support and empower the service user's capacity for growth and development and act as an advocate, as required. The staff member also fulfils roles as a programme organiser and community facilitator.

▸ Personal outcomes from participation in a creative arts programme in IWA are the development of skills, experience of participating in a structured education programme that supports people to express their feelings and the transfer of skills to other areas of life.

▸ Interpersonal outcomes can include improved communication skills, working as part of a group and assuming leadership responsibilities, which in turn can enhance participants' ability to engage in a wider range of community activities, vocational or educational programmes as a citizen.

▸ The IWA's creative arts programmes always have a community integration outcome whereby participants are supported to participate as citizens in a mainstream context.

▸ Community-based creative arts programmes can support participants and the wider community to acquire a cross-cultural understanding between those who have a disability and those who do not.

▸ A wide variety of ancillary skills can be developed through the medium of a community arts exhibition, including organisational skills, development and design of promotional material, marketing and media engagement.

▶ Participants are partners in the post-programme evaluation and help to measure the effectiveness of the programme and its efficiency in relation to the objectives. Also analysed are the programme impact and sustainability and the levels of satisfaction among participants. The analysis of the information can inform future programme planning and decision-making.

SEVENTEEN

Finding the Balance: Drama and Mental Health

Gerry Morgan

SNAPSHOT

▶ Mental health and drama: a context; fears around creative work.

▶ Fear of the imagination.

▶ Concerns around feeling or appearing stupid.

▶ Problems around body image.

▶ The fear of being seen.

▶ Addressing these problems.

▶ Creating a safe space for the work.

▶ A sample activity.

▶ Participants' own comments on the work.

Introduction

This chapter looks at the area of mental health and the use of drama to increase confidence, self-esteem and general well-being for people with mental health difficulties. The method of using drama in mental health is described through the use of a practical example. This drama programme is based on the work of Keith Johnstone (1989), Augusto Boal (1992) and Sheila Yeger (1990) and on the author's own twelve years' experience as a professional theatre artist. The module, designed for the Threshold Training Network, is intended to give

participants the opportunity to engage with drama and to create, improvise and perform. It focuses on the concerns of participants with mental health difficulties regarding the imagination, creative activities and the body. Whilst reading the chapter you, as a caring professional, will gain some insight into the potential of drama as an intervention with people with mental health difficulties, and learn some new techniques for your professional toolbox.

Mental Health and Drama: A Context for the Work

My first experience of a potential crossover between theatre/drama and mental health was in 1993 when I was invited to direct a play called *Riders on the Storm* in the Dublin Theatre Festival. *Riders on the Storm* concerned the story of a young man who hears voices and who is diagnosed with schizophrenia later in the play. In the course of preparing the production I was fortunate enough to meet with a group of people with schizophrenia who agreed to talk with me about their experience. I later worked with this group as a drama facilitator.

In the early to mid-1990s there was a major movement towards the democratisation of culture in Ireland, that is a growth in the belief that the arts were for everyone, not just as audience members but as participants and artists. Many marginalised groups were afforded the opportunity to engage with creating art, drama and music through the efforts of such organisations as CAFE, City Arts Centre and Very Special Arts on a national level, and many others on a local and community level. The country was awash with arts facilitators, who provided workshops that gave many people an initial taste of creative work.

As a result, some people from those marginalised groups began to seek training to practise different art forms, including drama, as a profession, in the hope of making a career from it. Among those who sought to train were a number of the group with schizophrenia that I had worked with; however, they were unsuccessful in obtaining course places. In response to their continued exclusion, I approached Schizophrenia Ireland, the Abbey Theatre and Equity (the trade union that represents theatre artists) and suggested they apply collectively to the European Union for funding. The programme, designed by Declan Drohan and me, aimed to provide training for people with mental health difficulties as professional theatre performers and artists. It was designed to take into account the difficulties of this illness and to allow the maximum possible amount of flexibility. The application was successful, and it ran for two years as a pilot programme (1998 and 1999). It was called the Pathways Theatre Training Programme.

In reality, not everyone wanted to be an actor or earn a living through theatre; some participants just wanted to return to work after their illness. However, they experienced personal and societal barriers as a result of having a mental health illness. One organisation that aims to support people experiencing these barriers is the Threshold Training Network, based in Tallaght, Dublin, where I have worked for thirteen years. This chapter describes the approach to drama developed there, and its benefits for the participants.

Societal factors are indeed a problem, but it is the personal experience of mental health difficulties that can leave a person without any belief in their own abilities, without a sense of self-worth, without confidence and, worst of all, without hope. In short, it can leave them without the capacity to imagine change, or to imagine a better future, or to re-imagine their lives.

The Imagination, Reason, the Body and Being Seen

It is important to anticipate whatever anxieties a group might have around drama work and to reassure the group about those anxieties. Any group can experience anxiety about being creative, and a group with mental health difficulties *is no exception*, which is essential for them to hear. Anxieties about drama are *normal*. Unless someone has had a positive experience of drama in the past, he/she is likely to be anxious. Questions rattle around, for example:

> *Who is this person doing drama with us? What are they like?*
> *What will they expect of us?*
> *Will I have to stand in front of others and perform?*
> *Will I have to read out loud?*
> *Will I have to learn lines?*
> *Will I have to do acting?*
> *Will I look stupid or weird?*

Add to this any negative experience people have had of creative work and the anxiety level is almost always very high in the group as a whole. There are other concerns, too, that more specific to the area of mental health.

The fear of the imagination

The participants on a programme such as Threshold or a project such as Pathways have often come to fear their own imagination. For people with a history of schizophrenia, the line between the perception of the real and the non-real has in the past disappeared, and as a result any journeying into imaginary realms and fictional characters needs to be handled gently and with assurances of safety. Verbal assurances of safety are not enough. Gradual steps towards the symbolic world are needed and the experience of making such small steps safely is actually what enables the participant to begin to trust his/her creative capacity again. People with other forms of mental illness can also have difficulties with imagination. One man who described his symptoms as 'hypo manic' told me that he had to be careful with imagination as he got carried away a lot into flights of fancy as part of his condition.

Anxiety is rooted firmly in the imagined outcome or the many imagined catastrophes. Lack of confidence is based on a fear of failing in the future. Paranoia, whether mild or acute, is an act of imagination. Therefore, many of these participants are understandably wary of the imagination, whether or not they are conscious of the reason for that wariness. What they are wary of is the negative or shadow side of the imagination. Unfortunately, their capacity to have a positive experience using imagination or creativity has also been reduced or damaged. A few have been left with very little capacity for symbolic or imaginative work at all. As a result, some of these participants appear to have a restricted imagination in certain areas, and this can be a challenge for a facilitator.

The body

A person who has had the fragmenting experience of mental illness emerges from that experience profoundly altered. Their relationships with friends or family are either fractured or barely surviving. Often roles have altered completely and they may become more cared for than carer. As a result, people's perceptions have changed, impacting on how they perceive themselves, and the longer the experience, the greater the change. Medication can also add to this.

The drugs used in the treatment of mental illness, particularly anti-psychotic drugs, are beneficial in the treatment of the symptoms, but can nonetheless have various side effects of different degrees of strength. Many of these have a physical manifestation, from uncontrollable tremors to weight gain and fluid retention; the body can be affected by the treatment of the mind. The client's own awareness of their body is affected, too. Posture can change and there is often a reluctance to be looked at, or to look at others and maintain eye contact. Physical movement can change, affected by low energy levels. All in all, the physical drama work contains the same measure of anxiety and discomfort as we saw with the imaginative. To overcome this, the facilitator requires the same need for safety and a gradual *movement towards movement*.

Reason vs unreason

Another thing to bear in mind is that a person with mental health difficulty always wants to be regarded as *normal*. Such people are acutely aware of the stigma attached to the illness and are striving to overcome it. Therefore for this group the question 'Will I look stupid or weird?' takes on an added importance.

The experience of being marginalised and stigmatised heightens their desire to experience normalcy. Drama, by its nature, is about a move towards freedom and an exploration of heightened moments in life. These explorations involve the imagination and the body. These are, as we have seen, areas of difficulty and challenge for the participants. Even a seasoned drama practitioner can, from time to time, cringe at the apparent weirdness or silliness of an exercise that is *foisted* upon them by a facilitator. The feeling of '*what if anyone were to see me now, doing this undignified thing?*' is not uncommon in quite ordinary drama settings. However, the presence of an *expert* and our longing to improve can mean that we go ahead with the exercise unquestioningly. This is even more of an issue for someone who has had a long experience of mental illness. The shadow of *non-compliance* still hangs over the sector. The participant may feel they have no choice but to co-operate and may be reluctant to question the wisdom of the *expert*.

The fear of being seen or being the focus of attention

As a result of the stigma still associated with mental health difficulties and the change in a person's circumstances due to those difficulties, confidence and self-esteem are greatly damaged. The actual physical changes mentioned above or the change in how self is perceived (self-image) combine with that damage and can leave the person afraid of being noticed, wanting to hide from view.

The notion of being the centre of attention becomes anathema. In fact, for some, if not many, being the focus of anyone's attention for any period of time becomes unbearable. Therefore the idea of drama, with its notions of the stage, audience and a public performance, can be terrifying. Even the seasoned actor can be prone to nightmares about forgetting their lines. What is the level of anxiety, then, for the ordinary person coming from an experience of mental illness and trying to re-engage with the world, work and society in general? Every group I have worked with has expressd this concern almost as soon as I raise the question of how they feel about drama during the first session. However, in order to re-engage with the world these fears must be faced. Drama approached in the right way can be the perfect medium to allow people to overcome these fears in a gradual and safe way.

It is vital to deal with these concerns early by placing the work in context and being clear about its nature and its purpose. These concerns need to be acknowledged in the first session. The group needs to know that their anxieties are being taken into account and that the work will be gradual and safe. Thereafter, any concerns are addressed within the work itself, week by week, gradually and gently moving into new areas of challenge.

Addressing these Concerns

Fear of the imagination

This is tackled by gradually engaging in small acts of safe imagination. In the very first session the group are given a sentence: 'He walked up to the door.' They are asked to think of it as the first sentence in a book. Then they are asked to visualise the door, the person walking up to the door, the weather, the time of day, to guess at the person's mood, etc. As each person responds with how they see the door, the person approaching, etc., a unique story begins to emerge from each person in the room. If there are twelve participants, we are left with the beginnings of twelve different scenes.

The word *imagine* is replaced in the early sessions by words or phrases like *guess* or *what do you reckon?*, emphasising all the time that there is no right or wrong. In another session they *guess* the life story of a person they have actually seen. It is only on completion that they realise that this is an act of the imagination and that the life story they have *guessed* is a new story, most likely completely unlike that person's actual life. They have used their imagination to create something new and invariably quite moving. They are realising their dormant powers of imagination and they are also discovering that it is safe. This exercise is described in detail at the end of the chapter.

The body

Each session begins with a short warm-up. After a while the group become used to the warm-ups, which they can relate to because the exercises are always explained in relation to their use by professional actors. The next step is to extend the use of the body through working with imaginary objects passed around the group as they stand in a circle. Then we have people crossing the circle briefly with those objects to give them to another. This brief journey across the circle also helps people with the fear of being seen.

After the body work the group are introduced to the concept of emotions. Short scenes written on a flip chart describe characters in various moods or emotional states. Then the idea of a script is introduced, which is described as a set of instructions for an actor so that they can display an emotional state. The possibility of performing an emotion even when it isn't being felt is discussed. The notion that we can *act* assured and confident even when we *feel* otherwise is introduced.

Further on in the process the group is divided into pairs to engage in an exercise called *sculpting*. One participant (the sculptor) sculpts a statue using their partner as the *clay*. The statue displays a physical and emotional state and the other sculptors have to guess at the emotion being represented. The important thing here is that the statue does not have to think about their physical action. That is the sculptor's job. This takes away the fear of embarrassment as it *was not their fault*. The fact that all the emotions are usually immediately clear to the onlookers helps the group realise that the body, too, is expressive. We then move on to group sculpts, followed by group sculpts that are animated, where the participants are allowed to move. Supporting all of this we have mirroring work and Boal-type exercises, such as 'Colombian Hypnosis' (Boal, 1992).

Reason vs unreason

Participants with mental health issues need to know that all exercises are 'normal', have a 'purpose' and are safe. I have found a regular discussion with the participants about their thoughts on the purpose of the exercise is very worthwhile. Also, if the facilitator can link any exercise back to its 'professional' use, that is its actual use by practising actors, writers, directors, or artists, it helps the participants to feel empowered. They are gaining access to at least one inner sanctum, and its mysteries are being unveiled. The process feels more reasoned. They are gaining tools that ultimately can make the creative process, the imagination and artistic expression less mysterious to them, more in their control and therefore safer. This empowers the safe exploration of the positive side of the imagination. As Levine notes, 'the healing of the imagination by the imagination' is a by-product (Levine, 1997:2).

The fear of being the focus of attention

In the early stages all work is conducted as a group with the possibility of contributing to the group creative process (a line of the story, a suggestion here and there) or passing and allowing the next person to continue. Eventually the group is split in two and this allows the opportunity for each group to look in on the other while it works. There is a subtle distinction between someone looking in on your work and *presenting* your work to someone. The former is a far safer notion. The next phase was working in pairs, with the pairs looking in at other pairs. This then moved to half the group 'showing' work to the other half and then to pairs showing work to other pairs and eventually to pairs showing work to the whole group. Always the option to opt out remained so that the element of choice and the safety inherent in that was always preserved.

The guiding principle is the gradual movement from low focus work, where the participant is just another member of the group, making their contribution from the relative safety of numbers, to shared focus work where a number of sub-groups are working simultaneously, to high focus where the whole group witnesses the work of one or two participants. There is a good discussion of this process in Christine Poulter's *Playing the Game* (1987).

Creating a Space where it is Safe to Imagine, be Heard and be Seen

As the imagination is the focus of our work and as it seems that most adults use their imagination far less than young children, it could be argued that at some point something negative caused us to use our imagination less. This may have been a negative comment or experience in school, possibly in tandem with interaction with peers or an authority figure (Johnstone, 1989). It is essential that the drama session be a place free from negative comment or ridicule. Funny things can be created, fun can be had, but it is important that we laugh *with* others and not at them. The groups generally accept and follow this principle. Only on one occasion did someone breach this rule and the other person with whom they were working left the room. But the person who breached the rule realised immediately what had happened and at the break apologised without any intervention from the facilitator. The person who had left returned to the session quite happy and their input was unaffected for the rest of the session.

There is no such thing as a bad idea in the creative space—there are only ideas. There is no right or wrong way to approach the work of the imagination. This is reinforced every time the group works on anything where the ideas of all members of the group are pooled. What is outside the room at the time of the session is left outside, and what was created in the room is left behind in the room. This is achieved through focusing and concentration exercises during the warm-up phase and time being allowed for closure and discussion at the end of the session.

Personal material is not explored. The emphasis is constantly on creation and the boundary between fiction and reality is constantly observed and reinforced. In all improvisations, participants are asked to name the characters they are representing with names other than their own. Even in sculpts or image theatre (Boal, 1992) the participants are made aware that the group member in the image is playing a character that is not themselves. This gives the group both a safety in role/self separation and more creative freedom as the character might behave in ways different from the participant. This is particularly useful in representations of conflict. The separation is constant. Self and character must never be confused. Eventually the group comes to habitually name the people they are representing. Any discussion of the characters is always in the third person: 'What do you think she/he might want?', 'What might he/she say now?', 'How do you think he/she felt then?'

An Example of an Activity

Imagining the other

Part 1: Creating a character/life story

This exercise was based on a suggested writing exercise in *The Sound of One Hand Clapping* (Yeger, 1990:86).

Goals

- Work with observation and recall.
- Accurate description.
- Activating the imagination.
- Creating a character.

Aims

Creating a life story containing all the raw materials of drama: relationships; life difficulties; memories; triumphs and disappointments; wishes and dreams. Looking beyond the self; imagining the other; empathy.

Method

Participants are asked to think of a person they saw recently who caught their attention and made them curious about that person's life. Some examples are given of persons who made the facilitator curious: a busker; a child begging; the lady who dances on O'Connell Street; a woman crying in a restaurant. Time should be allowed for each participant to think of someone. The encounter could be recent or from any time back to the participant's childhood. The only stipulation is that they know nothing of the chosen person's life.

Some participants may find it difficult to think of someone. Work with them quietly, trying to jog their memory of people they might have seen. At this point some participants may want to check that they are *doing it right*. Take the time to reassure them. The only criterion is that they don't know anything about the person's life. This is really important. The exercise really only works if this is the case. Despite this, someone may choose a person that they know of, or talked to, or were told more about. If this happens, accommodate it. That is obviously a story the person wants to tell, but only do so after really trying to communicate the importance of choosing an unknown person.

Ask about them to write down where they saw the person and why he/she caught their attention.Participants are then guided through a series of factual questions about the characteristics of the person: clothes; appearance; hair; demeanour; voice; posture; skin, etc. Wait until all have finished before moving on to each next question.

Ask about as many of these details as you can think of or as there is time for. You can also give examples: stooped, red-faced, wrinkled, weather-beaten, tanned. The exact clothes mightn't be remembered, but what type of clothes were they—old, new, trendy, posh, well-cut, etc.? When it comes to the voice, if they never heard it, ask them to guess what it might be like and give some suggestions: accent, deep, high, stammer, rough, sweet.

Then they are asked a series of 'do you think' questions.

- What age do you think the person is?
- What month might he/she have been born in? Write down the date of birth.
- Where do you think the person was going to spend the night?

At this stage it is common to hear *but I don't know* from some participants. Tell them sure it's only a guess so there is no right or wrong. This is a key moment. If someone moves beyond this point, they're with you for the rest of the exercise.

> *Just have a guess at the sort of place they might have been sleeping.*
> *Do they have any family?*
> *When did the person leave school? Did they ever go to school?*
> *Did they have a happy childhood?*
> *Were they ever in love?*

The series of guessed or imagined answers ends with the following questions:
> *What was the happiest day of this person's life?*
> *What was the saddest day of the person's life?*
> *What is their biggest regret?*
> *If they were granted a wish what would it be?*
> *If they were in a crisis who would they contact/write to?*

Participants are invited to share what they have written. Each is listened to in silence. When all have read, the facilitator discusses the fact that the life they have written about is probably completely different from the actual life of the person they started to write about. Each of them has created a completely new character and imagined a very rich story.

Have a discussion about the surprising amount that the participants have written. Time is spent validating each story. The facilitator picks strong points in each story. Note points of curiosity, pathos, comedy and tragedy. The participants are encouraged to see the potential of the characters in terms of forms they are familiar with.

The sessions ends with congratulations on their achievement, possibly a round of applause for each others' stories, and the facilitator takes questions and indicates that this will be taken a bit further in the next session.

Part 2: Writing a letter

Goals

- Recall of characters from last session.
- Finding the other's voice and words.
- A quick look at form.
- Writing as the other.
- Offering your work to the group.
- Affirmation of achievement.

Method

Participants are asked to return to the characters they had created in the previous session. After looking over them they give a brief reminder to the group of the person they had seen and chosen to work with. The facilitator intervenes with something he/she remembered from each one as a way of validating the creativity (showing the stories made an impression).

The participants are asked if they have chosen the person the character would write to in a crisis. If not, they do so now.

The group is then told the next task, which is to write the letter the character would write to that person to ask for help.

A discussion of letters follows. *What is the form of a letter? How do we address different people? How do children write letters? What are the ways of signing off?* The facilitator notes these on a flip chart for all to see.

Attention is turned to the voices and vocabularies of the characters, and also their education, and their relationship with the person they are writing to. *Was it formal or informal? Would they get straight to the point or beat around the bush?*

The participants are given time to write the letter. The facilitator moves around the room discreetly, in case of questions or a need for reassurance that a participant is 'doing it right'.

Time is left open, and some will finish very quickly as their letters are short. Others will keep writing and writing. The facilitator reassures participants about spelling and writing, stating that the only person who needs to be able to read it is the writer her/himself. When all are finished, participants are invited to read the letters. Each one is prefaced with a reminder of the character and the person they would write to, but *not* the problem.

The facilitator finds a way to affirm each contribution. When all have read, the group examines what possibilities the letters open in terms of the future of the story and the characters (for by now there are at least two in each story and possibly many more). What are the questions the listener is left with? Discussion of the fact that questions are what keep us interested in the drama. Tie this into forms that the group are familiar with: soaps, cinema.

Tell the group about theatre and films where the letter is used as a speech. Tell the group they have just written their first speeches for theatre. Congratulate them. Session ends with applause for each others' creations and mention of the next session.

The Benefits of the Work

'Drama gives you more confidence in yourself, it improved my communication skills, opened up my imagination and gave me more energy and enjoyment.'

'It has boosted my self-esteem and boosted my confidence.'

'The exercises and games are fun and help you be less introverted.'

'It has helped me restore focus, imagination and motivation. It's great for self-esteem and confidence.'

'It was great fun and gave me more confidence.'

'It made my mind wake up and think! It helped with confidence and concentration and helped activate my memory.'

'It was good fun, I especially liked role-play and story-writing.'

'It gives you energy, builds confidence, motivates you and is a great deal of fun.'

'It gave me a sense of fun and enjoyment and it was confidence building.'

(Comments from participants on the Threshold Training Network Course,
August 2009–February 2010.)

These comments came as feedback during a mid-course evaluation at the beginning of November 2009. One of the elements in the evaluation is a section where the participants can enter what they consider negative about the drama sessions. In the case of the above group, ten out of the twelve participants said that they wanted to do more 'acting' or 'role-play'. This from a group where the same number said they would never have the confidence to act or do anything in front of a group when we met for the first time.

It is clear a shift had taken place. While the focus of the facilitator was on a safe and enjoyable experience of drama and the imagination, the comments above show that that experience has had an impact on confidence, self-esteem, energy and motivation. These are the by-products of the safe, fun engagement with creativity and imagination through the medium of drama as identified by the participants themselves.

Chapter Summary

▶ There are particular issues around creative work with people who have experienced mental health difficulties.

▶ There is a fear of the imagination as those with metal health difficulties have often struggled with the negative or shadow side of the imagination.

▸ There is also often an inability to re-imagine their lives or possibilities for change.

▸ Like any group, they will have concerns about feeling or appearing stupid. However, their experience of marginalisation due to the stigma of their difficulties heightens those concerns.

▸ The illness and the necessary treatment can result in physical change or a change in body image that leaves the person reluctant to engage in the physical action that drama involves.

▸ Mental heath issues reduce confidence and self-esteem, leading to the person wishing to avoid being noticed or being in any way the focus of attention. This leads to difficulties in many situations, from interviews in the workplace to speaking out for oneself. It also means that aspects of drama or creative work could be quite terrifying.

▸ The acknowledgment of these worries and concerns and an approach that deals with them gently is vital if any use of drama is to be successful.

▸ Where a balance can be found between the participants' concerns and the challenges of drama, in a space where the participants feel safe, the participants themselves have identified benefits in terms of increased confidence, self-esteem, energy, motivation and communication.

SECTION 3

Example Activities

Title of Workshop: Kites and Planes

Author: Keiran Blunt

Suitable Group Details: this activity is aimed at children between the ages of five and twelve.

Duration: 30–60 minutes, depending on the decorations used.

Materials needed:

1. A4/A3 sheets of paper.
2. Colouring pencils/pens/crayons.
3. Ribbon and string.
4. Two wooden dowels/BBQ skewers.
5. Tape/glue.
6. Bin bag/plastic shopping bag.

Instructions:

The Kite

In order to make the kite, you take your two wooden dowels or skewers, whichever you prefer, and make a cross shape with them. Ensure the shorter piece goes across the middle, and then tie around the middle to attach each dowel/squire to one another. Then at each end of the dowel/squire make a notch for the next step.

Take your string and tightly pull around the kite, attaching the string to the notches at each end of the dowels/skewers. So the cross-shaped kite now has a diamond shape to it with the introduction of the string. The purpose of this string is to give the kite its shape and strength.

Place your kite on a piece of paper: the size of the paper will depend on the size of the kite. You can also use plastic bags or black bin bags and in some cases clingfilm. Draw around the kite's shape on the paper, and remove the kite so you have a diamond shape on the paper. Cut out this shape and fold it around the kite's string, right around the whole diamond, and glue or even tape the paper around the string to finish off the kite.

Flip the kite over so the reverse side is facing you, then take a piece of string long enough to reach each end of the kite. Make a loop in the middle of the string and tie each end of the string tightly and securely to each end of the kite. The purpose of this loop we will find out in the next step.

Take a piece of string of any length (if you want the kite to go high, take a long piece; if not, take a shorter piece), then loop one end of the string through the loop at the middle of the kite and tie securely. The other end is for you to hold on to. Now it's time for the fun part: you get to decorate your kite in any way you feel like, and in any way you feel looks great. So there you have it, go and test your new kite.

The Plane

Take a piece of paper of any size you like. Fold the paper horizontally across the middle. Take the two corners of the top of the page and bring into the middle so the paper looks like a triangle. Then fold the sides into the middle again so that the paper now looks like a tall, narrow triangle.

Now fold the paper in half so both sides of paper meet. You should now have what looks like a triangle with one straight side, which is going to be the bottom of your plane. Then fold down one side of the paper to create the wing and do the same with the other side of the paper. When you have done this your paper should look like a plane.

All that's left now is decoration, for example flames along the sides. But it's up to you how you decorate it. Now you have a plane that you can race with or play with.

Title of Workshop: Mini Carnival Time

Author: Kerri Byrne

Suitable Group Details:

Making the carnival: suitable for youth groups aged 14–18 years.

Playing in the carnival: suitable for youth groups aged 4–10 years.

Duration: To make the carnival: 30 minutes each session.

To paint balls and to play in the carnival: 30 minutes.

Materials needed:

- Newspaper/gift-wrapping paper or any kind of left-over paper.
- Balloons.
- Flour and water.

- Clay balls.
- Fifteen recyclable tin cans.
- Tables to lay out the games in the mini carnival.

Instructions for a youth group aged 14–18 years:

1. Divide the group into fours.
2. Give out old paper that has been recycled.
3. Get each group to blow up one balloon.
4. Begin by stirring three parts water into one part flour until you get a smooth and creamy mixture.
5. After stirring it all together properly, the papier mâché paste is ready for use.
6. Dip each piece of paper in the liquid mixture and then apply each paste-covered piece of paper to the balloon. Leave an opening between the sheets of paper. You should end up with a circular head shape with an open mouth big enough to throw balls into.
7. Then pop the balloon through the hole in mouth of the papier mâché face.
8. Take tin cans of the same shape and size and set them up in the shape of a pyramid.

Instructions for a youth group aged 4–10 years:

1. Give each young person a ball of clay to paint in whatever colour or style they would like.
2. There will be a tin can display set up and the children will have to throw one ball to see how many tins they can knock down.
3. When playing with the papier mâché head, the aim is to throw the ball into the mouth of the head.

Title of Workshop: Beautiful Bodies

Author: Rebecca Byrne
Suitable Group Details: teenagers.
Duration: 1 hour.

Materials needed:
All that is required for this activity is clay.

Instructions:
Each person is given a lump of clay and asked to replicate to the best of their ability a part of their body which they really like, for example a foot, nose, eye or hand.

When they have formed their body part, they will then say what the body part they have created is and why they like this particular body part. For example: 'This is my nose and the reason I have made this is because even though it is a bit bumpy I would not be able to smell my lovely candles without it' or 'I have recreated my legs as I think they are lovely and long and they look great in my favourite dress.'

Finally, after everyone has shown their piece and said a little bit about it, they must all merge their body parts together to create a model that will represent the love of our beautiful bodies.

Title of Workshop: Recycle Runway

Author: Jennifer Carberry

Suitable Group Details: this activity is suitable for ages 10–18 years and would be mainly for youth groups and other groups dealing with young people.

Duration: two to three hours, depending on the number of people in the group.

Materials needed:

- Recyclable materials, including cardboard, plastic bags, packaging, tinfoil, string, tin cans, plastic, old cloths, paper, etc.
- Paints, colours, markers.
- Sticky tape, glue, stapler and scissors.
- Radio.

Instructions:

1. Ask the group to collect any recyclable materials and bring them in on the chosen day of the activity.
2. Split the group into smaller teams of two or three.
3. The team will chose one person to be the model for the activity.
4. The team will then work together using the recyclable materials to create a costume or outfit and showcase it for the group.
5. When each team has created their costume, they will take turns to showcase it to the rest of the group with some background music to make it more fun.
6. The most creative outfit will be chosen at the end of the activity.

Title of Workshop: Getting to Know You

Author: Gary Coleman

Suitable Group Details: 8–12 years of age. This game can be played in groups of ten and sixteen people. You can change the number of questions according to the number of people playing in the game.

Duration: 40–60 minutes.

Materials needed:

- Paper.
- Pen.
- Bottle.
- Chairs.
- Tables.

The Warm-up: What do you Like?

For this game we split the group members into Group 1 and Group 2. In the groups everyone must introduce themselves and tell everyone something about their life. Then we start at the first person, who goes through everyone and tries to remember all their names, then we move on to the second and third person and repeat the sequence, so that by the end everyone knows their group's names as well as they can. You can make this even easier for the kids to remember by putting something fun in front of your name when saying it, for example Dangerous David or Great Gary.

After this a blank A4 sheet is given to everybody. Everyone's page is torn into five strips, and each person writes down five questions they would like to be asked. In this part you can increase or decrease the amount of questions depending on the size of the group. Then the group will compare questions and if there are two questions the same, one is thrown away and the other is kept. When this is done, all the questions are folded and placed into an empty box.

Name Game:

The participants are still kept in two separate groups, and they are all sitting at two different tables, both in the shape of a circle. The names of those in Group 1 and in Group 2 are written down on a single page, with a space left underneath each name for their final score. We then place an empty bottle on the table and the first person on the table spins the bottle. When the bottle stops, the person at whom it is pointing takes a question out of the box, stands up and reads the question out loud, and then answers the question in front of the group. An example: John picks out the question, what football team do you like? John then answers: Leeds United. John sits down and keeps his question beside him, and the others in the group must take a mental note of his answer. After this John spins the bottle again. This is repeated until there are no more questions in the box.

Final Part:

For this part of the game, the first person in the group reads out the question he/she was asked in the game when the bottle had pointed in his/her direction. If the group work as a team and can answer the question correctly, they score a point for their group, which is written down on the page with the names. This is repeated until all the questions are asked. The group who has the most points at the end wins the game and they all get first prize, as they showed the best group work and then worked as a team to remember the answers.

Title of Workshop: Bowling with Bottles

Author: Mary-Jane Crowe
Suitable Group Details: this game is suitable for many different groups, but would work best for individuals with intellectual disabilities.
Duration: one hour.

Materials needed:

- Ten plastic Coca-Cola bottles (or similar).
- Sand for the bottles to make them sturdy.
- One tennis ball.
- Space.
- Masking tape.
- Pen and paper.

Instructions:

To complete this activity, you must first get ten plastic Coca-Cola bottles or other similar bottles, such as Fanta bottles, etc.

1. Put a small bit of sand in the bottom of the bottles to keep them standing and to prevent them from falling over easily.
2. Next the bottles must be laid out on the ground in the shape of a triangle, evenly spaced. One bottle is to be put in front, two bottles beside each other behind that, three bottles behind the two bottles and the final four bottles placed behind the three bottles.
3. About 5 m to the front of the triangle make a straight line on the ground using the masking tape so the players do not cross the line.

4. The players then write their names in a list on the paper so they know whose go it is and what score they're on.

5. The players should then begin to play by rolling the tennis ball along the ground and trying to knock over as many bottles as possible.

6. The winner is the first person to reach 100 points. You win one point for each bottle you knock over. At each go, you have two chances to knock down all ten bottles.

Title of Workshop: Islands

Author: David Cullivan

Suitable Group Details: mostly suitable for groups of young people aged 12–25 years.

Duration: 15–20 minutes.

Materials needed:

- Cushions.
- Paper.
- Pens.

Instructions:

- Clear a space, roughly the size of a penalty box, in the middle of the room.
- Put three or four cushions in the middle of the room and a sheet of paper beside each cushion giving each cushion a name, e.g. Spring, Summer, Winter and Autumn. These places are designated 'safe islands' that people can run for when they hear the instructions. Participants must not put a foot on the floor as these waters are shark infested.
- The facilitator calls out options for each of the islands under various headings and people move as quickly as possible to the island that represents their choice. For example, foods, TV programmes, etc. For example, 'All those who like *Coronation Street* go to Spring Island.'

Title of Workshop: Cats and Dogs

Author: Lynn Daly

Suitable group details: children aged 4–8 years.

Duration: as this game can be played by any even number of players, the time duration may vary. It also depends on the size of the play area and the amount of materials used.

Materials needed:

- Two mats used as a dog's house and a cat's house.
- One basket or box.
- A number of plastic fish and bones.

Instructions:

Although this game can be played with any even number of children, I will explain it using the example of a group of eight six-year-olds.

1. First, the space must be prepared. Place a mat on the opposite sides of the room or play area. Clear the space around the room. In the centre of the room and at an equal distance from each mat, place a basket or box containing as many plastic fish and bones as you want. There must be an even number of each. The amount of fish and bones will determine the length of the game.
2. The children are split into two teams of four. There will be four cats and four dogs. Each team must wait on their mat.
3. When the game begins, one child from each team must crawl on all fours as quick as possible to the basket and find whichever object suits their animal (fish for cats, bones for dogs). They must then crawl back to their mats, let the next player go and wait for their next turn. The second person goes and so on until one team has no objects left.
4. The first team to finish must bark or meow to show they have won.

Extra suggestions: this game can be changed to accommodate larger groups; other animals could be used for extra teams; children could make the materials, i.e. the bones and fish, in an art class beforehand, by painting and cutting out fish and bones and, if possible, laminating them so they can be wiped clean and will last longer.

The game can also be made more challenging for older children if each child gives themselves funny pet names and when each child returns to the mat, the other team members must shout out the pet name for that player before the next player can go. Another way of making the game more challenging would be if the players had to balance their collected item on their head while returning to the mat.

Title of Workshop: Find Your Path

Author: Leanne Fagan
Suitable Group Details: this activity is suitable for any group of adolescents between the ages of fifteen and seventeen years, in small groups of five to ten people.
Duration: one to two hours.

Materials needed:

- Large sheets of paper.
- Pens and pencils.
- Colouring pencils/paint.
- Appropriate workspace.
- Illustrations, e.g. photographs.

Instructions:

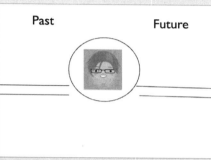

1. Draw a circle in the middle of the page.
2. Draw two paths coming out from the circle, one to represent the past and one for the future.
3. In the circle draw a picture of yourself.
4. In the past path use words, stories or pictures to illustrate your life up to the point you're at now.
5. Then take a few minutes to reflect on your past: what made you happy, sad, etc., and what you want for your future.
6. In the path for the future use words, stories or pictures to illustrate what you want to be in your future.
7. When this is completed share with the group.

Title of Workshop: Blind Snowballs

Author: Lisa Fennelly
Suitable group details: this workshop is suitable for people aged between eight and twenty-five years and with groups of five to fifteen people.
Duration: 15–40 minutes.

Materials needed:

- 5–15 pages.
- 5–15 pens.
- A scarf.

Instructions:

1. Get everyone to write three things about themselves on a piece of paper.
2. Crush the pages up into separate little balls (like snowballs).

3. Throw all the balls in the air.
4. Then each person takes turns in being blindfolded with a scarf while the rest of the group directs them towards one of the snowballs.
5. When they pick it up they can remove the scarf and read what the snowball says.
6. That person then has to guess which person in the group wrote the snowball.

Title of Workshop: Trust in Me

Author: Eabha Geraghty
Suitable Group Details: for participants from the age of seven up.
Duration: 20–30 minutes.

Materials needed:
- Blindfold.
- Objects to find (keys, scarf, etc.).

Instructions:
1. Divide the group into pairs.
2. The pairs must then name themselves as A and B.
3. Person A will be blindfolded.
4. Person B will guide them.
5. An object will be placed on the floor.
6. Person A must find this object while person B guides them.
7. However, person B is unable to use words. They must just use sounds.
8. Person B must stand in front of A .
9. A must follow the sound of B until the object is found.
10. The teams are timed.
11. Repeat this until all teams have gone.
12. The fastest team at the end are the winners.

Title of Workshop: Human Connect 4

Author: Jennifer Higgins
Suitable Group Details: suitable for people of all ages, but in this case a class of children aged 5–8 years.
Duration: 30 minutes.

Materials needed:

- A set of two different-coloured bibs.
- A huge sheet of paper and markers to draw a grid, or it can be done on the ground using chalk.
- Coloured paper.

Instructions:

1. Split up into two groups using the bibs to distinguish the groups.
2. Divide the children in the team into those who will answer the question and those who will be the human Connect 4 pieces.
3. Use coloured paper to associate with animals, vegetables, and other categories or just make up a set of questions if no coloured paper is available.
4. Place or draw the grid on the floor.
5. Every time a team answers a question correctly they can place a person on the grid from their team until they connect four people.
6. A team can connect a line sideways, upwards, downwards or diagonally.

Title of Workshop: Paper Bag Ballet

Author: Rachel Horan

Suitable Group Details: this activity is suitable for anybody over the age of six years. I think it would be most suitable for young people in a youth club between the ages of six and seventeen.

Duration: 10–15 minutes.

Materials Needed:

- Paper bag.
- Scissors.

Instructions:

1. Gather the group together.
2. Stand in a circle around the bag.
3. Get the group to do some light stretching (explain which muscles are being stretched, e.g. calf).
4. Place the bag open side up in the middle.
5. Each person gets a chance to pick up the bag with their mouth.
6. Hands cannot be used to help pick up the bag, but can be used for balance.

7. One foot must be on the floor at all times. The other can be either in the air or on top of the other foot. It just can't be touching the floor.
8. Hands cannot touch floor either.
9. Give each player a chance to try.
10. If any person cannot pick up the bag, they are out.
11. Then use the scissors to cut off the area they touched with their mouth (for sanitary reasons!).
12. The bag gets lower and lower as the game goes on and it gets harder and harder!
13. The person who picks it up when it is closest to the ground wins.

Title of Workshop: Music, Memory and Reflection

Author: Terry Jones
Suitable Group Details: specifically for use with the aged, but can be adapted for any group.
Duration: 45–60 minutes, depending on group.

Materials needed:
- Deck of playing cards with no face cards.
- List of *Hit Singles* book or *Guinness Book of Hit Singles*.
- Laptop, if available (for YouTube content).

Instructions:
One suit of cards are shuffled and a person picks out a card from 1 to 10: this is the number of things they have to remember about a particular song. This can be anything from where they were when they first heard the song, to who the singer was, what club they first heard it in, or what the song means to them and so on.

You can use the deck of cards for more music questions, for example the year in a particular decade of your choice, or what number a song rose to in the charts. A laptop can provide visual clues and reminders via YouTube.

(For example, my favourite singer from the 1960s is Françoise Hardy, who recorded continuously from 1962 to 2007, a lot of which is available on YouTube. In the years to come Ireland's aged are going to be from all nationalities, so the YouTube content is perhaps where the game will logically be played and adapted.)

Title of Workshop: Animal Squeeze

Author: Deirdre Jordan
Suitable Group Details: children aged 7–12 years.
Duration: as long as they want.

Materials needed:

- A spinner similar to the one used in Twister, but with animals on it—a cat, a lion, a fish, a frog, a snail.
- Different-coloured rubber mats.
- CD player and CD.

Instructions:

1. The rubber mats are all lying on the floor in a circle with one child standing on each.
2. Turn on the music.
3. Spin the spinner and see which animal it lands on.
4. Tell the kids which animal it is and let them run around the room acting like this animal.
5. Turn the music off and shout 'squeeze'.
6. At this point, all the kids will have to go running back to their own personal rubber mat and squeeze close to each other.
7. As the game progresses, the mats can be put closer to each other.
8. They may take turns spinning the spinner.
9. This can be repeated as many times as wished.

Title of Workshop: Exploring Status

Author: Kate McCarthy
Suitable Group Details: for ages 12+ and for groups of between ten and twenty people. Some elements of this workshop can be adapted for younger age groups.
Duration: 90 minutes.

Materials needed:

- Ten juggling balls.
- A deck of ordinary playing cards, minus the jokers.

The warm-up:

Here is a sample list of warm-up games.

Observing the Space

Begin by asking the participants to walk around the space, asking them to notice the physical features of the room, where the natural light sources are, how many radiators are present, etc. Encourage the group to 'change direction' to keep participants moving randomly in between one another. Once the group have been walking for a minute or so, ask them to 'freeze'. Ask the group to close their eyes and point to an object, e.g. a radiator. Once everyone has taken a guess, participants open their eyes to check if their guess was correct. The same process is repeated until the group become more at ease with each other and the space.

Opposite Call

I learned this game at a workshop facilitated by Augusto Julian Boal in Dublin in April 2008. Participants perform the opposite of the actions that the facilitator calls out. In this version the opposite of 'stop' is go, and 'go' is stop. When the facilitator says, 'Put your hands in the air', participants touch their knees, and when they hear 'touch your knees', participants put their hands in the air. As the facilitator says, 'name', participants jump, and on hearing 'jump', they say their names.

Name Game

Invite the group to stand in a large circle, ensuring that everyone can see each other. The facilitator (A) calls out participant B's name, and throws a juggling ball across the circle to B. B chooses another participant (C), calls out C's name and throws the same ball across the circle. C chooses another participant, and so the pattern continues. The final participant (Z) throws the ball back to the facilitator (A), and the sequence is complete. Play the sequence a few times until the group becomes at ease with the pattern; the facilitator then introduces a second, third, and fourth ball, as many as the group can handle, all to be thrown from participant to participant in the same sequence.

Mime it Down the Alley

If there is a large number in your workshop, invite the group to split into two parallel lines. If there is an odd number, join in. In this game every participant, except the participant at the top of the line, closes his or her eyes. Participant A performs a sequence of three simple actions. When ready, participant A taps participant B on the shoulder, and B opens their eyes to face A. A shows their sequence once and B copies the sequence as precisely as possible. Then, B taps participant C on the shoulder, and the process continues down the line until it reaches the last participant. Once the last participant (Z) has received the sequence of actions, s/he and participant A meet in the centre, facing their line. Z shows the sequence of actions s/he has received, and participant A shows the sequence that began the whole activity. The sequence of actions, inevitably, will have changed.

May I? (Emotions)

The members of the group stand in a circle. This game can also be grouped in the name game category; however, it moves beyond saying the name by allowing the participants to play with vocal qualities as they cross the circle. The facilitator stands in the middle of the circle, makes eye contact with someone in the circle and asks, 'James, may I?'. Once the facilitator has asked, she moves towards James's place. As she moves James must ask another participant, 'Nick, may I?', and James moves towards Nick's place, and so on. Once the group have established a rhythm and an ease with the rules of the game the facilitator suggests an emotion, which participants must use when asking, 'may I?' This game can also be used in the rehearsal process to allow participants to explore the emotional range of their characters or the play.

Main activities: exploring status

Status Game, Variation One

The facilitator shuffles a deck of cards and allows each participant to choose a card. Each card number indicates how high or low the participant's status in the space will be; therefore, if we play stereotypically, the ace being the lowest card might represent a beggar on the street. The highest card is the king, so this character might be a president. Each participant chooses a card and looks at it without telling what number they have. They must quickly decide what type of status is indicated by their card number, e.g. an eight might indicate a businessperson. At first, invite the group to play stereotypically. Explain that as you count backwards from ten to one their status, based on their card number, must begin to emerge as their character moves around the space.

The participants' objective is to try to guess the status, i.e. card number, of the other participants depending on how they move in the room, and how they treat other characters.

After a few minutes invite the participants to group together with characters they think are of similar status. Once this is completed, check the cards. Allow the group to discuss their guesses.

Status Game, Variation Two

Reshuffle the deck of cards. In this variation the participants choose a card, but must not look at it, but hold it to their forehead face out. The participant's objective in this version is to guess their card number by interpreting the reactions towards them. Invite the characters to begin to vocally engage with one another, e.g. ask the group, 'how might this character say hello?'. Once participants have grouped together, invite them to guess their status without looking at their card. Once everyone has listened and guessed, allow them to look at their cards.

This variation provides a stimulus for further discussion of stereotyping, and gives the group the opportunity to reflect on how we treat people in society, and how it feels to be treated in a positive or negative way. As discussed in Chapter 6, it can be useful to discuss the notion of status in relation to the world of drama and theatre in continuing to further the participants' knowledge of the art form.

Status Game Three: The Party

Again, invite each participant to choose a card, but allow them to decide how to interpret their card, i.e. their chosen status. In this way they are interpreting the inferred meaning of the card number from the previous games and discussions, and applying this knowledge to the fictitious world of the party. The facilitator plays the party host to keep the scene in motion.

Participants enter the party as individuals. They are all friends of 'John' or 'Mary', the facilitator's elusive husband or wife, who is late home from work. The host indicates the (imaginary) refreshments and drinks table to each guest, so there is always something for participants to do, and always someone, 'John' or 'Mary', about whom they can inquire. As the game continues invite participants to try to find out the various statuses at play in the room, but this time the conversation contains information too. At some point 'John' or 'Mary' calls and has had to go to accident and emergency; the party must come to an end. Encourage a discussion in which participants discuss their guesses, how they came to this or that conclusion, what other characters said or did not say and how we can use this exercise to reflect on our own behaviour.

Winding-down and Reflection

Depending on the type of drama session facilitated, the winding-down might need to be based on more physical exercises, such as stretches, breathing, etc. or further discussion might be needed on a challenging topic before the workshop ends. It is important to allow sufficient time for this final section in the workshop plan. With regards to this session I asked the group to stand in the circle format, standing shoulder to shoulder. I asked the participants to put their right hand into the circle but look over their left shoulder. As we move towards each other we 'find a hand'. The group is close together, and so we (slowly) bring the left hand into the circle, find another hand and shake hands with each other while making eye-contact with everyone. Finally, I ask each participant to disclose something they liked, and something they did not like, about the workshop.

Title of Activity: Memory Lockets

Author: Karl McLoughlin
Suitable Group Details: this activity is aimed at elderly service users. This activity is for groups of between ten and fifteen people. This workshop could also be adapted for children service-user groups.
Duration: 1 hour.

Materials needed:

- 2 bottle caps per person.

- A piece of ribbon 1 inch wide and 3 inches long.
- Photo of a family member, a place where the service user lived, a place they liked or went on holidays to, etc. —something that will trigger memories.
- A small circle of paper to fit inside the bottle cap with a message on it or a second photo.
- Spray paint.
- Paint.
- Pencil.
- Lace.
- Glue.
- Scissors.

Instructions:

1. Remove the rubbery part from the inside of the bottle caps. Then spray paint the bottle caps. Gold or silver are good choices as they give a nicer look to the final product but it can be whatever colour the service user chooses. Let dry for a minute or two.
2. Paint a picture on the outside of one bottle cap or stick a picture on it.
3. Put lace in the centre of the ribbon. Then fold the ribbon over the lace. Glue both ends of the ribbon inside the two bottle caps.
4. Cut photos to fit inside the bottle caps. The easiest way to get photos to fit is to put the bottle cap down on the photo and draw around it and then cut the part of the photo out.
5. Glue the picture on the inside of one bottle cap. This will be the bottom part of the locket. In the other bottle cap, which will be the top part of the locket, glue on a message or another picture.
6. Tie the ends of the lace together. Now it's finished and service users have a memory locket they made themselves.
7. Go around the room and give everyone in the room a chance to discuss their picture in the locket and the memories associated with it.

Suitability:

This activity is very suitable for elderly people and is very easy to do. The lockets are very simple to make. All items are cheap and easy to find items. Bottle caps can be got for free by asking a local restaurant or pub for them or instead of throwing them out they can be reused for the activity. This activity is also very environmentally friendly as it reuses bottle caps. The first step, which involves spray painting the bottle caps, could possibly be done by the care-giver or supervisor of the activity beforehand as spray paint gives off strong fumes. The step with the spray paint should be done outside because of the fumes.

Title of Workshop: The Guess Who? Game

Author: Elaine McNamara
Suitable Group Details: this workshop is suitable for people in their early teens to the elderly, in a group of seven to ten people.
Duration: 20–30 minutes.

Materials needed:

- Picture of each individual from when they were young.
- Name tags (if needed).
- Paper and pens or pencils.

Instructions:

(Give details in easy stages, and you can include illustrations.)

1.   Ensure everyone in the group has a picture of themselves from when they were young.
2.   Write your name on the back of your picture.
3.   Place all of the pictures facing upwards on a table or pin them up on the wall.
4.   Place a Post-it beside each picture, numbering them 1 to 10.
5.   Everybody has a piece of paper in front of them, and number down the side of the page 1 to 10 (name tags can be worn if needed).
6.   Then everyone writes down who they think is the child in the first picture, etc.
7.   The person who gets the most right wins a prize.

Title: Words, Feelings and Stuff

Author: Daire Ni Bhraoi
Suitable Group Details: this workshop is suitable for teenagers or adults. People who have an interest in music enjoy this but people who have shown no interest in music may surprise you. It can be done in a group as big as fifteen, but it works better with smaller groups. This can be used with anyone who can write for themselves. I would recommend it for groups who are comfortable with each other—this is when it is most effective.
Duration: this activity is best done on a weekly basis for two or three months. Each session should be 45–60 minutes. (This might seem too long at the start, but as time goes by it might seem not long enough.)

Materials needed:

- Paper.
- Pens.

- Space for people to work (this is important for when people break up in groups/on their own to write. I've found people like their own space when they are writing).
- Laptop with internet connection.
- Musical instruments (optional).
- A facilitator who isn't afraid to push people out of their comfort zones.

Instructions:

1. Gather everyone together in a comfortable setting and play a popular song everyone knows.
2. Now play the music only version of this song and perform your own lyrics. (For example, P!nk's 'Who Knew' and Avril Lavigne's 'Tomorrow'.)
3. Now get the group to pick a song they would like to write their own lyrics for.
4. Once you've picked your song, decide what your song is to be about. In the early days it's best to pick a funny theme rather than a serious/emotional theme as people find it easier.
5. Use a mind map to show everyone's ideas.
6. Now you can go in one of two directions: you can write the song as one big group or break people into smaller groups. At the start it works better as a big group.
7. Once everyone is happy with the new lyrics, you can talk about performing it.
8. Once you have the first song done, you can move on to giving the group a theme and seeing what they can come up with.
9. This goes on every week and as time goes by and people feel more comfortable in their abilities and around each other, they may open up and explore other issues.
10. At the end, you could have a show with everyone performing. Some people love this idea while others are more hesitant. I think the performance is good as it gives people a chance to show what they've done, but keep it voluntary.

Title of Workshop: Balls and Buckets

Author: Paula Noyes
Suitable Group Details: this game is suitable for people with intellectual disabilities in a group of three or more.
Duration: 20–40 minutes.

Materials needed:

- Sponge balls.
- 16 small buckets.

- Pens.
- Paper.

Instructions:

1. Cut paper into squares and on each piece of paper write a question. For example:
    How many people in your family?
    What's your favourite colour?
    Where do you live?
2. Number the buckets from 1 to 8, place four questions in each of the first eight buckets.
3. Place the other eight buckets on the floor in a circular shape.
4. Each person takes turns to throw a sponge ball into a bucket.
5. Whatever numbered bucket the sponge ball lands in, the service user will then answer a question in the corresponding numbered bucket.
6. The balls being used in the game are made of sponge which makes them light and easy to throw; they are also soft, which makes them easier to grip and if someone is accidentally (or purposely) hit with one it will not cause any harm. They are available in many different sizes and colours so each person can pick whatever size ball they feel comfortable using. Depending on the service user's disability they can stand closer or further away from the buckets, and the buckets used can be larger or smaller in size, reducing the level of difficulty if required. There is not much material needed to play the game, which makes it very cost effective, and the materials required can be bought cheaply and can be used time and time again. It can be played indoors or outside and does not require a lot of space.

Title of Workshop: Goggle Gaze

Author: Naomi O'Donnell
Suitable Group Details: this workshop is suitable for all young people from the ages of six to twenty-one years, arranged into groups of three.
Duration: 20–30 minutes.

Materials needed:

- Plastic swimming goggles.
- Box of random objects including things like feathers.
- Glitter.
- Coloured and plain paper.
- Paper/plastic animal ears/wings.
- Stuffed stockings.

- Pritt stick.
- Sticky tape.
- Elastic bands.
- Paper clips.
- Balloons.
- Cotton wool.
- String.
- Straws.
- Fake facial features.
- Shapes.
- Plastic telephone.
- Shell.
- Scissors.
- Any other art and craft pieces which may be of interest.

Instructions:

1. Divide the larger group into smaller groups of three people per group.
2. They are given a pair of goggles each and a small box filled with the objects mentioned above. They should share the contents among themselves.
3. Each person must think about who or what they would like their creation to be.
4. When they have thought about what they might want to be they then begin to create this creature or formation using the box of materials.
5. They may create anything that makes them happy but their creation must be physically attached to the goggles in some way. For example, if one person decided to be an elephant he/she could use the stuffed sock, an elastic band to attach this to their goggles and maybe some type of animal ears.

6. When their creation is ready to wear they can act whatever way they want for the next 3–4 minutes, obviously without breaking any house rules. If they have decided that their elephant wants to act like a donkey they must do as they please.
7. They can come into contact with people from all of the other groups or they can even create their masks to act together as a group.

Title of Workshop: Sharing a Rainbow

Author: Mark O'Sullivan

Suitable Group Details: children with intellectual disabilities from the ages of four to thirteen.

Duration: 40 minutes.

Materials Needed:

- Paint.
- Paint brushes.
- Water in cups (for cleaning the paint brushes).
- Coloured crêpe paper.
- A2 sheets of paper (one for each child).
- Crayons.
- Glue.
- Colouring makers.
- Pastels.
- Coloured chalk.
- Felt.
- Sandpaper.
- Tinfoil.

Instructions:

1. Draw out sections of the rainbow on several sheets of paper.
2. Get children to select their piece.
3. Show the children the material they can use to colour their section of the rainbow and get them to choose the material they would like to use.
4. A helper is available to give the children guidance, regarding glueing, painting and use of the materials.
5. Each section of the rainbow is given time to dry.
6. During this time the group is split up into teams to tidy up. Use music to make tidy-up time fun.
7. The rainbow is then pieced together by the children and placed on a wall in the classroom using Blu-Tack.
8. When the picture is complete the children should be given praise and encouragement for their efforts.

Title of Workshop: Hands On!

Author: Susan Parkes

Suitable Group Details: the size of the group unlimited, but the size of the inner groups would have to be between five/six and ten people. It would suit ages five years to adults, but is not suitable for toddlers or the elderly.

Duration: approx. 2 hours.

Materials needed:

- Get as many items as there are people.
- Markers, crayons, coloured pencils, paint.
- Large sheet of paper (or Sellotape small pieces of paper together).
- Glitter, stickers to decorate (optional).
- A sizeable space.

Instructions:

1. Place the large piece of paper on the floor. (If you don't have a large sheet, you can Sellotape small pieces of paper together.) Depending on the group size, each person could have a piece of paper, and Sellotape them together so they are touching in some way.
2. Give everyone a marker, crayon, coloured pencil or paint, depending on what's available.
3. Everyone picks a small section of the paper. In that section, the person will draw a body without the arms. So they will draw, head, torso, legs and feet.
4. Then within that body, they will write or draw their interests, hobbies or just experiences.
5. When everyone is finished, they will look at each body in the group and look for similarities in interests, hobbies or experiences.
6. Then each person at a time will draw an arm coming out of their body and linking the hands together with the person with whom they had similar interests, hobbies or experiences. A person can have more than two arms on their body.
7. If it's a small enough group, some people may not find similarities, which is why you need big enough groups within the group for this activity. If a person doesn't match up with anyone in the group, they will draw two arms hugging their body, around their interests, hobbies or experiences.

Title of Workshop: Our Story

Author: Niamh Sludds
Suitable group details: most suited to children between five and ten years, but can be adapted for ages older than this.
Duration: 1 hour.

Materials needed:

- A hat.
- Pieces of paper with questions on them.
- A blank page.
- Colouring pencils, markers.

Instructions:

The group should sit in a circle with one person (usually the social care worker) sitting outside the group. A hat is filled with questions, such as what is your name, age, where do you live, what is your favourite hobby, etc. This hat is passed around the circle, with each person answering one question. The social care worker should take note of each answer, so that when the activity is finished the children can write up a story. Each of the children should then write their part of the story on a big page. When every child has completed his/her part of the story, a communal story will have been made. The story should then be decorated with pictures of the person they have made together and the things that they like to do, etc.

Title of Workshop: What's the Length of a Piece of String?

Author: Emma Smith
Suitable group details: 8–12 years, for groups of between ten and twenty people. It could be adapted to suit younger and older groups.
Duration: this activity can take as long as possible, but generally between one and two hours.

Materials needed:

- String
- Paper.
- Glue.
- Paint.
- Paint brushes.

- Wool.
- Material.
- Crêpe paper.
- Cotton wool.
- Chalk.
- Oil pastels.

Instructions:

1. Use a piece of string to measure the height of the child; the child will later use this piece of string in a picture.
2. The child can now chose a place, person, animal, food, etc. that they love or is a happy thought or feeling.
3. The child can draw a picture of their choice and use any materials they like to make the picture.
4. When they are finished they then use their piece of string to add to the drawing in any way they like.

Title of Workshop: Let's Go Fishing

Author: Niamh Steele
Suitable Group Details: this activity is suitable for eight or more children between the ages of four and eleven and working in groups of four.
Duration: 1 hour.

Materials needed:

- 4 sheets of white A4 paper per child.
- 2 sheets of coloured A4 paper.
- 6 paperclips per child.
- A pencil per child.
- A bottle of PVA glue per group.
- A roll of Sellotape.
- A pair of scissors per child.
- Different-coloured markers.
- One strong magnet per group.
- Some long thread or string.
- Blu-Tack.

Note for Carer: using the coloured A4 paper and a pair of scissors, cut out four or more (depending on the number of young people playing) square cards. Write a different question on each of these cards. Ask personal information about anything from family members' names to favourite colours, but make sure the questions are not too personal. Example one: How many people are in your family? Example two: What is your favourite kind of music?

Instructions:

1. Give four white A4 pages and six paperclips to each young person participating in the activity.
2. Ask each young person to fold one of the white A4 pages in half. Then ask them to draw an oval on the folded page with the pencil and cut it out: this is the body of the fish.

3. With the other white A4 page ask the young people to draw a triangle for the tail of the fish and cut it out.
4. Now it is time to decorate. Using the different coloured markers allow each young person to decorate one side of each of the ovals and both sides of the triangle.
5. Turning the ovals over so the white side faces up, ask the young people to tape 3 paper clips in a line on to one of the ovals.

6. Glue half of the triangle on to the end of the oval with the paperclips on it, leaving the other half of the triangle to hang over the edge of the oval.
7. Glue the other oval on top of the paperclips, covering them. The fish is now made.
8. Repeat steps 1 to 7 using the other pages and paperclips to make another fish.
9 . Tie a long piece of thread or a piece of string to a magnet; you can secure it with Sellotape if you cannot tie it securely. The fishing rod is now made.
10. The carer should Blu-Tack one question on to one side of all of the fish. Then spread them out, question side down, on the floor.

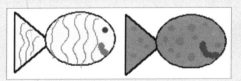

11. Now the game begins. Separate the children into two or more groups of four and ask them to take turns fishing for a fish and asking their other group members the questions on the fish they have caught. Place the fish to the side after the question is answered.
12. When there are no more fish left the groups should swap fish and ask the questions on the other fish.

Title of Workshop: Musical Cards

Author: Mariora Stoica

Suitable group details: ages 7+ and for groups of between four and six people. Some elements of this workshop can be adapted for younger age groups.

Duration: 40 minutes.

Materials needed:

- Picture of musical instruments.
- Set of musical cards.
- Definition cards (strings, brass, percussion and woodwind).
- Piece of music (CD).

Instructions:

Select a piece of music with different solo instrument parts (violin, flute, piano and saxophone). The musical cards are in the musical box. The participants sit in a circle. Get the children to close their eyes and listen together to a piece of music. They have to guess how many instruments they can hear. The children have to pick four different pictures of instruments from the box. In each case four children will pick the definition cards and will lay them out horizontally (strings, brass, percussion and woodwind). Now, the children have to listen again to this piece of music. This time they have to match the musical cards to the definition cards. They have to think about how the sound is made by those instruments they have picked (the sound is made by blowing into—brass and woodwind instruments; by using the bow—stringed instruments; by beating the instrument—percussion) and think about what kind of material is used to make that instrument. The children will read one definition card at a time and the other participants in the group will check if they match the cards. The musical cards and definition cards have colour codes on the back. At the end children can enjoy singing songs ('I am the Music Man') and doing the action for each instrument.

Title of Workshop: Shortest Straw

Author: Aideen Tierney

Suitable Group Details: all groups. This workshop is intended to be for a group of young people between 12 and 18 years who are just getting to know each other. It should be carried out with a group no bigger than twenty and should include five people to each subgroup.

Duration: 15–30 minutes.

Materials needed:

- Scissors.
- 20 straws.
- Sticky labels.

Instructions:

1. Divide the twenty straws into four groups of five.
2. Cut into different sizes so that each group of five has five straws of different sizes, e.g.:

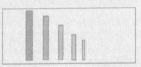

3. Divide the group up into groups of five.
4. Using the sticky labels, give each member of the group a name tag.
5. Tell each member of the group to pick a straw.
6. When all the straws have been drawn the group member with the longest straw has to tell the group one thing about themselves, excluding their name (as name tags have been provided) and so on until the member with the shortest straw has to tell the group five things about themselves.

Bibliography

Adair, C., *Women and Dance: Sylphs and Sirens*, London: Macmillan, 1992.

Adamson, P., *The Child Care Transition: A League Table on Early Childhood Education and Care in Economically Advanced Countries*, Florence: UNICEF Innocenti Research Centre, 2008.

Ainsworth, F. and Fulcher, L. (eds), *Group Care for Children: Concepts and Issues*, London: Tavistock Publications, 1981.

Amabile, T.M., *Growing up Creative – Nurturing a Lifetime of Creativity*, Buffalo, NY: The Creative Education Foundation Press, 1989.

Amabile, T.M. and Tighe, E., *Questions of Creativity*, New York: Touchstone, 1993.

Anglin, J.P., Denholm, C.J., Ferguson, R.V. and Pense, A.R. (eds), *Perspectives in Professional Child and Youth Care*, London: The Haworth Press, 1990.

Anning, A. and Ring, K., *Making Sense of Children's Drawings*, England: Open University Press, 2004.

Ansdell, G.P.M., *Beginning Research in the Arts Therapies*, London & Philadelphia: Jessica Kingsley Publishers, 2001.

Arnheim, R., *Art and Visual Perception: A Psychology of the Creative Eye*, California: California University Press, 2004.

Arts Council, *Arts and Wellbeing Programme: Arts in Disability, Arts in Health*, Dublin: Arts Council, 2005.

Artz, S., *Feeling As a Way Of Knowing*, Toronto: Trifolium Books Inc., 1994.

Asperger, H., 'Die "aunstisehen Psychopathen" im Kindesalter', *Archiv für Psychiatrie und Nervenkrankheiten* 117 (1944), pp. 76–136.

Attwood, T.

– *Asperger's Syndrome: A Guide for Parents and Professionals*, London: Jessica Kingsley Publishers, 1997.

– *The Complete Guide to Asperger's Syndrome,* London: Jessica Kingsley, 2007.

Baird, G., Simonoff, E., Pickles, A., Chandler, S., Loucas, T., Meldrum, D. and Charman, T., 'Prevalence of disorders of the autism spectrum in a population cohort of children in South Thames: the Special Needs and Autism Project (SNAP)', *Lancet*, 15, 368(9531) (2006), 210–15.

Baker, D., 'To Play or Not to Play', in N. McCaslin (ed.), *Children and Drama* (2nd edn), New York: Longman, 1981.

Baldwin, S. and Carlisle, J., 'Living with Disability: The Experiences of Parents and Children', in Allan, G. (ed.), *The Sociology of The Family. A Reader,* UK: Blackwell Publishers Ltd, 1999.

Bamford, A., *The Wow Factor*. Germany: Waxmann, 2006.

Baron-Cohen, S.,

— *Mindblindness: An Essay on Autism and Theory of Mind,* Boston: MIT Press, 1995.

— *Targeting Autism: What We Know, Don't Know, and Can Do to Help Young Children with Autism Spectrum Disorders* (3rd edn), London: University of California Press, Ltd, 2006.

Baron-Cohen, S., Leslie, U. and Frith, A.M., 'Does the autistic child have a "theory of mind"?' *Cognition* 21(1) (1985), 37–46.

Batchelor, J. and Boutland, K., 'Patterns That Connect opportunities for Reflective Practice in Network Placements', in N. Gould and I. Taylor, *Reflective Learning for Social Work,* Aldershot: Ashgate Publishers, 1996.

Bedding, S. and Sadlo, G., 'Retired people's experience of participation in art classes', *British Journal of Occupational Therapy* 71(9) (2008), 371–8.

Benari, N. *Inner Rhythm,* Switzerland: Harwood Academic Publications, 1995.

Benson, C, *The Place of the Arts in Irish Education,* 1979, retrieved from http://www.artscouncil.ie/Publications/The_Place_of_the_Arts_in_Irish_Education.pdf on 10 August 2009.

Best, D.,

— *Feeling and Reason in the Arts,* London: Allen & Unwin, 1985.

— 'Education of the emotion: rationality of feeling', *Oxford Review of Education,* Vol. 14, No. 2 (1988).

— *The Rationality of Feeling,* Oxford: The Falmer Press, 1992.

Biklen, D., *Autism and the Myth of the Person Alone,* New York: New York University Press, 2005.

Birch, A., *Developmental Psychology from Infancy to Adulthood,* London: Macmillan, 1997.

Bleuler, E., *Dementia Praecox or the Group of Schizophrenias* (trans. J. Zinkin), New York: International University Press, 1950. (Originally published in 1911.)

Blom, L.A. and Chaplin, L., *The Moment of Movement,* London: Dance Books, 2000.

Boal, A.,

— *Theatre of the Oppressed,* London: Pluto Pres,1979.

— *Games for Actors and Non-Actors,* London: Routledge, 1992.

— *The Rainbow of Desire: The Boal Method of Theatre and Therapy,* London: Routledge, 1994.

Bogdashina, O.

— *Communication Issues in Autism and Asperger Syndrome: Do We Speak the Same Language?* New York: Jessica Kingsley Publishers, 2004.

— *The Theory of Mind and the Triad of Perspective on Autism and Asperger Syndrome: A View from the Bridge,* New York: Jessica Kingsley Publishers, 2005.

Bolton, G.,

— *New Perspectives on Classroom Drama,* London: Simon & Schuster, 1992.

— *Acting in Classroom Drama: A Critical Analysis,* Stoke-on -Trent: Trentham Books, 1998.

Boud, D., Keogh, R. and Walker, D., *Reflection: Turning Experience into Learning,* London: Kogan Press, 1995.

Bowkett, S., *100 Ideas for Teaching Creativity.* London: Continuum, 2005.

Boyatzis, C.J. and Watson, M.W. (eds), *Symbolic and Social Constraints on the Development of Children's Artistic Style*, San Francisco: Jossey-Bas, 2000.

Brown, H. and Smith J., *Normalisation: A Reader for the Nineties*, UK: Routledge, 1994.

Brown, J., *Developing a Strategy for Crisis Intervention in Youthreach*, Ireland: Co. Donegal Vocational Education Committee Adult Education Services Youthreach & STTC Programmes, 2005.

Bruner, G.C., 'Music, mood and marketing', *Journal of Marketing*, 54 (1990), 94–104.

Byrne, J. and McHugh, J., 'Residential Childcare', in P. Share and N. McElwee (eds), *Applied Social Care: An Introduction for Irish Students,* Dublin: Gill and Macmillan, 2005.

Byrne, L., *Practice Placement in Social Care Worker Education*, Unpublished Master's Thesis, Cork Institute of Technology, 2000.

Carroll, N., *Philosophy of Art*, London and New York: Routledge, 1999.

Cast, A.D. and Burke, P. J., 'A theory of self-esteem', *Social Forces* 80(3) (2002), 1042.

Cattanach, A., *Drama for People with Special Needs* (2nd edn), London: A&C Black Publishers, 1996.

Central Statistics Office, *Quarterly National Household Survey, Quarter 3, 2007*, retrieved from http://www.cso.ie on 10 October 2009.

Chriss, J.J., *Counselling and the Therapeutic State*, New York: Aldine De Gruyter, 1999.

Citizens' Information Bureau, *Early Start Programme,* retrieved from http://www.citizens information.ie on 10 October 2009.

Clark, G.A., 'Judging children's drawings as measures of art abilities', *Studies in Art Education*, 34(2) (1993), 72–81.

Cochrane, P., *Are we Really Serious about Creativity?* UK: Arts Council England, 2006. Available online from: http://www.capeuk.org/publications/html. Accessed on 15 June 2009.

Cockett, Mike, *What Contribution can Creativity and Creative Learning Make to Social Inclusion?* UK: Arts Council England, 2006. Available online from: http://www.capeuk.org/publications.html. Accessed on 17 June 2009.

Cohen, J., *Statistical Power Analysis for the Behavioral Sciences*, NY: Academic Press, 1969.

Cohen, L.J., *Playful Parenting*, New York: Random House/Ballantine Books, 2001.

Collins, M.A. and Amabile T.M., 'Motivation and Creativity' in R.J. Sternberg, *Handbook of Creativity*, Cambridge: Cambridge University Press, 1999.

Commission on the Status of People with Disabilities, *A Strategy for Equality*, Report of the Commission on the Status of People with Disabilities, Dublin: Stationery Office, 1996.

Conn, C., *Using Drama with Children on the Autism Spectrum*, Brackley: Speechmark Publishing Ltd, 2007.

Cook, E., *Let's Play, Psychologies* (UK edn), 2009.

Cooke, G., Griffan, D. and Cox, M., *Teaching Young Children to Draw; Imaginative Approaches to Representational Drawing*, Washington: Falmer Press, 1998.

Corbin, M.R.J., *The Importance of Play*, ITB journal (online) (2007) (16), 43–53,retrieved from http://www.itb.ie/site/researchinnovation/itbjournal/ITB_Journal_December_ 2007 .pdf.

Courtney, D., *Social Care Education and Training: Towards a National Standard,* Conference Paper, Cork: IASCE Conference, 2003.

Cox, M.,

– *Children's Drawings of the Human Figure*, London: Psychology Press, 1993.

– *The Pictorial World of the Child*, Cambridge: Cambridge University Press, 2005.

Craft, A., Jeffrey, B. and Leibling, M., *Creativity in Education*, London & New York: Continuum, 2001.

Cronin, J. (ed.), *Irish Youth Theatre Handbook: A Guide to Good Practice in Youth Drama*, Dublin: National Association for Youth Drama, 2001.

Cropley, A.J., *More Ways Than One: Fostering Creativity*, Norwood, NJ: Ablex Publishing, 1992.

Croton, J., 'The Assessment of Professional Competence' in R. Pierce and J. Weinstein (eds), *Innovative Education and Training for Care Professionals,* London: Jessica Kingsley Publishers, 2000.

Crowther, J., *Oxford Advanced Learner's Dictionary*, Oxford & New York: Oxford University Press, 1995.

Cumine, V., Leach, J. and Stevenson, G., *Asperger Syndrome – A practical guide for teachers,* London: David Fulton Publishers, 1998.

Curtis, A. and O'Hagan, M., *Care and Education in Early Childhood: Student's Guide to Theory and Practice*, London: Routledge Falmer, 2003.

Dale, N., *Working With Families of Children with Special Needs. Partnership and Practice,* London: Routledge, 1996.

Damasio, A.R., *Descartes' Error: Emotion, Reason and the Human Brain,* New York: Vintage Books, 2006.

Damasio, A.R. and Damasio, H. 'Musical Faculty and Cerebral Dominance', in M. Critchley and R.A. Henson (eds), *Music and the Brain*, London: Heinemann, 1977.

Daniels, H., Cole, M. and Westsch, J.V. (eds), *The Cambridge Companion to Vygotsky,* New York: Cambridge University Press, 2007.

D'Arcy, F., Flynn, J., McCarthy, Y., O'Connor, C. and Tierney, E. 'Sibshops: An evaluation of an interagency model', *Journal of Intellectual Disabilities* 9(43) (2005), 43–57.

Darden-Brunson, F., Green, A. and Goldstein, H., 'Video-Based Instruction for Children with Autism', in J. K. Luiselli, D.C. Russo, W.P. Christian and S.M. Wilczynski (eds), *Effective Practices for Children with Autism: Educational and Behavioral Support Interventions that Work*, New York: Oxford University Press, 2008.

Dawson, J., *Learning Disabilities and Sibling Issues,* USA: GreatSchools Inc., retrieved on 24 November 2005 from www.greatschools.net/cgi-bin/showarticle 2334.

Denholm, C.J., Ferguson, R.V. and Pense, A.R. (eds), *Perspectives in Professional Child and Youth Care*, London: The Haworth Press, 1990.

Department of Education and Science,

– *Curriculum for Irish Primary Schools*, Dublin: The Stationery Office, 1999.

– *The Report of the Task Force on Autism,* Dublin: The Stationery Office, 2001a.

– *Youth Work Act*, Dublin: Government Publications Office, 2001b.

– *National Youth Work Development Plan 2003–2007*, Dublin: Government Publications Office, 2003.

deSouza-Fleith, D., 'Teacher and student perceptions of creativity in the classroom environment', *Roeper Review* 22(3) (2000),149.

Devlin, M, 'Working with Young People', in P. Share and K. Lalor (eds), *Applied Social Care: an Introduction for Students in Ireland,* 2nd edn, Dublin: Gill and Macmillan, 2009.

Dewey, J., *Art as Experience*, New York: The Penguin Group, 1934.

Di Leo, J.H., *Young Children and their Drawings,* London: Psychology Press, 1996.

Dissanayake, E., *Homo Aestheticus. Where Art Comes from and Why*, Seattle & London: University of Washington Press, 1995.

Donaldson, M., *Human Minds. An Exploration*, New York: Allen Lane, The Penguin Press, 1992.

Dorn, C.M., *Mind in Art: Cognitive Foundations in Art Education*, New Jersey: Lawrence Erlbaum Associates, 1999.

Douglas, F.G. and Horgan, M.A., 'The Light Beneath the Bushel – A Discussion Paper on Early Years Education and Care in the Republic of Ireland', *Irish Journal of Applied Social Studies,* 2(2) (Summer 2000), 186–210.

Doyle, J. and Lalor, K., 'The Social Care Practice Placement: A College Perspective', in P. Share and K. Lalor (eds.), *Applied Social Care*, 2nd edn, Dublin: Gill and Macmillan, 2009.

Duffy, B., *Supporting Creativity and Imagination in the Early Years*, New York: Open University Press, 2006.

Dunlap, G., Iovannone, R. and Kincaid, D., 'Essential Components for Effective Autism Educational Programs' in J.K. Luiselli, D.C. Russo, W.P. Christian and S.M. Wilczynski (eds), *Effective Practices for Children with Autism: Educational and Behavioral Support Interventions that Work*, New York: Oxford University Press, 2008.

Ebbeck, M. and Waniganayake, M., *Early Childhood Professionals: Leading Today and Tomorrow,* Chatswood, New South Wales: Elsevier Australia, 2003.

Edwards, L.C., *The Creative Arts. A Process Approach for Teachers and Children*, New Jersey: Pearson, Merrill Prentice Hall, 2006.

Egan, J. and Walsh, P., 'Sources of stress among adult siblings of Irish people with intellectual disability', *Irish Journal of Psychology* 22(1) (2001), 28–38.

Eisenberg, L. and Baker, B.L., 'Siblings of children with mental retardation living at home or in residential placement', *Journal of Child Psychology and Psychiatry,* 39(30) (1998), 355–63.

Ekman, P. and Friesen, W., *Unmasking the Face,* Englewood Cliffs, NJ: Prentice Hall, 1972.

Elder, L.M., Caterino, L.C., Chao, J., Shacknai, D. and De Simone, G., 'The efficacy of social skills treatment for children with Asperger Syndrome', *Education and Treatment of Children,* 29(4) (2006), 635–63.

Eurostat, *Living in Ireland Survey 2001.*

Fahlberg, V., *A Child's Journey through Placement*, Indianapolis: Perspectives Press, 1991.

Feldman, D.H., 'Creativity: Dreams, Insights, and Transformations' in D.H. Felman, M. Csikszentmihalyi and H. Gardner (eds), *Changing the World: A Framework for the Study of Creativity*, Connecticut: Praeger Publications, 1994.

Feldman, D.H. and Piirto, J., 'Parenting Talented Children', in M.H. Bornstein, *Handbook of Parenting; Practical Issues in Parenting*, New Jersey: Lawrence Erlbaum Publishers, 2001.

Ferszt, G.G., Heineman L., *et al.*. 'Transformation through grieving: art and the bereaved', *Holistic Nursing Practice* 13(1) (1998), 68–75.

Fewster, G., 'Growing Together: The Personal Relationship in Child and Youth Care', in J.P. Anglin *et al.*, *Perspectives in Professional Child and Youth Care*, 1990.

Fiske, E. (ed.), *Champions of Change: The Impact of the Arts on Learning*, Washington DC: Arts Education Partnership and the President's Committee on the Arts and the Humanities, 2000.

Fitzgerald, M., *Autism and Creativity: Is there a Link Between Autism in Men and Exceptional Ability?*, London: Bruner-Routledge, 2004.

Flanagan, F., *The Greatest Educators Ever*, Continuum Books, 2006.

Fleming, M., *Starting Drama Teaching*, London: David Fulton Publishers Ltd, 1994 (2nd edn, 2003).

Florida, R., *The Rise of the Creative Class*, New York: Basic Books, 2002.

Fowler, C. (1988), *Can we Rescue the Arts for America's Children? Coming to our Senses 10 Years Later*, New York: American Council for the Arts, 1988.

– 'Strong arts, strong schools', *Educational Leadership*, 52(3) (1994), 4.

Fowler, W., *Infant and Child Care*, Boston: Allyn and Bacon Inc., 1980.

Frank, J.D. and Frank, J.B., *Persuasion and Healing*, Baltimore and London: Johns Hopkins University Press, 1993.

Freeman, B.J., Cronin, P. and Candela, P., 'Asperger Syndrome or autistic disorder?: The diagnostic dilemma', *Focus on Autism and Other Developmental Disabilities,* Vol. 17, No. 3 (2002), 145–51.

Freeman, N.H., 'Children's Human Figure Drawing', in R.L. Gregory (ed.), *The Oxford Companion to the Mind* (2nd edn), Oxford: Oxford University Press, 2004, pp. 159–64.

Freud, S., *Civilization and its Discontents*, London: W.W. Norton, 1961.

Frith, U.,

– *Autism and Asperger Syndrome*, Cambridge: Cambridge University Press, 1991.

– *Autism. Explaining the Enigma* (2nd edn), Oxford: Blackwell, 2003.

Gannon, B. and Nolan, B., *Disability and Social Inclusion*, Ireland: ERSI.

Gardner, H.,

– *Artful Scribbles*, New York: Basic Books, 1980.

– 'Seven Creators of the Modern Era', in J. Brockman, *Creativity*, New York: Simon & Schuster, 1993.

Garfat, T., 'Questions about self and relationship', *Journal of Child and Youth Care,* 13(2) (1999), iii–vi.

Garvey, C., *Play: The Developing Child,* UK: Fontana/Open Books, 1977.

Gersie, A. and King, N., *Storymaking in Education and Therapy*, Sweden: Stockholm Institute of Education Press, 1990.

Gibbs, L. and Gambrill, E., *Critical Thinking for Helping Professionals: A Skills-Based Workbook*, New York: Oxford University Press US, 2009.

Giddens, A., *Sociology*, 6th edn, UK: Polity Press, 2009.

Gillberg, C., *A Guide to Asperger Syndrome*, Cambridge: Cambridge University Press, 2002.

Ginnott, H. G., *Between Teacher and Child: A Book for Parents and Teachers*, New York: Macmillan, 1972.

Golan, O. and Baron-Cohen. S., 'Systemizing empathy: Teaching adults with Asperger syndrome or high-functioning autism to recognize complex emotions using interactive multimedia', *Development and Psychopathology*, 18(2) (2006), 591–617.

Golomb, C. *The Child's Creation of a Pictorial World* (2nd edn), New Jersey: Lawrence Erlbaum Associates, 2004.

Goodway, D., *Herbert Read Reassessed*, Liverpool: Liverpool University Press, 1998.

Gould, J., 'What is the autistic spectrum?' *GP Magazine* (22 May 1998), 56–8.

Government of Ireland,

– Employment Equality Acts 1998–2004, Dublin: Stationery Office.

– Equality Act 2004, Dublin: Stationery Office.

– Equal Status Act 2000, Dublin: Stationery Office.

– *Local Development Social Inclusion Programme 1994–1999*.

– *National Anti-Poverty Strategy 2001*.

– *Programme for Economic and Social Progress*, 1991.

– *Towards 2016: Ten Year Framework Social Partnership Agreement 2006–2015*. Dublin: Stationery Office.

Graffiti Theatre Company homepage (nd), retrieved from http://www.graffiti.ie/home.htm on 10 August 2009.

Gray, C.,

– *Comic Strip Conversations: Illustrated Interactions that Teach Conversation Skills to Students with Autism and Related Disorders*, London: Future Horizons, 1994.

– *The New Social Story Book*, London: Future Horizons, 2000.

Gray, C. and White, A. L., *My Social Stories Book*, London and Philadelphia: Jessica Kingsley Publishers, 2002.

Greenspan, S. and Wieder, S., *Engaging Autism: Helping Children Relate, Communicate and Think with the DIR Floortime Approach*, Cambridge: Da Capo Press, 2006.

Gutstein, S.E. and Whitney, T., 'Asperger syndrome and the development of social competence', *Focus on Autism and Other Developmental Disabilities*, Vol. 17, No. 3 (2002), 161–71.

Hadley, L.B., 'Expressive Arts Playdough', in H. Kaduson and C. Schaefer (eds), *101 Favourite Play Therapy Techniques*, Oxford: Rowman and Littlefield Publishers, Inc., 1997.

Hahlo, R., and Reynolds, P., *Dramatic Events: How to Run a Successful Workshop*, London: Faber & Faber, 2000.

Hanlon, N., McWilliams, A. and Quinlan-Cooke, S. 'Practice Teaching and Learning in Social Care: Reflections on a Course Development', in T. O'Connor and M. Murphy (eds), *Social Care in Ireland: Theory, Policy and Practice*, Cork: Cork Institute of Technology Press, 2006.

Happe, F.G.E., *Autism: The Introduction to Psychological Theory*, Hove & New York: Psychology Press, Taylor & Francis, 1994.

Hargreaves, D.J. and North, A.C. (eds),*The Social Psychology of Music*, Oxford University Press, 1997.

Hayes, N.

– *The Case for a National Policy on Early Education*, Dublin: Combat Poverty Agency, 1995.

– 'Quality in Early Education', *Irish Educational Studies,* Vol. 15 (Spring 1996), 1–13.

Heflin, L.J. and Alaimo, D.F., *Students with Autism Spectrum Disorders: Effective Instructional Practices*, New Jersey: Pearson Education, Inc., 2007.

Helpguide, *Playing Together for Fun: Creative Play and Lifelong Games*, Santa Monica, CA: Center for Healthy Aging, 15 December 2004.

Hevner, K.,

– 'The affective character of the major and minor modes in music', *American Journal of Psychology*, 47 (1935a), 103–18.

– 'Expression in music: a discussion of experimental studies and theories', *Psychological Review*, 42 (1935b), 186–204.

– 'The affective value of pitch and tempo in music', *American Journal of Psychology*, 49 (1936), 621–30.

– 'Experimental studies of the elements of expression in music', *American Journal of Psychology*, 48 (1937), 246–68.

Higher Education Training Awards Council, *Draft Document for the Award Standards on Social Care Work*, Dublin: HETAC, 2009.

Hill, E.L., 'Executive dysfunction in autism', *Trends in Cognitive Sciences,* 8(1) (2004), 26–32.

Hippler, K. and Klicpera, C., 'A retrospective analysis of the clinical case records of "autistic psychopaths" diagnosed by Hans Asperger and his team at the University Children's Hospital, Vienna', *Philosophical Transactions of the Royal Society of London. Series B, Biological Sciences*, 28:358 (1430) (2003), 291–301.

Horgan, M. and Douglas, F.G., 'Where angels fear to tread', *Irish Journal of Applied Social Studies,* Vol. 1, No. 1 (Summer 1998), 13–36.

Hornbrook, D.,

– *Education and Dramatic Art* (2nd edn), London: Routledge, 1989.

– (ed.), *On the Subject of Drama*, London: Routledge, 1998.

Howard, M., 'An Art Therapist Looks at Her Professional History', in E. Ulman and C.A. Levy, *Art Therapy Viewpoints*, New York: Schocken Books, 1980.

Howard, P.J., *The Owner's Manual for the Brain: Everyday Applications from Mind-Brain Research*, New York: Bard Press, 2000.

Howlin, P., *Children with Autism and Asperger Syndrome: A Guide for Practitioners and Carers*, Oxford: Wiley Blackwell, 1998.

Hunt, C. and West, L., 'Learning in a border country: Using psychodynamic ideas in teaching and research', *Studies in the Education of Adults* 38(2):165 (2006).

Hutt, S.J., Hutt, C., Lenard, H.G., Bernuth, H.V. and Muntjerwerff, W.J., 'Auditory responsivity in the human neonate', *Nature*, 218 (1968), 888–90.

Irish Wheelchair Association, *Your Life—Your Way: A Strategy for the Future, 2008–2011*, Dublin: IWA, 2008.

Ives, M. and Munro, N. *Caring for a child with Autism,* UK: Jessica Kingsley Publishers, 2002.

Jackson, A. (ed.), *Learning through Theatre: New Perspectives on Theatre in Education*, 2nd edn, London: Routledge, 1993.

Jackson, L., *Freaks, Geeks and Asperger Syndrome: A User Guide to Adolescence*, London: Jessica Kingsley Publishers, 2002.

Jackson, N., 'Assessing students' creativity: synthesis of higher education teacher views', *Higher Education Academy*, 23-3-07 (2005).

Jarvis, P., 'Learning Practical Knowledge', in L. Kydd, M. Crawford, and C. Riches (eds), *Professional Development for Educational Management*, Buckingham: Open University Press, 1997.

Jennings, S.,
– *Creative Drama in Groupwork*, Bicester, Oxford: Winslow Press, 1986.
– *Introduction to Dramatherapy: Ariadne's Ball of Thread,* London: Jessica Kingsley Publishers, 1998.
– *Introduction to Developmental Playtherapy*, London: Jessica Kingsley Publishers, 1999.
– *Creative Play and Drama with Adults at Risk*, Bicester, Oxford: Speechmark, 2005.
– *Creative Puppetry with Children and Adults*, Bicester, Oxford: Speechmark, 2008.
– *Embodiment Projection, Role,* Workshop at Athlone Institute of Technology, 19 February 2008. Retrieved from http://www.suejennings.com/epr.html.
– Workshop in Creative Care, Ballymore, Co. Westmeath: Children's Theapy Centre, 17–22 February 2009.

Jennings, S. and Stagnitti, K., 'From little things big things grow', *EQ Australia*, Issue 7 (Autumn 2007), 32–24.

Johnson, C. and O'Neill, C., *Dorothy Heathcote: Collected Writings on Drama and Education*, USA: North Western University Press, 1991.

Johnston, C., *House of Games: Making Theatre from Everyday Life*, 2nd edn, London: Nick Hern Books, 2005.

Johnstone, K.,
– *Impro, Improvisation and the Theatre*, London: Methuen Drama, 1989.
– *Improv for Storytellers*, London: Faber & Faber, 1999.

Joint Committee on Social Care Professionals, *Report of Joint Committee on Social Care Professionals*, Ireland. (n.d.)

Jolley, R.P., 'Children and Pictures: Drawing and Understanding', in *Understanding Children's Worlds*, Vol. 6, Wiley-Blackwell Publishers, 2009.

Jones, G., *Educational Provision for Children with Autism and Asperger Syndrome: Meeting Their Needs*, London: David Fulton Publishers, 2002.

Jordan, R., 'Managing autism and Asperger's syndrome in current educational provision', *Pediatric Rehabilitation,* 8(2) (2005), 104–12.

Jordan, R. and Powell, S., *Understanding and Teaching Children with Autism,* New York: Wiley, 1995.

Jourdain, R., *Music, the Brain, and Ecstasy: How Music Captures Our Imagination,* Harper Perennial, HarperCollins, 1997.

Kagan, J. and Lewis, M., 'Studies of attention in the human infant', *Merrill-Palmer Quarterly, Behavioural Development,* 11 (1965), 95–127.

Kanner, L., 'Autistic disturbances of affective contact', *Nervous Child,* 2 (1943), 217–50.

Kaufman, B.N., *Son-Rise: The Miracle Continues,* Tiburon: H.J. Kramer, 1994.

Keating, S., 'Is art fit for society?' *The Irish Times,* 2008.

Kellogg, R., *Analyzing Children's Art,* Palo Alto, CA: Mayfield Publishing Company, 1970.

Kelly, D.D., *Uncovering the History of Children's Drawing and Art,* California: Greenwood Publishers, 2004.

Kennefick, P., 'Training the person', *European Journal of Social Education FESET,* (4) (2003), 91–4.

Khalfa, S., Peretz, I., Blondin, J.-P. and Manon, R., 'Event-related skin conductance responses to musical emotions in humans', *Neuroscience Letters,* Vol. 328 (2002), 145–9.

Kindler, A.M., 'Researching Impossible? Models of Artistic Development Reconsidered', in E.W. Eisner and M.D. Day (eds), *Handbook of Research and Policy in Art Education,* Mahwah, NJ: Lawrence Erlbaum, 2004.

Kindler, A.M. and Darras, B., 'Maps of Artistic Development', in A.M. Kindler (ed.), *Child Development in Art,* Vancouver: National Art Education Association, 1997.

Klin, A. and Volkmar, F.R., *Asperger Syndrome: Treatment and Intervention. Some Guidelines for Parents,* New Haven, CT.: Yale Child Studies Centre, 1996.

Krasny, L., Williams, B.J., Provencal, S. and Ozonoff, S., 'Social skills interventions for the autism spectrum: essential ingredients and a model curriculum', *Child and Adolescent Psychiatry Clinics,* 12 (2003), 107–22.

Krueger, M., 'Presence as Dance in Work with Youth', *Journal of Child and Youth Care,* 13(2) (1999), 59–72.

Kuppers, P., *Community Performance: An Introduction,* London: Routledge, 2007.

Laban, R. von, *Modern Educational Dance,* Suffolk: Chaucer Press Ltd, 1963.

Lacey, P. and Ouvry, C. (eds), *People with Profound and Multiple Learning Disabilities: A Collaborative Approach to Meeting Complex Needs,* London: David Fulton Publishers, 1998.

Lalor, K. and Doyle, J., 'The Social Care Practice Placement: A College Perspective', in P. Share and N. McElwee (eds), *Applied Social Care: An Introduction for Irish Students,* 2005.

Lazarus, R.S., *Emoton and Adaptation,* New York: Oxford University Press, 1991.

Lee, S.S., Theng, Y.L., Goh, D.H., 'Creative information seeking Part! a conceptual framework', *Aslib Proceedings: New Information Perspectives* 57(5):463 (2005).

Leekam, S., Libby, S., Wing, L., Gould, J. and Gillberg, C., 'Comparison of ICD-10 and Gillberg criteria for Asperger syndrome', *Autism* 4(1) (2000), 11–28.

Levine, S.K., *Poiesis: The Language of Psychology and the Speech of the Soul*, London: Jessica Kingsley, 1997.

Lowenfeld, V. and Brittain, W.L., *Creative and Mental Growth*, New Jersey: Macmillan Publishing Company, 1987.

Luquet, G.H., *Children's Drawings*, trans. A. Costall, London: Free Association Books, 2001.

Luria, A.R., *The Higher Cortical Functions in Man*. New York: Basic Books, 1966.

Lynch, M.D. and Harris, C.R., *Fostering Creativity in Children*, Needham Heights, MA: Allyn & Bacon, 2001.

Lyons, D.,

– *Drama as an Intervention for Challenging Behaviour in Residential Care*, Dublin: Dublin Institute of Technology: Unpublished Thesis, 1998.

– *The Benefits of Using the Creative Arts in Education and Practice*, Conference Paper, Dublin: IASCE Conference 2008.

MacGiollari, D., *Developing Social Care Students' Creativity through an Art Therapy Approach; Change, Learning & Self-actualisation*, Cork: Art Therapy Department, Cork Institute of Technology, Unpublished MA Thesis, 2008.

Madsen, C.K., 'Emotion versus tension in Haydn's Symphony no. 104 as measured by the two-dimensional continuous response of digital interface', *Journal of Research in Music Education*, 46 (1998), 546–54.

Malchiodi, C.A.,

– *Understanding Children's Drawings*, New York: The Guilford Press, 1998.

– *The Art Therapy Sourcebook*, New York: McGraw-Hill Professional, 2006.

Maley, A. and Duff, A., *Drama Techniques: A Resource Book of Communication Activities for Language Teachers*, Cambridge: Cambridge University Press, 2005.

Marks, S.U., Matson, A. and Barraza, L., 'The impact of siblings with disabilities on their brothers and sisters pursuing a career in special education', *Research and Practice for Persons with Severe Disabilities*, 30(4) (2005), 205–18.

Marsh, D.T., *Forgotton Family Members*, USA: Westchester Community Network, 2001. Retrieved on 24 November 2008 from www.westchestercommunitynetwork.com/family_ties/FamTies/FamTiesArchives/Siblings/siblings.html.

Maslow, A., *Abraham Maslow on Creativity* (1980–89). Retrieved on 30 September 2009 from http://www.slideshow.net/rsm/abraham-maslow-on-creativity.

Maslow, H.A., *The Farther Reaches of Human Nature*. Arkana: Penguin, 1971.

Markwick, A. and Parrish, A., *Learning Disabilities*, New York: Butterworth Heinemann, 2003.

Matthews, J.,

– *Drawing and Painting; Children and Visual Representation,* London: Sage Publications, 2003.

– 'The Art of Infancy', in E.W. Eisner and M.D. Day (eds.), *Handbook of Research and Policy in Art Education*, Mahwah, NJ: Lawrence Erlbaum, 2004.

May, R., *The Courage to Create*. New York: Bantam Books, 1980.

Mayesky, M.,

– *Creative Art and Activities*, Florence: Cengage Learning, 2004.

– *Creative Activities for Young Children*, Florence: Cengage Publishers, 2009.

McCarthy, M., *The Arts and Irish Education: Some Lessons from the USA*, 2004, retrieved from http://nayd.ie/research/show/learning_through_drama on 30 July 2009.

McCaslin, N.,

– (ed.), *Children and Drama* (2nd edn), New York: Longman, 1981.

– *Creative Drama in the Classroom and Beyond*, Cambridge: Cambridge University Press, 2005.

McMahon, L., 'Working at Understanding and Helping Troubled Children', in A. Ward and L. McMahon (eds), *Intuition is not Enough: Matching Learning with Practice in Therapeutic Child Care*, London and New York: Routledge, 1998.

Meador, K.S., *Creative Thinking and Problem Solving for Young Learners*, Englewood, CO: Teacher Ideas Press, 1997.

Mesibov, G.B., Shea, V., Schopler, E., *The TEACCH Approach to Autism Spectrum Disorders*, New York: Springer, 2004.

Meyer, D. (ed.), *Views from our Shoes*, USA: Paul H. Brookes Publishing, 1997.

Meyer, D. and Vadasy, P., *Sibshops: Workshops for Siblings of Children with Special Needs*, USA: Paul H. Brookes Publishing, 2007.

Morgan, N., and Saxton, J., *Teaching Drama: A Mind of Many Wonders*, Cheltenham: Stanley Thornes Publishers Ltd, 1989

Morris, D., *People Watching: The Desmond Morris Guide to Body Language*, Britain: Vintage Publishing, 2002.

Moustakas C.E., *Creative Life*, Van Nostrand Reinhold Company, 1977.

Nadeau, R., 'Using the Creative Arts to Expand Personal Creativity', in B. Warren, *Using The Creative Arts in Therapy and Healthcare*, New York: Routledge, 2008.

National Council for Curriculum and Assessment (O'Sullivan, C., Leahy, M., Howard, M. and Corr, M.), *Arts Education (Drama): Curriculum Guidelines for Teachers of Students with Moderate General Learning Disabilities*, Dublin: NCCA, 2002.

National Council for Curriculum and Assessment, *Primary School Curriculum*, Dublin: NCCA, 1999, www.curriculumonline.ie/en/Primary_School_Curriculum.

Navior, A. and Prescott, P., 'All about my brother', *Community Care* 1538 (2004), pp. 34–5.

Negus, K. and Pickering, M., *Creativity, Communication and Cultural Value*, London: Sage Publications, 2004.

Nesse, R.M., 'The evolution of hope and despair', *Social Research*, 66(2) (1999).

Nicholson, H.,

– *Applied Drama: The Gift of Theatre*, Hampshire: Palgrave Macmillan, 2005.

– *Theatre and Education*, UK: Palgrave Macmillan, 2009.

Nickerson, R.S., 'Enhancing Creativity' in R.J. Sternberg, *Handbook of Creativity*, Cambridge: Cambridge University Press, 1999.

North, A. and Hargreaves, D., *The Social and Applied Psychology of Music*, New York: Oxford University Press, 2008.

O'Brien, J., *A Framework for Accomplishment*, Decatur, IN: Responsive Systems Associates, 1987.

O'Brien, J. and Lovett, H., 'Finding a way towards everyday lives: A contribution of person centred planning', *Office of Mental Retardation*, USA: Pennsylvania, 1989.

O'Connor, T. and Murphy, M. (eds), *Social Care in Ireland: Theory, Policy and Practice*, Cork: Cork Institute of Technology Press, 2006.

O'Neill, C., *Drama Worlds*, Portsmouth, NH: Heinemann, 1995.

O'Neill, C. and Lambert, A., *Drama Structures: A Practical Handbook for Teachers*, Cheltenham: Stanley Thornes Publishers Ltd, 1990.

O'Neill, C., Lambert, A., Linnell, R. and Warr-Wood, J., *Drama Guidelines*, London: Heinemann Educational Books, 1976.

O'Neil, J.L., *Through the Eyes of Aliens*, London: Jessica Kingsley Publishers, 1998.

Osman, B., *How Learning Disabilities Affect a Child's Siblings*, USA: GreatSchools Inc., 2001. Retrieved on 24 November 2008 from www.greatschools.net/cgi-bin/showarticle2334.

O'Sullivan, C. and Williams, G., *Building Bridges—Laying the Foundations for a Child-Centred Curriculum in Drama and Education*, Birmingham: National Association for the Teaching of Drama, 1998.

O'Toole, John, *The Process of Drama: Negotiating Art and Meaning*, London: Routledge, 1992.

Owen-DeSchryver, J.S., Carr, E.G., Cale, S.I. and Blakely-Smith, A., 'Promoting social interactions between students with autism spectrum disorders and their peers in inclusive school settings', *Focus on Autism and Other Developmental Disabilities*, 23(1) (2008), 15–28.

Ozonoff, S., 'Executive Functions in Autism', in E. Schopler and G.B. Mesibov (eds.), *Learning and Cognition in Autism*, New York: Plenum Press, 1995.

Parhan, L.D., *Play in Occupational Therapy for Children*, St. Louis: Mosby Printing, 1997.

Paxton, S., *Touchdown Dance*, 2003. Available online from: http://www.touchdowndance.co.uk/graphic/contact_improvisation.html

Pearson, J., *Discovering the Self through Drama and Movement*, London: Jessica Kingsley Publishers, 1996.

Peter, M., *Drama for All: Developing Drama in the Curriculum for SEN Students*, London: David Fulton Publishers, 1994.

Piaget, J., *The Child's Conception of the World*, London: Routledge and Kegan Paul, 1928.

Playing Together for Fun: Creative Play and Lifelong Games, in *Helpguide*, Center for Healthy Aging (15 December 2004), California.

Porter, L.M., *Professional Collaboration with Parents of Children with Disabilities*, London: Whurr Publishers Ltd, 2000.

Poulter C., *Playing the Game*, London: Palgrave Macmillan, 1987.

Prentki, T. and Preston, S., *The Applied Theatre Reader*, London: Routledge, 2009.

Preston–Dunlop, V.,

– *Dancing and Dance Theory*, London: Laban Centre for Music and Dance, 1979.

– *A Handbook for Dance in Education*, London: MacDonald and Evans Ltd, 1980.

Prior, M., *Learning and Behaviour Problems in Asperger Syndrome*, New York: Guilford Press, 2003.

Qualifications and Curriculum Authority, *Creativity: Find it, Promote it*, London: QCA publications, 2004.

Ramsey, B., *The Male Dancer: Bodies, Spectacle, Sexualities*, London: Routledge, 2007.

Raymond-Nolan, R., *The Role of Creative Practice in Social Care (Drama)*, Conference Paper, Tralee: 5th Annual IASCE Conference, 20–21 October 2005.

Richards, R., 'Frank Barron and the study of creativity: a voice that lives on', *Journal of Humanistic Psychology* 46(3) (2006), 353.

Ricks, F., 'Self-awareness model for training and application in child and youth care', *Journal of Child and Youth Care* (1989).

Ricks, F. and Charlesworth, J., *Emergent Practice Planning*, New York: Kluwer Academic/Plenum Publishers, 2003.

Riley, J. and Reedy, D., 'Communication, language and literacy: learning through speaking and listening, reading and writing', in J. Riley (ed.), *Learning in the Early Years 3–7*, London: Sage Publications, 2007.

Rinehart, N.J., 'Autism and Asperger's disorder: A neurobehavioural approach to clinical definition', *Australian Journal of Psychology*, 58 (Supplement) (2006), 186.

Ritossa, D.A. and Rickard, N.S., 'The relative utility of "pleasantness and liking" dimensions in predicting the emotions expressed by music', *Psychology of Music*, 32 (2004), 5–22.

Rogers, C.R., *On Becoming a Person*, London: Constable, 1961.

Rotatori, A.F., Wahlberg, T., Obiakor, F.E. and Burkhardt, S.A., *Autistic Spectrum Disorders: Educational and Clinical Interventions*. London: Elsevier, 2001.

Russell, J., 'How executive disorders can bring about an adequate "theory of mind"', in J. Russell (ed.), *Autism as an Executive Disorder*, Oxford: Oxford University Press, 1997, pp. 256–304.

Sawyer, K.R., *Explaining Creativity. The Science of Human Innovation*. Oxford & New York: Oxford University Press, 2006.

Scarlett, W.G., Naudeau, S., Salonius-Pasternak, D. and Ponte, I., *Children's Play*, Sage Publications, 2005.

Schaefer, C.E., Jocobson, H.E. and Ghahramanlou, M., 'Play group therapy for social skills deficit for children', in Schaefer and Kadusan (eds.), *Short Term Play Therapy for Children*, New York: Guilford Press, 2000.

Schaffer, R., *Social Development*, Oxford: Blackwell Publishing, 1996.

Schon, D.A.,
– *The Reflective Practitioner*, London: Temple Smith, 1983.
– *Educating the Reflective Practitioner*, San Francisco: Jossey-Bass, 1987.

Schonbrun, M., *The Everything Music Theory Book: A Complete Guide to Taking Your Understanding of Music to the Next Level*, Cincinnati, USA: Everything Book Company, 2006.

Schreibman, L., *The Science and Fiction of Autism*, Cambridge MA: Harvard University Press, 2005.

Schubert, R., 'Modelling perceived emotion with continuous musical features', *Music Perception*, 21 (2004), 561–85.

Schultz, R.T., 'Developmental deficits in social perception in autism: the role of the amygdala and fusiform face area', *International Journal of Developmental Neuroscience* 23 (2005), 125–41.

Schutzman, M. and Cohen-Cruz, J. (eds), *Playing Boal*, New York: Routledge, 1994.

Seidel, S. (2000). '"Stand and unfold yourself": A Monograph on the Shakespeare & Company Research Study', in E.B. Fiske (ed.), *Champions of Change: The Impact of the Arts on Learning* (pp. 79–90), Washington DC: Arts Education Partnership and the President's Committee on the Arts and the Humanities, 2000.

Seligman, M. and Darling, R.B. *Ordinary Families, Special Children. A Systems Approach to Childhood Disability* (2nd edn), New York: Guilford Press, 1997.

Seltzer, G.B., 'Informal supports for aging mentally retarded persons', *American Journal of Mental Deficiency*, 90 (1985), 259–65.

Share, P. and McElwee, N.,

– 'What is Social Care?' in *Applied Social Care: An Introduction for Irish Students,* Dublin: Gill and Macmillan, 2005a.

– 'The Professionalism of Social Care in Ireland', in *Applied Social Care: An Introduction for Irish Students,* Dublin: Gill and Macmillan, 2005b.

– (eds), *Applied Social Care: An Introduction for Irish Students,* Dublin: Gill and Macmillan, 2005c.

Sharp, D., *C.G. Jung Lexicon. A Primer of Terms and Concepts*, Toronto: Inner City Books, 1991.

Sheratt, D. and Peter, M., *Developing Play and Drama in Children with Autistic Spectrum Disorders*, London: David Fulton Publishers Ltd, 2002.

Sherborne, V., *Developmental Movement for Children* (2nd edn), London: Worth Publishing, 2001.

Sheridan, C., *Reminiscence: Uncovering a Lifetime of Memories*, San Francisco: Elder Press, 1991.

Shulman, L., 'Groupwork practice with hard to reach clients: a modality of choice', *Groupwork,* Vol. 1(1) (1988), 5–16.

Sicile-Kira, C., *Autism Spectrum Disorders: The Complete Guide*, London: Vermilion, 2003.

Singer, D., Golinkoff, R., Hersh-Pasek, *Play Equals Learning*, Oxford: Oxford University Press, 2006.

Skovholt, M., 'The cycle of caring: a model of expertise in the helping professions', *Journal of Mental Health Counselling*, Vol. 27(1) (2005), 82–8.

Slade, P.,

– *Child Drama*, New York: Philosophical Library, 1954.

– *Child Play* (2nd edn), London: Jessica Kingsley Publishers, 1995 and 2001.

Sloboda, J.A., *The Musical Mind: The Cognitive Psychology of Music*. New York: Oxford Science Publications, Oxford University Press, 1985.

Sloboda, J.A. and Juslin, P.N., 'Psychological Perspectives on Music and Emotion', in P.N. Juslin and J.A. Sloboda (eds), *Music and Emotion: Theory and Research* (pp.71–104), Oxford: Oxford University Press, 2001.

Smilansky, S. and Shefataya, L., *Facilitating Play: Promoting Cognitive, Socio-emotional and Academic Development in Young Children,* Gaithersburg, MD: Psychological and Educational Publications, 1990.

Smith, V., *Sophie's Story: Raising a Chimp in the Family,* Somerset: Butler & Tanner Ltd, 2003.

Smith-Autard, J.M., *The Art of Dance in Education,* London: A&C Black, 2002.

Special Education Support Service (SESS) Ireland, *Signposts: Resource Pack for Teachers,* 2008.

Spolin, V.,
– *Theatre Games of the Classroom: A Teacher's Handbook,* Evanston Illinois: Northwestern University Press, 1986.
– *Improvisation for the Theatre: A Handbook of Teaching and Directing Techniques* (3rd edn), Illinois: Northwestern University Press, 1999.

Stagnitti, K., 'Workshop notes' for *Learn to Play* Conference at All Hallows College, Dublin, 16–17 June 2009.

Stagnitti, K. and Jellie, L., *Play to Learn: Building Literacy in the Early Years,* Melbourne: Curriculum Corporation, 2006.

Staples New, R. and Cochran, M., *Early Childhood Education: An International Encyclopedia,* Vol. 1, California: Greenwood Publishing Group, 2007.

Sternberg, R.J., *Handbook of Creativity,* Cambridge: University of Cambridge Press, 1999.

Sternberg, R.J. and Lubart, T.I., 'The Concept of Creativity: Prospects and Paradigms' in R.J. Sternberg, *Handbook of Creativity,* Cambridge: Cambridge University Press, 1999.

Sternberg, R.J. and Williams, W.M., *How to Develop Student Creativity,* 1996. Retrieved on 29 September 2009 from http://www.ascd.org/readingroom/books/sternberg96book.html.

Storr, A., *The Art of Psychotherapy,* New York: Methuen, 1980.

Strock-Lynskey, D. and Keller, D.W., 'Integrating a family centred approach into social work practice with families of children and adolescents with disabilities', *Journal of Social Work in Disability and Rehabilitation* 6(1, 2) (2007), 111–34.

Strohm, K.,
– *Siblings: Brothers and Sisters of Children with Special Needs,* Adelaide: Wakefield Press, 2002.
– 'Sibling project', *Youth Studies Australia* 20(4) (2001), 48–52.

Sunderland, M., *Using Story Telling as a Therapeutic Tool with Children,* Bicester: Speechmark Publishing Ltd, 2000.

Sylwester, R., 'Art for brain's sake', *Educational Leadership,* 56(3) (1998), 31–5.

Tarbox, R.S.F. and Najdowski, A.C., 'Discrete Trial Training as a Teaching Paradigm' in J.K. Luiselli, D.C. Russo, W.P. Christian and S.M. Wilczynski (eds), *Effective Practices for Children with Autism: Educational and Behavioral Support Interventions that Work,* New York: Oxford University Press, 2008.

Task Force on Child Care Services, *Final Report to the Minister for Health: Task Force on Child Care Services,* Dublin: Government Publications Office, 1980.

Taunt, H.M. and Hastings, R.P., 'Positive impact of children with developmental disabilities on their families: a preliminary study', *Education and Training in Mental Retardation and Developmental Disabilities*, 37(4) (2002), 410–20.

Taylor, C. and Taylor, J., *Psychology of Dance*, Yorkshire, UK: Human Kinetics Europe, 1995.

TEAM Educational Theatre homepage (nd), retrieved from http://www.teamtheatre.ie/ on 15 July 2009.

Thomas, H. *Dance, Modernity and Culture*, London: Routledge, 1995.

Todd, S. and Shinzato, S., 'Thinking for the future: developing higher-level thinking and creativity for students in Japan—and elsewhere', *Childhood Education*, Vol. 75(6) (1999), 342–5.

Tomkins, G.M., Gelehrter, T.D., Granner, G., Martin, D., Jr., Samuels, H.H. and Thompson, E.B., 'Control of specific gene expression in higher organisms', *Science*, 19 December 1969, 166(3912):1474–80.

Torrance, E.P., *Guiding Creative Talent*, Englewood Cliffs: Prentice-Hall, 1962.

Trachtenberg, S.W. and Batshaw, M.L., 'Caring and Coping: The Family of a Child with Disabilities' in M.L. Batshaw (ed.), *Children With Disabilities* (4th edn), USA: Paul H. Brookes Publishing Co., 1997.

United Nations Convention on the Rights of the Child (1989), UN: General Assembly Document, retrieved from http://www.cirp.org/library/ethics/UN-convention/ on 30 October 2009.

Vais, D., *Dancing with Down Syndrome*, 2008. Available online from http://www.down Syndromecentre.ie/news/2008/sep/02/dancing-down- Syndrome/

Vander Ven, K., 'You are what you do and become what you've done: the role of activity in development of self', *Journal of Child and Youth Care*, Vol. 13(2) (1999), 133–48.

Veenema, S., Hetland, L. and Chalfen, K. (eds), *The Project Zero Classroom: New Approaches to Thinking and Understanding*. Cambridge, MA: Harvard Project Zero, 1997.

Vinter, A., 'How meaning modifies drawing behaviour in Children', *Child Development*, Vol. 70, 1 (33–49), New Jersey: Blackwell Publishing, 1999.

Vygotsky, L.S., *Mind in Society: The Development of Higher Mental Processes* (trans. and ed. M. Cole, V. John-Steiner, S. Scribner and E. Souberman), Cambridge, MA.: Harvard University Press, 1978, original publication 1930–35.

Wagner, B.,
– *Dorothy Heathcote: Drama as a Learning Medium* (2nd edn), Portland, ME: Calendar Island Publications, 1976.
– (ed.), *Building Moral Communities through Educational Drama*, London: Ablex Publishing Corporation, 1999.

Walsh, P.N., Conliffe, C. and Birbeck, G., 'Permanency planning and maternal well-being: a study of caregivers of people with intellectual disability in Ireland and Northern Ireland', *Irish Journal of Psychology* 27 (1993), 176–88.

Ward, A., 'An inner world and its implications', in A. Ward and L. McMahon (eds.), *Intuition is not Enough: Matching Learning with Practice in Therapeutic Child Care*, London and New York: Routledge, 1998.

Way, B., *Development through Drama*, Atlantic Highlands, NJ: Humanities Press, 1967.

Whelan, F., *The Complete Guide to Irish Dance*, Belfast: Appletree, 2000.

Wilderdom Store: Gear for Adventurous Learning, (nd), *Icebreakers, Warm-ups, Energizers, & Deinhibitizers*, retrieved from http://wilderdom.com/games/Icebreakers.html on 25 August 2009.

Willats, J., *Making Sense of Children's Drawings*, New York: Lawrence Erlbaum Associates, 2005.

Williams, D. and Lalor, K., 'Obstacles to the professionalisation of residential child care in Ireland', *Irish Journal of Applied Social Studies*, Vol. 2(3) (2000).

Wing, L.,

– 'Asperger's syndrome: a clinical account', *Psychological Medicine* 11 (1981), 115–29.

– *The Autistic Spectrum*, Oxford: Pergamon, 1996.

Wing, L. and Gould, J., 'Severe impairments of social interaction and associated abnormalities in children: epidemiology and classification', *Journal of Autism and Developmental Disorders* 9 (1979), 11–29.

Winner, E. and Hetland, L. (eds), 'The arts and academic achievement: what the evidence shows', *Journal of Aesthetic Education*, 34(3–4) (2000).

Wood, E. and Attfield, J., *Play, Learning and the Early Childhood Curriculum* (2nd edn), London: Sage Publications, 2008.

Yamagata, K., 'Representational activity during mother–child interaction: the scribbling stage of drawing', *Journal of Development*, 15 (1997), 355–66.

Yeger, S., *The Sound of One Hand Clapping*, Oxford: Amber Lane Press, 1990.

Youth Work Ireland, *Annual Report*, Dublin: Youth Work Ireland, 2008.

Index